STRATEGIES FOR INDUSTRIALISATION
IN DEVELOPING COUNTRIES

STRATEGIES FOR INDUSTRIALISATION IN DEVELOPING COUNTRIES

by

GYÖRGY CUKOR

ST. MARTIN'S PRESS
NEW YORK

338.09
C 966

Published in Hungary in 1971 by Akadémiai Kiadó, Budapest,
as *A feljödö országok iparositásának néhány kérdése*

This translation © 1974, C. Hurst & Co. (Publishers) Ltd., London

AFFILIATED PUBLISHERS: Macmillan Limited, London—
also at Bombay, Calcutta, Madras and Melbourne

CONTENTS

ANNEXES

TABLES

PUBLISHERS' NOTE

The publishers record with great regret that Dr György Cukor died on 4 January 1972, at the age of fifty-four. He was deputy director of the Institute of Economics, Hungarian Academy of Sciences, and was highly regarded both in his profession and as a man.

Owing to Dr Cukor's death, the final stages of preparing the book for press were supervised by György Hajdu. The index was compiled by Miss Zsuzsu Jozsits. Below are printed the author's own acknowledgments and a further note written by Mrs Katherine Cukor, the author's widow.

ACKNOWLEDGMENTS

I should like to express my thanks here to B. Martos, who was kind enough to check the mathematical relationships used in Chapters II and III; to B. Végsö who wrote the program for the trend calculations used in Chapter V for prognostical purposes; to S. Balázsy, S. Gosztonyi and L. Kismarty for their advice concerning certain industries; to Gy. Erös, Gy. Tallós, G. Kertész and K. Réti for having made available Hungarian experience in the trade with developing countries, and to Éva Zsolnay for preparing the major part of the statistical tables.

Special thanks are due to B. Forgács for the most careful typing and the help rendered in ordering the manuscript.

Budapest   GYÖRGY CUKOR
May 1971

This work by György Cukor was published in the original Hungarian early in 1971 by the Publishing House of the Hungarian Academy of Sciences. Directly afterwards the author began to prepare the English edition. His sudden illness and tragically early death, however, prevented him from concluding the work and so his book reaches English-speaking readers with some delay, though still in good time.

A*

Only three years have passed since the first Hungarian edition, but nonetheless János Timár, one of the closest friends and associates of the author, has re-examined the original manuscript in the light of the most recent results and developments in the field. This has convinced him that György Cukor's work and findings are still valid. Only minor revisions were justified in small matters of detail. I wish to thank him for taking care of this book, as he did of so many other things. The English edition has, for instance, been brought up to date by supplementing the tables with the data which have become available since the closing of the manuscript in September 1969. I also wish to express my warmest thanks and acknowledgment to the staff of the Afro-Asian Research Centre of the Hungarian Academy of Sciences, who were instrumental in making the additions to the tables. All this help was given freely and unasked – in devotion to the book and its author.

Budapest
April 1973   KATHERINE CUKOR

FOREWORD

Strategies of Industrialisation in Developing Countries, now presented to the English-speaking public, analyses in a concrete way actual problems which economic policy-makers in developing countries are confronted with in their responsibility of making major decisions on the speed, orientation and priorities in the industrialisation process. It reflects the experience accumulated during the various steps of György Cukor's career and the considerable analytical work he realised to organise the variety of facts collected through that experience. It reflects also the conviction of the author that the research worker cannot be content with writing for himself and for a reduced circle of colleagues and students. In his study he has not only to describe and analyse the world but to help in transforming it by providing tools which could serve those primarily responsible for this transformation. No doubt the book will be widely used since it gives the possibility to apply the same basic principles to a great variety of specific situations. While he concentrates on the economic aspects of the industrialisation strategies, the author cautions the reader that this is only part of the overall phenomenon. Social and political aspects may be equally or predominantly important.

The rich substance of this book cannot be analysed in a few pages. I would like only to underline a few points on which I have found Cukor's contribution particularly interesting. In the introduction on economic growth and industrialisation the present unfavourable conditions of the developing countries are rightly stressed. The so-called 'advantage of the late-comer', based on the possibility to have access to already available technologies, is more than offset by many other adverse conditions internal as well as external. To overcome these difficulties, industrialisation should be a major tool. In this connection, Cukor devotes a stimulating chapter to the relations of agriculture and industry in economic growth. He rejects as a false dichotomy the question of 'sectoral priority', as it is often put. The problem is not to choose one of the two sectors, but to see how both can be developed and benefit from each other. The question to answer is where the surplus can be generated and how it can be channelled and utilised. In doing so, present conditions different from those of the past should be considered so that the lessons of history cannot be decisive for developing countries.

In other crucial matters related to industrialisation, Cukor's stimulating and unconventional views are worthy of being considered. For instance, in an issue which is presently so widely discussed, namely that of technology choices, Cukor states that the more important is not the choice of technology to be adopted for a given project, since there are relatively few cases where several feasible alternatives actually exist. Of more relevance is the question of choice of priority industries to be developed, and in that connection he stresses again the importance of the engineering industries to which he devoted an interesting study a few years ago. One could mention also a balanced approach on the relative roles of large-scale and small-scale units in the process of industrialisation, underlining that it is not proved that in all cases the capital intensity grows as the size increases.

These few examples show that this book comes at an opportune time when many aspects of the industrialisation process are widely discussed and the need is felt for a reassessment of the role of industry in economic development. It will support those who think that applying the principle of comparative advantage in a static way could not be a solution for a more adequate distribution of industries at the world level and that new forms of international division of labour in the field of industry should be actively looked for, and negotiated among interested parties.

The more we appreciate Cukor's contribution at this juncture the more we have a feeling of regret and frustration in having to admit it will stop here and that we will no more benefit from this exceptional combination of a strongly articulate conceptual framework with a great attention to a multiplicity of facts collected through a wide and diversified experience. A number of avenues for reflection are open in this book in which no doubt Cukor himself, with his intelligence, energy and devotion, would have progressed much further. It is to be hoped that, stimulated by his ideas, more research workers will follow up in the field he has so eminently contributed to explore.

Vienna, 31 August 1973   FRANÇOIS LE GUAY
                               Director, Industrial Policies and
                               Programming Division, UNIDO

INTRODUCTION

This study deals with the industrialisation of developing countries, which is an important problem of their economic growth. The method and purpose of the study will be outlined in the Introduction, while the problem itself and its framework will be described in Chapter I. Chapter II will discuss the interrelation between the development of agriculture and industry and economic growth, as well as the mutual relations between the two sectors. Chapter III will analyse three fundamental problems of industrial development strategy, namely size of plant, the choice of technology and the complex problems of import substitution and export promotion. Chapter IV deals with the role of government and planning in economic development. Chapter V briefly reviews the past and expected further development of industrialisation in developing countries, devoting a separate section to drawing up a forecast up to 1985. The experience in industrialisation of the European socialist countries, particularly Hungary, which may be useful from the viewpoint of developing countries, is treated in Chapter VI.

As can be seen, the study does not discuss – if only for lack of space – every aspect of industrialisation in the developing countries. It does not treat, for example (beyond the general framework of export promotion and import substitution), the problems of foreign trade, foreign credits and aid, or the various forms of technical aid and other problems.

For an easier survey of the discussion, the statistical data and other information that are not indispensable for following the argument and for judging its correctness, are to be found in the Annexes. This material serves as a broader background to the study and may be useful for illustration; it provides information about the sources used and may be of interest to those more closely involved in the problem. Statistics cover in general the data that could be collected up to the end of 1968. The data that more immediately support the argument are contained in Tables within the text.

I made efforts to cover the relevant literature as extensively as possible. In particular, I have tried to use every printed publication of international organisations that is closely related to the subject. In addition, I have had the opportunity to use several studies of international organisations, particularly of U.N.I.D.O., available only in a mimeographed form. Owing to the rich literature dealing with developing countries, a full coverage would be out of the question.

ON THE METHOD OF THE INVESTIGATION

The method of the study is determined by the intention of the author to give a picture of the process of industrialisation and its essential aspects from the viewpoint of economic decisions influencing this process and from the aspect of economic policies. From the point of view of this method the present and past situations are interesting mainly to the extent that they influence what can be done and what will happen in the future. In the study, therefore, the descriptive, historical and statistical parts have a role only insofar as they are able to shed better light on development perspectives and possibilities of choice by drawing historical parallels; while the role of abstract verbal and/or mathematical models is limited to their direct relevance for an understanding of concrete developments or for the decision-making process. A relatively bigger role will be accorded to a critical and polemical review of various ideas about industrialisation in general and about some of its key problems (e.g. the application of labour-intensive or capital-intensive technology, the development of small-scale or large-scale plants, etc.). A review of the arguments about these questions will facilitate the presentation of the development alternatives.

In addition, I am guided by the principle that the proof of any theoretical standpoint or method is practice. In our case this commonplace general statement means the following: the best methods for the economic development and industrialisation of backward countries have not so far been established. The trouble is not only that mistakes are made which could have been recognised and avoided in the light of science (though this is no rarity) – practical examples thus not always being examples of correct behaviour or correct economic policy. Yet the correctness of any theoretical standpoint cannot be judged of itself in some abstract model, but by relying on the experience of many countries over many years. Thus the real problems of economic growth cannot be judged only on the basis of theoretical models, but rather also by confronting them with practical experience; but even practical experience and facts are of limited value in themselves, if they are lacking the systematising force of theory and its power of illuminating the future.

However much this study intends to discuss the subject from the point of view of possible economic decisions and from the aspect of economic policy, it should be obvious that it can treat only the more general interrelations of industrialisation, and cannot be related to a concrete situation in any given country. It can only offer help in solving such problems, and even that not so much from the viewpoint of the concrete measure to be taken as from that of the preliminary analysis.

In connection with the method of investigation, a few further remarks seem justified as regards both the standpoint to be explained and the interpretation of this standpoint. When analysing a part of any major complex of economic problems, however important, the author runs the danger of *being* one-sided, and much more of *looking* one-sided. For instance, productivity or technological development are highly important factors in economic growth, but the concentration of all energies would clearly not solve every problem unless productivity or technological progress is so widely interpreted as to include everything into this category, even the international division of labour and the system of economic control and management, as well. From the viewpoint of agricultural development, the use of fertilisers or irrigation are obviously highly important, but they do not exhaust the whole problem of development. If someone is investigating a limited subject for years, no particular distorting eyeglass is needed to see everything as bigger that stands nearer to the subject and as smaller that is farther from it. Under such conditions the author may easily believe that he is holding in his hands the only key to the solution of the major complex of problems, or at least the main method of solution. Even more easily, the reader may obtain the *impression* that the author believes so; since, as a matter of fact, he treats in detail only a part of a major complex of problems. Most likely, the author of the present study is not fully armed against either of these dangers. I believe industrialisation is the decisive question of economic growth in the developing countries, but I think it correct to stress that I do not consider it the only means of development that would solve every problem in itself.

It is well known that developing countries differ greatly from the point of view of their national economies. There are developing countries with one or two million inhabitants and there are others with several hundreds of millions. There are countries whose internal market is already large now and even larger potentially, and others where the domestic market is small even in a longer perspective. Nor does *per capita* income alone – which may vary from $50 to almost $1,000 per year – characterise the developing countries. The differences are equally great with regard to other factors generally considered to indicate economic development level. The ratio of people engaged in agriculture is high in comparison to industrial countries, but while in some developing countries it amounts to only 30–40 per cent, in others we find 80–90 per cent. The cultural level also shows such deviations: the ratio of illiterates is 25–30 per cent in one country and 90–95 in another. As regards the health service, the number of doctors may range from 0·1 to 12–15 per 10,000 of population. From the viewpoint of climate, the picture is somewhat more uniform: most of the developing countries lie in a warm or hot climate. It should thus be clear that in respect of the developing countries excessive generalisation should not be made. Even in professional literature we find frequent examples of phenomena which appear only in some countries being considered as general ones, or solutions being proposed for general use which have been tested or may be useful only in some of the countries. There are, however, certain justified generalisations. It is justified, for example, to treat industrialisation in the developing countries globally as a first approach and to characterise this process, similarly as a first approach, with the relevant index number of growth, although this will probably not exactly reflect the situation of any country–particularly not in the long run.

In the above, we have mainly mentioned economic circumstances and differences in economic development. Economic growth and industrialisation are, however, affected not only by these but by important political and social factors as well. It should be clear that the differences in the socio-political situation of the developing countries (feudal aristocracy or tribal organisation, etc., uniform national language and culture or linguistic fragmentation, long traditions or only a few years of independent nationhood) will have, in addition to the colonial or half-colonial past, an influence on the whole direction and feasibility of economic development and industrialisation within it.

At least as important are the differences which are rooted not in the past but in the objectives set by the present political power, and are reflected mainly in the extent to which they wish to restrict or to develop the capitalist sector of the economy or precisely its non-capitalist (government or co-operative) sector, to what extent they aim at comprehensive economic planning (where capitalist enterprise also has its place) or to what extent they consider planning a tool for making way for capitalist enterprises.

In this study, however, I am going to deal with the *economic problems* of industrialisation and will not treat the social and political aspects. Concentration on economic problems is intentional, although I am far from believing that industrialisation is an exclusively economic problem. I feel it is justified and correct in the course of this investigation to examine industrialisation as a central problem of economic growth; that a certain generalisation, a certain neglect of differences among the developing countries is necessary for discerning and understanding the essential phenomena; and that it is justified to put economic problems into the foreground.

I

ECONOMIC GROWTH AND INDUSTRIALISATION IN THE DEVELOPING COUNTRIES*

In historical perspective, the main cause of economic backwardness is the colonial system, that is, the form of international division of labour which made the greater part of the world economically dependent upon the industrially developed capitalist countries, and turned them into buyers of industrial articles and suppliers of raw materials – fundamentally by military and political domination. This circumstance is not affected by the fact that there are developing countries which have never been, or have been only for a short time, under direct foreign rule. But the example of Latin America proved long ago what the Asian and African countries after the Second World War have underlined, namely that the *existence of national independence* is only a necessary condition, but not a sufficient one, for *overcoming backwardness*. For further development we have to deal not with a single or even a main cause of backwardness, but with a whole system of causes. In developing countries, national income is low since accumulation is low, and this in turn results in a low rate of economic growth and a low national income. Or: in developing countries the standard of living is low, causing a low level of education (qualification); thus productivity is low, resulting in a low standard of living and in the very slow growth of such standards.

Obviously, such a 'vicious circle' is not sufficient as an explanation, and many other questions may be asked. For example: why do science and technology not help since, in order to achieve higher productivity, the developing countries only have to adopt the methods already implemented elsewhere? Scientific and technological progress, however, which are the basis of economic growth in industrial countries, are only a mixed blessing for the developing

---

* Developing countries in this study are, according to the usual terminology of international organisations, the countries of Africa, Latin America and Asia, without the Republic of South Africa, Japan and the Asian socialist countries.

countries. True, it is easier to adopt the technology tried out and tested elsewhere than to create new technology. However, under the present conditions it is one of the consequences of technological progress that the demand of developed industrial countries for the products of the developing countries is relatively limited. In respect of foodstuffs this is so because food consumption grows slower than consumption of industrial articles; and as regards industrial raw materials originating from the developing countries, demand for them rises more slowly than the production of processing industries. The explanation can be found partly in the introduction of various substitute materials (plastics, synthetic fibres), and partly in the effect of technological progress which reduces per unit material consumption. This is why the export market is limited and thus also import possibilities are limited. Owing to the progress of health services, mortality has declined in the developing countries and their population is rapidly increasing. This phenomenon, to be welcomed from humanitarian viewpoints, causes further concern, since the growing population consumes the increment of national income: on a *per capita* basis, consumption and accumulation are stagnating or increasing only very slowly.

The situation of developing countries is not particularly favourable in respect of natural resources either. Though they have valuable raw materials, the exploitation of these has come mostly under the influence of the leading capitalist countries. Presumably, this will remain so for some time to come. The problem is not only that the exploitation of raw material resources takes place with the aid of foreign capital, but also the raw materials have to be sold abroad, mostly in developed capitalist countries, independently of the fact of who owns the factory, mine or plantation, since, with their present economic structure the developing countries could hardly use a sufficient quantity of these raw materials. The disadvantages of natural conditions can be felt in a most pronounced manner in food production. Particularly in the densely populated developing countries, it is rather difficult to increase food production quickly.[1]

Rapid development also has *internal* social and political obstacles. In some countries the tribal system, in others feudalism, or the remnants of these and the related social system of values, or the general behaviour of people – these do not favour development. We have not touched here upon every obstacle to development in the backward countries. Nor was it our intention to do so, *but rather to present the proper subject of this book, industrialisation, in a more general setting of problems in the developing countries.* Economic backwardness is accompanied by a low level of industrial development, just as it is also accompanied by poor diet and a low cultural level.

Thus, industrialisation is a central problem of the economic development of backward countries, because it is in close interrelation with social and cultural development, with economic development as a whole and, within that, with the growth of the other branches of the economy, mainly of agriculture. Industrialisation is one of the major tools with the aid of which the vicious circle of backwardness and poverty can be broken. It can be proved that the closest relationship exists between general economic development and the development of industry, though opinions may differ as to what extent industrial development is the cause or the consequence of general economic development. The opinion is widespread today that the industries of the backward countries should be developed, but opinions differ widely as to how, at what rate and with what allocation of resources among various objectives this should be done.

There is no clear-cut answer to the question what precisely should be meant by industrialisation and industrial development. There exists also a view according to which industrialisation is the process through which an economy fundamentally relying on agriculture turns into a more advanced industrial economy, and the development of industry means the further growth of this already existing industry. Since, however, it is rather difficult to draw the line in this respect, the terms 'industrialisation' and 'industrial development' will be used throughout this study as synonyms, though in Chapter V, when we discuss a special problem, a certain distinction will be made between industrialisation and the various stages of industrial development. Opinions may also differ as to what should be understood by industrialisation. According to an earlier U.N. study, industrialisation is

... the permanent growth of the proportion of the non-agricultural sectors within the national economy running with the considerable increase of the total industrial production and that of the *per capita* industrial production as well as with the spread of application of the up-to-date technology.[2]

After a rather long discussion, the following definition was adopted in the U.N. Committee for Industrial Development:

Industrialisation is a process of economic development where an increasing proportion of the home resources is mobilised to establish a technically up-to-date and diversificated economic structure. This economy is characterised by a dynamical processing industry producing means of production and consumer goods, suitable for making the fast development of the total [whole] national economy and the economic and social progress sure.[3]

Like almost every definition relating to complex economic phenomena, this too is open to criticism. Its merit, at any rate, is that,
apart from having been adopted by an international forum, it stresses
the dynamic character of the process and the particular role played
by manufacturing industry. The terms 'industrialisation' and 'industrial development' will normally be used in the above sense.

THE NECESSITY OF INDUSTRIALISATION

Opinions about the perspectives of the economic development of
developing countries and, within that, about industrial development
have undergone profound changes in recent decades.

At the end of the nineteenth century and the beginning of the
twentieth, it was expected, particularly in the industrialised countries,
that the rate of growth would slow down in the economically developed world. Economic crises and the slow and uneven growth of
markets seemed unavoidable, and the narrowing of productive
capital investment possibilities was assumed. In the less developed
countries, on the other hand, it was assumed that unexploited natural
resources and potentially great absorbing markets are available,
together with the possibility of adopting the modern technology developed in the more advanced countries. These countries may thus
jump a few steps at a time, at least from the technological point of
view, and can use modern equipment at once. In the nineteenth
century and at the beginning of the twentieth, this actually happened.
Countries that were late in industrialising – particularly Germany
and the U.S.A. – made up for their lag behind the birthplace of the
first industrial revolution, i.e. England, and even overtook her.
It seemed that something similar would happen in the African,
Asian and Latin American countries.[4]

However, the world economy has actually developed along a different course. Since the Second World War, it has become obvious
that late-comers not only have advantages but also substantial
disadvantages in economic development and, particularly, in industrial development. Even in the 1950s and 1060s, the difference
between the developed and the developing countries has grown rather
than diminished in absolute terms, although it seems that for the
rate of economic growth in the developing countries, the middle of
the twentieth century is a turning-point.

Ideas about industrialisation in the developing countries have
undergone quite radical changes. Today in the literature on the
economic development of the developing countries, the question
whether *industrialisation is necessary or not* is no longer discussed.
What is discussed is *how* to industrialise. But the consensus mentioned
is of fairly recent origin and by no means complete. Many signs also

indicate that the differences in opinion on how to industrialise cover deeper differences of principle. Some of the authors, however, do not sound very convincing when they acknowledge the necessity of industrialisation. To deny the necessity of industrialisation would not be gratifying to public opinion in the developing countries. In many cases, the acknowledgment of the necessity of industrialisation occurred in the same way as with the definition of the group of the countries concerned. First came the term 'backward countries', and later, in order not to hurt the susceptibilities of the people or rather certain circles in these countries, it was changed to 'less developed' countries. At present, the generally adopted denomination is 'developing countries' so as to reflect not a static situation, or their being weakly developed, but the future, when development would be achieved. It would be a mistake to deny that an expression may also have political importance, but the substance of the matter is obviously not what name you use. For people of these countries the question is whether their economy does develop – at what rate and in what direction. From the viewpoint of economic analysis, however, the point is whether the phenomena and problems are correctly analysed and whether the conclusions are correct.

To simplify the complex reality, the development of ideas related to industrialisation may be divided into three main stages. In the theory prevailing in the developed (Western) countries, the belief in the benefits of free competition and in the *automatic materialisation of comparative advantages deriving from the international division of labour* was initially dominant. It was thought that the free play of market forces was the best or even the only way to arrive at economic progress. The best and quickest development could thus be achieved by leaving these forces alone, not just in a single country but also – through the comparative advantages – between countries. It followed that *there was no need for any special industrialisation policy*, and in many cases even industrialisation itself was superfluous, since, through foreign trade, specialisation in the production of raw materials would serve economic and social progress as well as, or even better than, domestic industrialisation.

The next stage of thinking was characterised by stressing *limited industrialisation*. The change has most likely been brought about by the demographic factor, that is by the realisation that there is no chance in the developing countries of employing the whole and rapidly increasing labour force in agriculture and other extracting branches alone. The main emphasis, however, was laid on the relative scarcity of labour and capital. According to this reasoning, it was in developing countries, where labour is abundant but capital is scarce, that small-scale industries (handicrafts) and light industry should be developed, and the products of heavy industry should be imported – even in the future. The appearance was given that this kind of industrialisation could promote development in the densely populated countries, which are relatively little developed, but that in other countries, where development is based on specialisation in agriculture, and a higher stage of development has already been achieved (e.g. Australia), the effect might be unfavourable. The reality was different: today there is no developed country without developed industry, and the contribution even of developed agriculture to national income is relatively small, and is declining. It is worth while to mention that several authors, mainly American, took a rather cautious standpoint in respect of industrialisation in developing countries *even in the 1960s*.

> Only a few of the smaller under-developed countries have got the actual possibility (chance) to become an industrial country inasmuch for most of them there is a comparative economic advantage to produce non-industrial products on the basis of their agricultural or other home resources.[5]

The same author is similarly 'cautious' when treating the development of heavy industry:

> Frequently, there were arguments, that the basis of the economic development in general and that of the industrial one in particular is the heavy industry and also, that this basis has to be established, regardless that it commands a high price.[6]

Many people, even immediately after the Second World War, viewed with suspicion the industrialisation efforts of developing countries (then mainly colonies); in these cases economic development was not justified. They were of the opinion that these efforts

> ... are the means of expression of that not quite sensible ambition that the country concerned could prove its capability to produce goods which used to be imported from Europe or from the U.S.A. in the past.[7]

The idea of the author quoted will be even clearer from his ironic remark that in industrialisation, as it were, national ambitions are satisfied if a country can operate a 'national' foundry or blast furnace of its own, or can produce its own 'national' nitrogen and 'national' matches.

This approach may be found even in the earlier studies prepared by the Secretariat of the United Nations. Thus, for example, in the first U.N. study dealing with the industrialisation problems[8] of the underdeveloped countries, the general tendency is indicated by the statement that the study does not treat the problem of whether an economy should industrialise or not. Though the study itself examines industrialisation in the framework of the more general process of economic growth, it does not consider it as economically fully justified, but as an objective justified to varying extent by national efforts at greater security and higher prestige.

This suspicious and reserved attitude towards industrialisation has changed. In connection with industrialisation for the developing countries the emphasis is put on the necessity of an economic policy directed towards *the creation of a diversified domestic industry* (which, of course, does not contradict the requirement of observing the importance of international specialisation). This idea is already reflected in a 1961 study of the United Nations: 'It is clear enough what the final aim of the underdeveloped countries should be: to create a versatile industrial economy like the ones existing in developed countries.'[9]

Obviously, in bringing about the latest attitude, i.e. the acknowledgement of the necessity of diversified industrialisation, the *foreign trade gap* also played a role. It has become obvious that with only the export of raw materials or with import substitution with light industrial products, foreign exchange revenues cannot be increased to the extent made necessary by the growing needs of the economy, mainly because of the import of capital goods. The main reason – though by no means the only reason – for this circumstance was in all likelihood the change in the pattern of utilisation, and the technological progress which brought about a more economic use of raw materials and created synthetic materials as substitutes for raw material, with the result that the consumption of raw materials imported from the developing countries is growing slower all over the world than that of manufactures.

It should, of course, be taken into account that influential circles in the developed Western countries were also suspicious of the industrialisation of developing countries because they believed that this could be detrimental to their economic interests. Obviously, the economic views on industrialisation also reflected and still do reflect such a belief. At the same time it would be incorrect to discover in every kind of critique on some method of industrialisation some special reactionary behaviour defending capitalist interests; the critique often has a grain of truth.

THE EXTENT OF BACKWARDNESS AND EFFORTS AT DEVELOPMENT

The problems of the developing countries, particularly the problems of their economic growth, have come into the foreground of world politics and world opinion mainly since the Second World War. In these countries live the majority of mankind; in comparison to the developed industrial countries they are poor and backward. Though their growth has accelerated in absolute terms, their backwardness in terms of *per capita* production in comparison to the developed countries has not diminished, but has even increased in recent years.

Literature treating the causes and criteria of backwardness is extremely rich. However, while we know plenty about the *criteria* of backwardness, our knowledge of its *causes* is far from satisfactory. This is particularly true if we analyse the causes from the aspect of their possible elimination, with the aim of abolishing backwardness; that is, if we think in terms of development, of the things to be done.

In analysing the problem, it causes a difficulty that the present economic levels of the developing countries and their rate of growth show great differences. A reliable comparison of development levels in different countries is, of course, rather difficult. The most generally used indicator, *per capita* national income, is not always a realistic basis for comparison if the patterns of production and consumption show great differences. Comparison is difficult even on the basis of physical units of measurement. For example, in respect of nutrition on the basis of *per capita* calorie consumption, the real differences in nutrition levels are underestimated; however, any other valuation of the foodstuffs used (e.g. on the basis of protein content or animal proteins) would involve rather voluntaristic weighting.

Let us survey the data in Table I/1, relating to the development of sixty-eight countries, classified into six groups, relying on U.N. sources. The basis of the classification is:

(*a*) *per capita* national income, which is the most comprehensive indicator of development levels. In addition,

(*b*) *per capita* energy consumption (in coal equivalent) as an indicator of industrial development;

(*c*) and (*d*) infant mortality and the number of inhabitants per physician, as an indicator of health services;

(*e*) the literacy ratio to characterise the level of education;

(*f*) *per capita* food consumption in calories, to characterise food supply; and, finally,

(*g*) rate of agricultural employment to characterise the relative importance of agriculture in the national economy, or in other words to characterise the structure of the economy by branches.

The group *averages* show identical tendencies, that is, higher national income is accompanied by a more developed industry, better nutrition and health service, smaller agricultural employment and higher educational levels. Thus from a global point of view, *per capita* national income provides good orientation. As regards details, the situation is different. If, for example, we examine the countries to be found in the same groups, we meet with several cases which contradict our general knowledge about economic development levels and raise doubts as to the suitability of categorisation by national income. The extreme cases seem unequivocal. Group I comprises the richest countries and Group VI generally the poor ones. Even Group II contains such countries as are known for their industrial development, with the natural exception of Venezuela whose high ranking may be explained by the income from oil – mostly later transferred abroad. It is, however, more difficult to explain why Chile and Uruguay should be more developed than Japan, or Costa Rica and Panama more developed than Romania. If we select for the fundamental criterion of classification some indicator other than national income, some of the countries – particularly those situated in the middle range – will obtain different ranking, which could even cause other groups to be formed. The coun-

Table I/1

AVERAGE INDICATORS OF ECONOMIC DEVELOPMENT AND STANDARD OF LIVING IN SOME COUNTRIES

(classified by per capita National Income)

Per capita national income in U.S. dollars by Country Groups I–VI *(see page 16)*	a	b	c	d	e	f	g
I. Above 1,000	1,366	3,900	24·9	885	98	3,153	17
II. Between 575–1,000	760	2,710	41·9	944	94	2,944	21
III. 350–575	431	1,861	56·8	1,724	81	2,920	35
IV. 200–350	269	536	97·2	3,132	70	2,510	53
V. 100–200	161	265	131·1	5,185	51	2,240	64
VI. Under 100	72	114	180·0	13,450	29	2,070	74

Key:

(a) *Per capita* national income (G.N.P.). (Average of 1956–8).

(b) *Per capita* energy consumption, in kilograms of hard coal equivalent (average of 1956–8).

(c) Infant mortality (average of 1955–8) per 1,000 live births.

(d) Inhabitant per physician.

(e) Ratio of those able to read and write from population aged above 15 years, estimate for 1950.

(f) *Per capita* food consumption in calories.

(g) Agricultural employment as percentage of total manpower (males only, estimate for 1956).

Country Groups referred to in Table 1/1

Group I: EUROPE, NORTH AMERICA, OCEANIA:
Australia, Canada, New Zealand, Sweden, Switzerland, U.S.A.

Group II: EUROPE, NORTH AMERICA, OCEANIA:
Belgium, Czechoslovakia, Denmark, Finland, France, West Germany, Netherlands, Norway, Soviet Union, United Kingdom
LATIN AMERICA:
Venezuela
ASIA:
Israel

Group III: EUROPE, NORTH AMERICA, OCEANIA:
Austria, East Germany, Hungary, Ireland, Italy, Poland
LATIN AMERICA:
Argentina, Chile, Cuba, Puerto Rico, Trinidad and Tobago, Uruguay
AFRICA:
Republic of South Africa

Group IV: EUROPE, NORTH AMERICA, OCEANIA:
Bulgaria, Greece, Spain, Turkey, Yugoslavia
LATIN AMERICA:
Guyana, Costa Rica, Jamaica, Mexico, Panama
ASIA:
Malaya, Japan

Group V: EUROPE, NORTH AMERICA, OCEANIA:
Albania, Portugal, Romania
LATIN AMERICA:
Brazil, Columbia, Dominican Republic, Ecuador, Honduras, Nicaragua, Paraguay, Peru
AFRICA:
Ghana
ASIA:
Ceylon, the Philippines

Group VI: LATIN AMERICA:
Bolivia
AFRICA:
Congo (Kinshasa)
ASIA:
Burma, Cambodia, Taiwan, India, Indonesia, Laos, Pakistan, Thailand

---

Source: Report on the World Social Situation, U.N., New York, 1961, pp. 41 and 48.

tries may, for example, also be classified according to a characteristic indicator of industrial development, i.e. *per capita* energy consumption. The U.N. study quoted uses the following classification:

*Per capita energy
consumption in
calories*

I.	Above 3,150	II.	1,675–3,150
III.	800–1,675	IV.	350–800
V.	120–350	VI.	below 120

According to this criterion some of the European countries and Japan would be placed in a higher category than on the basis of national income; e.g. Belgium, Czechoslovakia, West Germany and East Germany are transferred from Group II to Group I; Austria, Hungary and Poland from the third to the second; and Bulgaria and Japan from the fourth to the third. The ranking of several non-European, industrially underdeveloped countries would change: Uruguay would move from the third category to the fourth, and Turkey and Costa Rica from the fourth to the fifth. On the basis of classification by energy consumption, Venezuela would remain in the second group, but on the basis of living standards – especially on that of health and education – it would not. By infant mortality it would be placed into the fourth group, and by schooling into the fifth. Nor does the picture change if we examine these groups of countries by relying on later indices, partly deviating from those to be found in the U.N. study:

Table I/2

A FEW ECONOMIC INDICES AS A FUNCTION OF
ECONOMIC DEVELOPMENT LEVEL

Per capita G.N.P. in U.S. dollars of 1964	Gross investment in per cent of G.N.P.	Share of primary sector in G.D.P. per cent	Employment in industry as percentage of total employment	Ratio of urban population	Rate of school enrolment	Literacy rate of adults	Birth rate
I. Above 1,000	24–25	16–10	33–40	58–65	82–91	89–93	22–17
I. 600–1,000	22–23	22–19	28–31	52–55	74–79	80–85	28–25
I. 300–400	20–21	30–27	21–23	41–46	61–67	65–72	34–31
V. 200	18	36	17	34	53	55	37
V. 100	15	46	10	20	36	37	42
I. 50	12	58	4	7	18	15	47

ource: Hollis B. Chenery, 'Growth and Structural Change', *Finance and Development*, 1971, No. 3.

Three conclusions may be drawn from the above:

1. Economic development level is not a phenomenon of a single dimension, i.e. it cannot be measured and characterised on a single scale of measurement. The same holds good for the rate of economic growth.
2. The differences among the individual countries are very substantial by any scale. The ratio between the most developed and the most backward groups (I and VI) is 1 : 18 in the case of *per capita* national income, 1 : 34 in that of energy consumption characteristic of industrial development, and 1 : 15 as regards availability of physicians.
3. The richest and poorest countries are unequivocally distinguished from each other: that is, the West European and North American countries that were first to embark on capitalist industrial development, on the one hand, and on the other hand their former Asian and African colonies which still preserve feudal and pre-feudal conditions. But not every European country is rich, and there are substantial differences also among the former colonies and semicolonial countries. (Portugal is a poor country, although – or maybe because – it stubbornly insists on keeping its colonies.)

The question naturally emerges: when did polarisation start among the individual countries, leading to such differences in development?

The difference between the industrial and the underdeveloped countries is not of recent origin, though opinions differ as to when the *great difference* did, in fact, emerge. There is a standpoint according to which inequality started with the industrial revolution, since 'in the early nineteenth century there was – according to reliable sources – not much difference between the living standards of the British and the Chinese peoples.'[10] According to S. J. Patel[11] *per capita* national income in dollars in the industrial countries (Western Europe, North America, New Zealand and Australia, as well as the European socialist countries) was as follows in 1850 and 1960:

	1850	1960
Industrial countries	150	1100
Non-industrial countries	100	120

Thus, the ratio in the mid-nineteenth century was 1·5 : 1.

According to other opinions, the now developed countries were already much more developed in the nineteenth century than the developing countries are *now*. Kuznets made efforts to approach the problem from various aspects and with different methods. According to his simplest calculations, which are, of course only approximate, *per capita* income increased in the developing countries in the last century at most by 50 per cent, while in the developed (capitalist) countries it grew fourfold. According to his assumption – and in conformity with Table 1 – *per capita* national income in the poorest countries about the middle of the twentieth century was about $75 and in the most advanced $1,400, that is, the ratio was 1 : 18·5. Therefore, a hundred years ago the ratio was 1400/4 : 75/1·5, that is, 7 : 1. In this sense the present huge difference is considered relatively new also by Kuznets.[12] Of course, this is not essential from the point of view of the *present differences*, although it is not immaterial whether the polarisation took place in 150 or 300 – 400 years.

It is certain at any rate that the difference between the industrialised and the underdeveloped countries has come about mostly in the last 150 years, while the definite demand of the third world for development and for an acknowledgement by the developed countries of their duty to offer help is of relatively recent origin. This has several causes. A considerable part of the countries in question obtained *political independence* only after the Second World War, and the increased political role strengthened the wholly justified aspirations to higher living standards and to greater economic independence. Certainly, these claims existed even earlier, but the colonial system hindered their coming to light.

That the problems of the developing countries have come to the foreground is also related to the demographic situation of the world. Although, as far as can be established, the majority of the world's population has always lived in Asia, Africa and Latin America, that is in the areas now considered as 'developing', *the tendency of population growth has recently changed*. As can be seen from Table I/3, the population of Europe, North America and Oceania – that is, of the now developed world – increased from the middle of the eighteenth century to the beginning of the twentieth more quickly than that of the whole world. This rate was rather more than 21 per cent in the middle of the eighteenth century, but above 33 per cent in the twentieth century. Since then, the tendency has turned and at present the population in the developing countries is growing much faster than in the developed ones, and, according to prognoses, this trend seems to continue.

The form in which the problems of developing countries present themselves is also related to the emergence of *the socialist countries* and their growing strength. Through direct and indirect effects, first the weakening and then the virtual abolition of the colonial system is closely related to it. The mere existence of the socialist countries helps the developing countries to have more independent policies both in domestic and international problems.

The appearance of the problems of the developing countries be-

Table I/2

DISTRIBUTION OF THE WORLD'S POPULATION

	Europe*	North America	Latin America	Oceania	Asia	Africa	World total
1750	19·8	0·1	1·5	0·3	65·2	13·1	100
1800	21·2	0·7	2·1	0·2	65·9	9·9	100
1850	23·4	2·2	2·8	0·2	63·3	8·1	100
1900	26·3	5·0	3·9	0·4	56·9	7·5	100
1930	26·4	6·7	5·4	0·5	53·2	7·8	100
1950	22·9	6·7	6·5	0·5	55·2	8·2	100
1960	21·3	6·6	7·1	0·6	55·9	8·5	100
1970	19·4	6·3	7·8	0·5	56·6	9·4	100
1980	17·2	5·8	8·4	0·5	57·9	10·2	100

POPULATION GROWTH IN THE PERIODS INDICATED
(*per cent*)

1750–1800	5·9	43·1	11·6	—	4·7	1·1	4·5
1800–50	7·4	34·1	11·7	—	4·4	1·1	5·3
1850–1900	9·1	25·5	13·8	24·6	4·3	4·8	6·5
1900–30	7·9	18·6	20·0	20·1	5·4	9·4	7·8
1930–50	6·4	14·0	24·8	16·6	16·2	17·9	14·3
1950–60	11·1	19·8	30·9	26·9	21·7	24·2	20·0
1960–70	—	—	—	—	—	—	—
1970–80	8·9	15·0	32·7	26·3	25·5	32·8	22·7

* Including Russia and the Asian parts of the Soviet Union (prior to 1917, of Tsarist Russia).

Source: Simon Kuznets, *Modern Economic Growth: Rate, Structure and Spread*, Yale University Press, 1966 for 1750–1960 and U.N. *Monthly Bulletin of Statistics*, April 1971 and August 1972.

fore world opinion is influenced also by the existence and operation of *international organisations*, mainly the United Nations. Developing countries obtain a growing role in the functions of international organisations, and from a political viewpoint these organisations are becoming more and more a forum for the aspirations of the developing countries. Particularly in recent years, the practical activities of international organisations have increasingly shifted towards aiding the developing countries, in the forms of technical aid; health supply; primary, secondary and university education; vocational training; by means of world trade; in industrialisation, etc.

Thus, the basic problem is *how to industrialise* in the developing countries. The circumstances of industrialisation are determined by the political independence of the developing countries and the international environment that is more favourable in comparison to the past, by the existence and policy of the socialist countries and by the international organisations.

One crucial problem of 'how to industrialise' is the relation between agriculture and industry, and their interplay in economic growth. It is this problem we shall deal with in the next chapter.

REFERENCES

1. For details see Chapter II.
2. Simon Kuznets, *The Study of Patterns of Industrialization*. U.N. Department of Social Affairs, 1948 (mimeographed).
3. Committee for Industrial Development. Report of the Third Session. 13–31 May 1963, E.C.O.S.O.C. E/3781. U.N.
4. H. W. Singer, *International Development: Growth and Change*. McGraw-Hill, New York, 1964.
5. D. Bryce Murray, *Industrial Development*, McGraw-Hill, 1960, p. 14.
6. Ibid., p. 19.
7. John A. Adler, *The Underdeveloped Areas, their industrialization*, Yale Institute of International Studies, 1949.
8. *Process and Problems of Industrialization in Underdeveloped Countries*, U.N., 1955.
9. *World Economic Survey*, 1961.
10. Dr. J. Bognár, *A fejlődő országok helyzete és szerepe a következő évtizedek világgazdaságában* (Situation of the developing countries and their role in the world economy of the next decades), Inaugural Address at the Hungarian Academy of Sciences, 1965.
11. S. J. Patel, 'Economic Transition in Africa', *Journal of Modern African Studies*, 1964, No. 3.
12. Simon Kuznets, *Modern Economic Growth: Rate, Structure and Spread*, Yale University Press, 1966.

II

THE ROLES OF AGRICULTURE
AND INDUSTRY IN THE ECONOMIC
GROWTH OF DEVELOPING
COUNTRIES

1. *On Changes in the Structure of the Economy*

Economic growth is a complex process. Technological and cultural levels, the rise in standards of living and the growth of the individual branches of the economy – agriculture, industry, construction, transport, trade and other services – are closely interrelated. The role, relative weight and mutual interrelation of the two most important branches of the economy, which turn out the majority of material goods – namely agriculture and industry – are of special importance. Our study is mainly concerned with industrialisation of developing countries; however, we also have to discuss the relative roles and importance of agriculture and industry in the economic growth process, in the first place from the viewpoint of development strategy.

It is superfluous to lose much time on arguments whether *only industry* or *only agriculture* should be developed, or whether one or the other should be given absolute priority. Obviously, both must be developed. The essential problem is 'how to develop' and in what order, with what allocation of the means serving development and with what differences owing to various (economic, geographic and historical) circumstances. Let us briefly survey the relevant arguments.

Relying on the comparison of production and employment patterns of countries on different levels of development, industrialisation is frequently considered as the key to economic growth. As is known, the higher in general the economic development level of a country (in terms of *per capita* national income), the higher the share of manufacturing industry and the lower the share of agriculture, calculated either by output or by employment. Table I/1 in Chapter I shows an unequivocally negative correlation between *per capita* national income and the share of agricultural employment, and an unequivocally positive correlation between national income and energy consumption characteristic of industrial development.

It is usual to examine the structural changes accompanying development for the three main sectors of the economy: primary (agriculture, fishing, mining), secondary (manufacturing) and tertiary (services). It is typical in economic progress that, at first, the share of the secondary sector grows at the expense mainly of agriculture, and later the tertiary sector grows more quickly while the share of the primary sector essentially diminishes and that of the secondary also declines somewhat.[1]

This type of development may be explained in part by changes in consumption and in part by technological development. With increasing incomes, demand for the products of manufacturing industries increases in relative terms, both in final demand and in productive consumption; in the case of higher incomes, again, demand grows most quickly for services, while in services productivity increases more slowly (thus requiring relatively more manpower) than in manufacturing.

ONCE MORE ON COMPARATIVE ADVANTAGES

In economic literature we find the objection – though less frequently in recent years – that a higher growth rate in the secondary sector (manufacturing) than in agriculture is *not necessary* for economic growth. According to A. J. Robinson:

> Where the resource basis and market potentialities in the non-agricultural sector are not adequate for the development of viable industries, it may be preferable to retain the surplus above subsistence on the agriculture sector, investing it in further increases of agricultural output. The additional agricultural products could then be exchanged in world markets for imports of consumer goods, or for the purchase of equipment and materials for the further improvement of productivity and increases of output in the agricultural sector, thus leading to the *sustained increases in output . . . that constitute* the *sine qua non* of economic growth.[2]

According to this author, the surplus created in agriculture can be used to bring new land under cultivation and to diversify agricultural production (to produce meat, fruit, tea, coffee and non-food agricultural products).

The main point here is that once a surplus output above subsistence consumption in agriculture becomes available it may be invested in various ways, one of which is the development of manufacturing industry. Whether the surplus will in fact be used to develop manufacturing will depend, ceteris paribus, upon whether manufacturing yields higher returns to capital invested than do alternative forms of investment.[3]

In the final analysis, this reasoning is equivalent to the one-sided, static emphasis on comparative advantages, mentioned earlier. The world market prices of agricultural products, particularly of the tropical products that can be produced for export by the developing countries, have fallen in the past by comparison with the prices of industrial products. The market of the developed countries is limited or is only expanding slowly; stabilisation of the prices of some products has succeeded only at the expense of reducing production or with some other support. It is impossible to rely upon the tendency changing in future. A lasting specialisation in the production of agricultural raw materials would result for developing countries in permanent losses, difficulties in securing sales and, if the supply should grow considerably, the accumulation of unsaleable stocks.

A *complexity of development*, that is, the development of various stages of processing raw materials, and the related development in industry, transport, construction, etc., are unequivocally advantageous. This process generates direct and indirect connections which, partly through the flows of products, and partly through the spread of technological progress, mutually create and increase the markets of the individual branches, their productivity and the material bases for developing production. A one-sided specialisation in agriculture and renunciation of the development of manufacturing would mean forgoing these advantages. In that case, the industrial development due to agricultural development would occur abroad, and the typically colonial or semi-colonial situation would be perpetuated. It is not certain – nor is it likely in the present situation – that, by leaving the matter to the short-term rate of return on investment, or to the profit motive of private capital, industrial development would automatically follow.

It seems that for a successful development of agriculture a domestic industry is also needed and the supply of industrial inputs for agriculture cannot be *entirely* left to imports. The example of the last decade shows (see Table II/1) that, also considering population growth, the industrially developed countries were better able to increase their agricultural and food production, while the developing countries were relatively lagging behind in this respect.[4]

According to some authors, the examples of Australia and New

Table II/1
AVERAGE ANNUAL GROWTH RATE OF TOTAL AND
PER CAPITA AGRICULTURAL AND FOOD PRODUCTION
FROM 1959/61 TO 1969/71
(*percentages*)

	Total			Per capita	
	agri-cultural produc-tion	food produc-tion	popula-tion	agri-cultural produc-tion	food produc-tion
Western Europe	2·5	2·7	0·8	1·7	1·8
European Socialist countries	2·8	2·9	1·1	1·8	1·8
North America	1·7	2·1	1·3	0·4	0·8
Oceania	2·9	3·4	2·0	0·8	1·3
Other developed countries*	3·3	3·6	1·3	1·9	2·3
All developed countries	2·4	2·6	1·2	1·2	1·5
Latin America	2·6	3·2	2·9	−0·3	0·3
Far East (excl. Japan)	2·8	2·8	2·6	0·2	0·2
Near East (excl. Israel)	3·2	2·9	2·5	0·3	0·1
Africa (excl. South Africa)	2·5	2·3	2·6	0·0	−0·3
All developing countries	2·7	2·8	2·7	0·1	0·2
World total	2·6	2·7	2·0	0·5	0·7

* Israel, Japan, South Africa.

Source: F.A.O., *Monthly Bulletin of Agricultural Economics and Statistics*, January 1972.

Zealand, which are rich countries, prove that it is possible to special-ise in agriculture.[5] In reality, the contribution of agriculture to the Australian national income was 16·8 per cent in 1956 and 12·6 per cent in 1961, while the corresponding figures for manufacturing were 27·4 and 27·5 per cent.[6] In New Zealand, agriculture contri-buted 22 per cent to national income in 1954, while total industry (including construction), however, contributed 32·1 per cent and manufacturing 21·7.[7]

Manufacturing increased rather slowly in Australia: from 1950 to 1960 the annual average growth rate was 1·8 per cent, while it was relatively rapid in New Zealand at 5·5 per cent. Development was of the 'modern' type in both countries, that is, engineering and the chemical industry increased relatively faster and the light and food industries relatively slower.

True, the importance of agriculture is great in both countries. This can be seen also from investment: for example, in Australia in 1961 agriculture obtained 12 per cent and manufacturing 16 per cent of all investment. It is particularly true of foreign trade: both countries export mainly agricultural products. In 1965 about three-quarters of Australian exports and about nine-tenths of those of New Zealand were of agricultural origin.

Thus, the examples of Australia and New Zealand prove that an export pattern oriented to agrarian products is compatible with economic development (with high living standards), but it does not prove that it would be possible to orientate the whole economy towards agriculture. Of course, industrial development started in these two countries rather late and on the basis of high economic and living standards relying on agricultural exports. It is doubtful, however, whether the possibility of similar economic growth exists for the developing countries under present circumstances. The necessity of a structural change – that is, of reducing the share of agriculture and the growth of manufacturing – is mostly accepted today even by authors dealing with agriculture and emphasising its importance.

> . . . but this type of structural transformation of an economy seems to be a necessary condition for cumulative and self-sustaining growth. A mere change in the product-mix available for consumption obtainable up to a point entirely by means of international trade is apparently *not* a sufficient condition.[8]

HOW SHOULD WE INTERPRET THE HISTORICAL EXPERIENCE OF ECONOMIC GROWTH?

In stressing the importance of industrialisation one relies not only on the example of the now developed countries – namely, on the relative share of industry in the economy of these countries – but also on an evaluation of historical experience that considers the growth of industry the decisive factor in economic progress.

The above-outlined and, in my opinion, exaggerated and one-sided pushing into the foreground of comparative advantages challenges the correctness of the first aspect, which is the lesson to be drawn from the economic structure of the developed countries. We may meet with differing opinions also in respect of the experience of historical development. Some of the authors believe that heavy emphasis on industrialisation '. . . reflects a wrong evaluation of

European history as well as a tendency which attributes extreme importance to the industrial revolution in comparison with the overtaking agricultural revolution.'[9]

This idea is explained in detail by Buchanan and Ellis.[10] As is well known, it was England which first took the road to modern economic development. After describing British development, and precisely in the interest of conclusions to be drawn from the viewpoint of developing countries, these authors put the question whether historically it was first agriculture which changed and industry which followed suit, or *vice versa*.

> Was it, broadly speaking, the improvements in agricultural productivity that drove people off the land and so made possible the development of manufacturing? Or did manufacturing pull people out of agriculture and so pave the way for improvements and adjustment in agriculture? *Perhaps the more logical view is that improvement in agriculture came first*. But if the agricultural improvements tended to push people out of agriculture, the newly developing manufactures also pulled people into industry and commerce.[11]

In the eyes of Buchanan and Ellis, the development of other West European countries is very similar.

This statement, however, does not appear to be unequivocally proved. On the one hand, it looks as if the 'agricultural revolution' – that is, the development of agricultural techniques – had covered a much longer period than the industrial revolution, that is the appearance and spread of mechanised large-scale industry. It is as if no agreement existed among authors examining historical experience from the viewpoint of the present problems of the developing countries as to when the agricultural revolution took place. According to the renowned French agricultural economist, René Dumond:

> The great 'agricultural revolution' of western Europe which began in Flanders in the fourteenth century, and in England in the sixteenth century, consisted mainly of introducing the careful weeding of plants and later, a high level of fertilisation. Briefly, this represented the application of horticultural techniques, and gardening methods in field. Next came the expansion of forage crops . . .[12]

Buchanan and Ellis put the English agricultural revolution at a later date, the eighteenth and partly the nineteenth centuries. According to them, the improved agricultural methods which took root first in England in the eighteenth century and spread from there to Western Europe, consisted partly in a more intensive utilisation of land and partly in the better performance of such traditional work as ploughing, sowing, harvesting and thrashing. The selective methods of animal husbandry (development of superior species) were also introduced. But, according to these authors, the propelling force of the agricultural revolution was trade, both foreign trade and that between town and countryside.[13]

If this is true, however, the primary role of agriculture in economic growth may also be challenged on a logical basis, since the birth of big towns and, particularly, the development of foreign trade required something beyond agricultural development. Towns paid something into the countryside for domestic agricultural produce, and it is not likely that foreign trade could have relied primarily on the export of domestic agricultural products. The book in question itself comprises sufficient data on the rapid development of industry in the second half of the eighteenth century, of an extent that could hardly be attributed to the development of agriculture. Imports of cotton increased, between 1776 and 1831, more than forty-fold. The price of cotton fibre fell, between 1779 and 1830, to about one-sixth of its former level; these two figures seem to prove the rather rapid growth of production and productivity in the textile industry. Output of coal increased, from 1770 to 1816, more than two and a half times – obviously also in consequence of industrial growth.[14]

Similar views, attributing some primary importance to agricultural growth, can be met with elsewhere. Accordingly, the *general* model of economic growth was that, after the stagnation characteristic of the pre-capitalistic era, the economy shifts within a relatively short time into the period of sustained development. This change is preceded by a rapid growth of agriculture, exceeding that of population. Thus, a surplus above self-consumption appears in the agricultural sector, and this is the key to the start of economic growth. From the point of view of the shift, agriculture has a 'generating' effect, bringing about the conditions for rapid industrialisation; therefore, industrialisation must essentially rely on agriculture.

In my opinion this generating effect of agriculture, and the postulation of its growth as the direct releasing cause of industrialisation in the countries now advanced have not been proved; it is obvious, however, that the development of agriculture, employing as it initially does the major part of the population, is highly important. (This is dealt with in greater detail in Section 2, page 34 ff.) Of course, historical statistics are deficient, existing data are inaccurate and the relationships between cause and effect cannot yet be proved on the basis of quantitative relationships. A relative growth of agricultural production may perhaps best be felt from the data on England. According to the calculations of Kuznets,[15] between about 1688 and 1770 the share of agriculture in the national product increased from 40 to 45 per cent, that of industry rose from

21 to 24 per cent, while the share of services declined. In the following periods the share of agriculture diminished. In France, from 1789/ 1815 to 1825/35 the share of industry increased while that of agriculture remained unchanged.[16] As regards other countries, although the data are available only from the 1860s, a considerable growth in industry at the expense of agriculture can be observed.

A surplus of agricultural products obviously cannot in itself be regarded as a sufficient condition of economic development. If this were the case, all the backward countries would be well advanced by now, as they were for a long time characterised by this agricultural surplus (of course, with a low living standard of the population) and by industrial imports. It could be objected that in the majority of developing countries, surplus thus appears in special tropical products – coffee, tea, cocoa, etc. – which are not foodstuffs of prime importance and, because of this, they are more subject to market fluctuations; furthermore, their domestic use is negligible. There is some truth in that. There are, however, also countries, like Argentina and Uruguay, which mainly produce foodstuffs of primary importance for export like wheat and meat – that is, products for which demand has been substantial, particularly in the last decades. These countries, however, although they had attained a quite high degree of development even before the First World War, did not start on a rapid development, though on the basis of their advanced agricultural production, they would have had the opportunity. Thus, agricultural 'surplus' is not sufficient to modernise the whole of the economy.

Up to now, historical experience has been examined from the viewpoint of the present problems of developing countries and their possible economic policies. It will be worthwhile to remember, in connection with historical experience, the analysis of Marx. He, of course, did not examine development from this viewpoint but from that of changes in relations of production, the emergence of capitalism from feudalism, the development of capitalist commodity production and the market, and the substitution of socialism for capitalism. He approvingly quotes one of his critics: 'For this it is quite enough, if he proves, at the same time, both the necessity of the present order of things, and the necessity of another order into which the first must inevitably pass over, and this all the same, whether men believe or do not believe it, whether they are conscious or unconscious of it.'[17]

However, Marx also states: 'the revolution called forth by modern industry in agriculture, and in the social relations of agricultural producers, will be investigated later on.'[18] He does not speak as if the development of agriculture (or the agricultural revolution) would have revolutionised industry, but rather presents the whole development process in its complex interrelations, in its long and diversified historical evolution. He also treats the transformation of agriculture, using the example of England, which he considers the classic form of development, though he indicates the differences in various countries, e.g. America and Italy.

In Marx' analysis the substance of the transformation of agriculture and industry is '. . . that [it] is based, so to say, on the fusing together of the isolated, independent labouring-individual with the conditions of his labour, is supplanted by capitalistic private property which rests on exploitation of the nominally free labour of others, i.e. on wages-labour.'[19]

The capitalist mode of production is more advanced than the old one, where forces of production stagnate or develop only slowly, owing to the fragmentation of land and the other means of production. The old system excludes the possibility of the division of labour; '. . . so also it excludes co-operation, division of labour within each separate process of production, the control over, and the productive application of the forces of Nature by society, and the free development of the social productive powers.'[20]

Of course, from the analysis of Marx it can be seen also that the growth of productive forces was no idyllic process either in industry or in agriculture. Transformation of agriculture is mainly dealt with in Chapter 24 of the first volume of *Capital*, where it is shown that the basis of the process of original accumulation was the expropriation of the peasant, his eviction from land, and the deprivation of great masses of people of their means of livelihood, throwing them on to the labour market as proletarians.

According to Marx, the beginning of the whole process long ante-dated the industrial revolution (which introduced quicker growth of the economy, the general application of machines, and large-scale investment). The immediate push had been given in England by the prosperity of the wool-manufactures in Flanders and the rise in wool prices at the end of the fifteenth century, as a result of which peasants were driven by landlords from the land and arable land was converted into pasture. The capitalist system, however, needed precisely this situation among the masses, with wage labourers from the countryside who, deprived of the means of production, could sell only their labour power and were forced to buy for money the goods necessary for their subsistence which they had previously produced themselves on small peasant farms. Transformation was slow: an independent peasantry was significant even at the end of the seventeenth century. The process was influenced by political strife and power relations, changes in the relative importance of plant cultivation and animal husbandry, the role of cottage industry and manufactures, the emergence of commercial and money capital, and other circumstances. Depriving the peasantry of land, the coercion of the exiled peasant population into the discipline of wage labour, and the reduction of the wages of agricultural and industrial workers took diverse forms.

Productivity increased in agriculture, and,

In spite of the smaller number of its cultivators, the soil brought forth as much or more produce, after as before, because the revolution in the conditions of landed property was accompanied by improved methods of culture, greater co-operation, and concentration of the means of production, etc., and because not only were the agricultural wage-labourers put under more intense strain, but the field of production on which they worked for themselves became more and more contracted.[21]

Transformation of agriculture took place at the expense of the peasant population, whose situation deteriorated more and more: 'In fact, usurpation of the common lands and the revolution in agriculture accompanying this, told so acutely on the agricultural labourers that, even according to Eden, between 1765 and 1780, their wages began to fall below the minimum, and to be supplemented by official poor-law relief.'[22]

By this time, the process of expropriating those who had earlier been independent peasant farmers, of liquidating the rural cottage industry, of the development of manufactures was well advanced. But for Marx, who analyses development primarily from the aspect of production relations, '. . . the period of the manufactures does not reach fundamental changes.' Manufactures rely on urban artisans and the rural cottage industry, and if they liquidate one form of the latter, they call it into being again in some other form, namely by creating small rural producers whose main occupation is industry (and who sell their products to the manufactures) and are part-time farmers. From the end of the fifteenth century, capitalist economy gained ground in the countryside, and the peasantry became ruined ever more quickly, but was always to be found again, since in England grain production or the breeding of animals predominated alternately, and peasant farming followed these fluctuations.

Modern Industry alone, and finally, supplies in machinery, the lasting basis of capitalistic agriculture, expropriates radically the enormous majority of the agricultural population, and completes the separation between agriculture and rural domestic industry, whose roots – spinning and weaving – it tears up.[23]

* * *

On the question of the arguments stressing the role of agriculture, *it is a wrong over-simplification of the historical experience of economic growth to state that it is only the growth of industry which, as if automatically, draws the other branches with itself;* it would also be especially incorrect to apply this to the present condition of the developing countries. Real interrelations are more complicated, and the growth of individual branches is affected by mutually 'generating' impulses. Beyond that, there is no definitely recognisable scheme of economic development that would be generally valid for every country; the transition from stagnation to an economically developed (industrialised) state varies according to historical periods, geographical regions and even by countries, depending on the relative importance of individual major – and, within those, minor – economic branches in starting the growth process. For instance, the textile industry had a greater role in English development than it had in Germany, while in the latter country railway building had an outstanding role. There are, however, several general phenomena too: for example, with economic growth the share of industry increases and that of agriculture diminishes in employment and in the production of national income.

Of course, *lessons of economic history – however interesting, useful and thought-provoking the analogies they offer – cannot be decisive for the present problems of developing countries.* Early capitalist development in England in the eighteenth century, and the following capitalist growth in Western Europe and Japan in the nineteenth century, in the era of free capitalist competition, cannot decide the possible strategies of developing countries in the power field of monopoly capitalism and the socialist world in the last third of the twentieth century.

HAS AGRICULTURE BEEN NEGLECTED IN THE DEVELOPING COUNTRIES?

One concealed or open critique of industrialisation efforts wants to find the cause of difficulties encountered in the past decade or two in the alleged overemphasis by the developing countries of the importance of industry and their neglect of agriculture, mainly in not investing enough in agriculture. In my opinion, this standpoint thus generally formulated is exaggerated and contradicts facts.

Agriculture, supposedly, has not obtained enough from total investment. According to a Hungarian author, Béla Kádár, agriculture in the developing countries received in the last two decades only 10–12 per cent of investment – that is, about the same proportion as in the advanced capitalist countries, where agriculture now plays a subordinate role. The neglect of agricultural investment has lead to a slow-down of agricultural growth already amounting to stagnation.[24]

In reality, agricultural production *increased* in the developing countries, according to F.A.O. data, by almost 3 per cent annually in recent years. At the end of the 1960s it was more than 70 per cent higher than the average before the war and 50 per cent higher than the average for 1948–53. This is hardly stagnation. However, *per capita agricultural production* almost stagnated, increasing only by 0·5 per cent in 15 years, owing to the quick growth of the population. Within that, there are significant differences between countries and even between major regions. In Asia, for example, *per capita* agricultural and food production increased, whereas in Africa it fell. The development of agriculture – as will be explained now – depends not only, and in certain periods not even mainly, on direct agricultural investment. But we have not succeeded in finding data whereby the developing countries could be shown to devote only 10–12 per cent of their total investment to agriculture. The national accounts statistics of the U.N. are not sufficiently detailed, and the F.A.O. reports have not contained such data. What is available, however, is a survey of the economic *plans* of the developing countries, based on a compilation by the U.N. (Obviously, the plan is not the same as realisation, but it at least reflects the intentions of the planners. We have no information that the implementation of agricultural investment would lag regularly and generally behind the average.) Let us now look at the data relating to industrial and agricultural investment.[25]

From among the twenty-seven developing countries in the survey, twenty-one published data on the rate of investment in agriculture. The proportions vary between 5 and 39 per cent, but only two countries have figures below 10 per cent. From one point of view, the percentage of government investments in agriculture is even more indicative of trends in economic policy. The figures vary from 5 to 45 per cent, with two of them below 10. No picture emerges of the developing countries regularly spending less on the development of agriculture than on manufacturing industry. Of course, the question to what extent the distribution of investments by sectors can be considered optimum or at least rational is a different matter.

Perhaps an even more characteristic picture is obtained of the weight of agriculture in the development plans from a compilation by the F.A.O. which groups the developing countries by the percentage share of government investment in agriculture. As can be seen from Table II/2, the picture is rather mixed: there are countries where this share is below 10 per cent, and others where it is above 30. At any rate, the number of countries with a share above 20 per cent in government investment is substantially greater than the number of those where the share of agriculture is lower than 10 per cent, although the latter group comprises such Latin American countries as Argentina, Brazil or Chile. Of course, it has to be considered again how large is the share of government investment within agricultural investment.

The view that in developing countries not enough is invested in agriculture also relies on a belief that agriculture is not a capital-intensive branch, that the capital/output ratio is lower in agriculture than in industry.[26] According to the F.A.O.,[27] however, the opinion that the capital/output ratio of agriculture is generally low cannot be supported by the analyses carried out. In fact, the capital/output ratio of agriculture – even if land is not accounted for – is generally higher than in industry, though it is lower than in public utilities (electricity supply or transport). However, this seems to be unequivocally so in the developed countries, where the capital-intensity of agriculture may be several times as high as that in industry, while in the developing countries – as will be explained later – there is a possibility of developing agriculture, at least in the initial period, in a less capital-intensive way.

It is obviously true that the agriculture of the developing countries has not developed satisfactorily, in comparison either to needs or to industrial growth. In many countries less care has been devoted to it than was necessary, but – at least in some of the developing countries – agriculture has in recent years come more to the fore. Whether agriculture was neglected because disproportionately more has been spent on industry is alone open to argument. In the following pages, however, we will be analysing not this question but the relations of agriculture and industry to each other and to the whole of economic growth.

2. *Development of Agriculture and Industry as Complementary and as Competitive Processes*

It is incorrect, or at least insufficiently exact, to contrast the development of industry and agriculture (or of other branches of the economy). Development of the various economic sectors has first of all a *complementary character*, growth of the one being a precondition and a cause of the other. It is true, of course, that they also compete for certain scarce resources, e.g. for investment, particularly in the short run, and to this extent it is necessary to contrast them. However, there are also resources in respect of which there is no such competition, since they cannot be used in any economic sector, and as regards these, contrasting is again unnecessary. Characteristic resources of this kind are land and – at least at the beginning of

Table II/2

SHARE OF PLANNED GOVERNMENT INVESTMENT SERVING AGRICULTURE

	Below 10%	10-14%	15-19%	20-29%	Above 30%
LATIN AMERICA	Argentina Brazil Chile Ecuador Honduras	Bolivia El Salvador	Haiti Mexico Panama Peru Trinidad Trinidad and Tobago Venezuela	Cuba Guatemala Jamaica	Nicaragua
ASIA	Japan Chinese People's Republic Malaysia: Singapore	Cambodia Taiwan Indonesia Laos Philippines Thailand	Burma South Korea Malaysia: Malaya South Vietnam	Ceylon India Nepal Malaysia: Sarawak Pakistan	
MIDDLE EAST				Afghanistan Iran Iraq Lybia Somalia Sudan U.A.R.	Cyprus Syria
AFRICA	Congo (Kinshasa) Sierra Leone Tanzania	Algeria Congo (Brazzaville) Gabon Ghana Kenya Malawi Nigeria	Ivory Coast Mauretania Senegal Uganda	Gambia Guinea Mali Mauritius Nigeria Tanzania: Tanganyika Zambia	Chad Madagascar Morocco Portugese colonies Tunisia

Source: F.A.O., *The State of Food and Agriculture,* 1965.

development – unskilled labour, which can almost always be used in agriculture while only to a limited extent and with varying efficiency in other branches.

It should be obvious that if initially a preponderant part of the population works in agriculture and the total population is unchanged or even growing, then in order to increase the proportion of non-agricultural workers in the population (i.e. for developing industry) it is necessary to raise productivity in agriculture so that agriculture can provide the other sectors with food (and perhaps with raw material for industrial processing). Of course, if food consumption declines, there is no need to increase productivity; but in developing countries this can hardly be the foundation of a growth policy. The need to increase agricultural productivity reveals nothing as yet about the relationship between cause and effect, about priorities to be applied in the development strategy; or whether it is the autonomous growth of agricultural production that makes development of other branches possible, or whether it is the growth of other branches that creates a market for the sale of agricultural surpluses; also whether it provides an impulse with the supply of industrial articles to increasing commodity production in agriculture.

Let us try to survey the most important interrelations systematically.

The role of any branch of the economy in economic growth may be viewed from the following aspects:

1. *Satisfaction of domestic needs* (consumption, current productive inputs and investments);
2. *Creation of a market*, partly within the branch, and partly for other branches of the economy – both for productive uses (further processing of materials, machinery, etc.) and for the consumption of the population employed in the branch in question;
3. *Savings* necessary for expanding production;
4. Production for *exports*, necessary as the countervalue of imports, and *substitution* of current imports or of new imports potentially necessary for economic growth;
5. *Creation of jobs, or the releasing of labour* for other sectors.

At the beginning of development, when the greater part of the population is engaged in agriculture, it is quite obvious that the role of agriculture is greatest, both for satisfying domestic supply and from the points of view of exports, of employing the labour force and, later, of releasing it; as well as – though not always or unequivocally – for savings necessary for expansion. On the other hand, the change in structure – that is, the relative decrease of the share of agriculture and the gradual growth of that of industry and the non-agricultural sectors in general – is a necessary condition of development.

GROWTH OF THE AGRICULTURAL AND THE NON-AGRICULTURAL POPULATION

In respect of the developing countries, we may start from the facts that population – the greater part of which is agricultural – rapidly increases, and that in its structure the shares of industry and the other non-agricultural sectors are growing, while that of agriculture is diminishing.

Let us examine the problem more closely, with the aid of a simple two-sector model interpreted from the viewpoint of the distribution of population by occupation.

The development of agriculture may be divided into two main stages. Let us call them here the *extensive* and the *intensive* stages. By this we mean now that only in the extensive stage does agricultural population increase in absolute terms, but its share relative to total population diminishes, while in the intensive stage it diminishes also in absolute terms. As will be proved later, the two stages differ not only from demographic viewpoints, but also in a rational development strategy, as well as in the character of relations between agriculture and industry.

Let total population at the start (in year o) be P_o, and agricultural production L_o, then in year t total population will be $P_t - P_o e\alpha t$ and non-agricultural population $L_t - L_o e^{\beta t}$ where α = population increase and β = the growth of non-agricultural population (both annual increases).

In year $t = o$ the ratio of non-agricultural population to total population is λ, and thus $L_o = \lambda P_o$. We assume that non-agricultural population is growing quicker than total population, that is $\alpha < \beta$.

Extensive growth of agriculture lasts until the growth of non-agricultural population absorbs the total increment of population, that is

$$\frac{dP_t}{dt} = \frac{dL_t}{dt}$$

after T years $P_o \alpha e^{\alpha t} = L_o \beta e^{\beta t} = \lambda P_o \beta e^{\beta t}$

$$\alpha e^{\alpha T} = \lambda \beta e^{\beta T}$$

$$ln\alpha + \alpha T = ln\lambda\beta + \beta T$$

$$(\beta - \alpha)T = ln\alpha - ln\lambda\beta$$

and the length of the extensive stage is

$$T = \frac{ln \dfrac{\alpha}{\lambda\beta}}{\beta - \alpha}$$

Accordingly, the length of the period when agricultural population grows in absolute terms (i.e. the 'extensive' stage) depends on the difference between and relative shares of the growth of total population and of non-agricultural population as well as on the initial proportions between total and non-agricultural population.

Let us analyse with the aid of the above fomula the length of the extensive period assuming certain realistic values of the parameters. The detailed calculations are to be found in Annexe II/1, but the comprehensive results are the following:

LENGTH OF THE EXTENSIVE PERIOD IN YEARS
($\lambda = 0\cdot2$)

β α	0·04	0·05	0·06	0·07	0·08
0·02	45·8	23·0	12·9	7·2	3·8
0·025	92·0	36·6	20·8	13·0	8·2
0·03	132·4	55·0	30·3	19·3	12·5

($\lambda = 0\cdot3$)

	0·04	0·05	0·06	0·07	0·08
0·02	25·64	9·5	2·6	—	—
0·025	48·8	20·5	9·4	3·9	0·7
0·03	91·6	34·6	17·1	8·9	4·5

Thus, agricultural population increases in absolute terms until a date determined by the growth of total population and of non-agricultural population. As shown by the data in the table, this period may be quite long. The ratio of non-agricultural population by the end of the extensive stage will be:

$$\frac{L_t}{P_t} = \frac{P_o \lambda e^{\beta t}}{P_o e^{\alpha t}} = \lambda \frac{e^{\beta t}}{e^{\alpha t}} = \lambda e^{(\beta - \alpha)t}$$

if

$$t = T = \frac{ln \dfrac{\alpha}{\lambda\beta}}{\beta - \alpha}$$

$$\frac{L_t}{P_t} = \lambda e \; ln \; \frac{\alpha}{\lambda\beta} = \lambda \frac{\alpha}{\lambda\beta} = \frac{\alpha}{\beta}$$

Thus, the ratio of non-agricultural to total population at the end of the period we call extensive depends only on the *ratios* to each other of the two growth rates. (Of course, the relation makes sense economically only if the growth rates α and β remain relatively stable for sufficiently long.) It is probably desirable that the share of non-agricultural population should not be too high at the end of the extensive stage – that is, the growth rate β should be high enough in comparison with population increase, expressing only in other forms that the extensive stage should not be too prolonged, the changes in structure should not take too much time.

The agriculture of developing countries is not uniform. To simplify greatly, from the organisational and technical points of view, the following types of farms may be distinguished:

Plantations. Specialised large-scale farms, producing generally with modern methods for export (frequently not foodstuffs necessary for the basic supply of the population). Thus, these are more a part of the industrially developed economies than of the developing country where they are situated geographically and whose soil, climate and cheap labour they use. Also as regards their supply with capital, their relations with the international capital market, their ways of management and the nationality of a greater part of their chief personnel, they are frequently large-scale plants belonging to the developed capitalist countries. Such are to be found mainly in Asia and Africa, but to smaller extent also in Latin America.

Latifundia. They are found mainly in Latin America, and are large-scale farms of feudal character. The methods of cultivation are usually not up-to-date, the owners try to invest as little as possible, withdrawing profits from the farms and transferring them frequently to a secure place (that is, abroad). Utilisation of the land is mediocre or poor. The range of production is broader, comprising also elements of subsistence economy.

Small-scale subsistence economy. The main purpose of production is to supply the family, that is, the agricultural population; production technologies are traditional, and not up-to-date. These farms are connected with commodity production and the monetary economy only to a small extent. This, however, does not exclude the possibility of investment and improvements based on investment. But investment is limited, because only the seasonal labour surplus can be used for simple constructions, or for improving the soil and conditions of cultivation. Even this possibility does not always exist, and for lack of proper markets – that is, because of the difficulty of selling surplus products and procuring industrial goods, etc., in exchange – even the proper incentives are missing.

Of course, the categories indicated above cannot be rigidly delimited, at least not from the viewpoint of every important criterion. The capitalist plantation and the feudal latifundium cannot be strictly delimited. The capitalist plantation is characterised by the fact that it produces for the market, mainly for export. This is also done in the latifundium, though, owing to lower productivity and a less specialised pattern of products, it is more self-sufficient. The majority of the small-scale subsistence farms do not produce mainly for the market, yet they have some market activity; and from the subsistence economy there gradually emerge the farms which, though not big as regards their land area, increasingly produce for the market. Yet the majority of the latter constitute rather part of the subsistence sector, owing to their size and much more because of the traditional technology of cultivation and within that, the labour-intensive character of investment.

For the purposes of further analysis we will simplify to the extent of neglecting the sector of agriculture in developing countries which produces for the market with modern, capital-intensive, large-scale methods. The conclusions hold as far as such simplification is permissible. In addition, we assume that the ratio of economically active to total population is the same in the agricultural and non-agricultural sectors. This assumption, for the most part, is likely to hold, but even a more exactly formulated assumption would not change the essential conclusions; only the calculations and the line of reasoning would become somewhat more complicated.

Let us, for the time being, disregard foreign trade, and examine the changes in the relations between agricultural and non-agricultural sectors as a function of changes in the ratio of agricultural population, assuming that agricultural population supplies the total population with food and other agricultural products at an unchanged level. The interrelations are shown in the table below.

The table illustrates eight successive stages of structural changes, assuming a gradual decrease in agricultural population from a proportion of 90 per cent to 20 per cent.

In order to supply the total population at an unchanged level, with the decrease in agricultural population and the growing ratio of non-agricultural population, there is a need to increase agricultural productivity and commodity production in agriculture. The growth rates of productivity and of commodity production change between two stages in an opposite sense.

If the difference between the growth rates of population increase and that of non-agricultural population $(\beta - \alpha)$ is 0·03, then the population of the non-agricultural sector will increase in about fifteen years from 20 to 30 per cent. Assuming an unchanged supply of agricultural products, agricultural productivity must grow in the same period by 14 per cent, that is, by about 1 per cent each year. This growth rate, however, significantly accelerates later; for example, the rate of non-agricultural population grows from 40 to 50 per cent in about eleven years, while productivity must grow at the same time by 20 per cent, that is by 1·7 per cent annually. Thus, if both population increase and that of the non-agricultural population are uniform – which of course is not necessarily so in reality – the requirement for productivity growth brought about by structural changes is accelerating, i.e. it is initially lower, owing to the initially large share of agricultural population, and it increases later. The growth of commodity production, however, will be quicker in the beginning, while diminishing later. According to the above example, in the first case it is about 2·75 per cent annually and in the second it is about 2 per cent.

Agricultural population, as percentage of Total	Total population, per agricultural population	Percentage increase over the preceding period		
		in agricultural productivity	in agricultural commodity production	in commodity output per agricultural worker
1	2	3	4	5
90	1·11	—	—	—
80	1·25	12	100	226
70	1·43	14	50	72
60	1·66	17	33	56
50	2·00	20	15	49
40	2·50	25	20	50
30	3·33	33	17	55
20	5·00	50	14	72

In the case of quick population increase and a low rate of non-agricultural population, the number of those employed in agriculture will first grow in absolute terms, initially rather quickly. If, for example, population growth is 2 per cent and the non-agricultural population increases at the annual rate of 5 per cent, while the share of the agricultural population is 80 per cent, in ten years the agricultural population will rise by almost a quarter. It is thus obvious, even without deeper analysis, that in *this stage agriculture does not primarily need labour-saving investment, since it could not be satisfactorily utilised.*

3. *Technology conforming to the Development of the Agricultural Population*

From the point of view of the main directions of development possibilities, the extensive period may be divided – logically, at least – into two sub-periods.[28]

Initially there are unused resources in agriculture which make it possible to produce more with more labour, even with the old technologies. This possibility depends mainly – though not exclusively – on population density, i.e. on whether new areas can be brought under cultivation within the framework of identical circumstances. As far as can be established, this situation does exist in various areas of Latin America and Black Africa, while – owing to greater population density – this is not characteristic of Asia.

However, because of the growth of agricultural population in absolute terms, this possibility sooner or later ceases, and production can be increased either not at all or only very little and with unchanged technology. Still being in the extensive stage, population increase continues and the large-scale application of labour-saving investment is not yet appropriate; rather, yield-increasing technology is needed. Finally, in the period when agricultural population is declining in absolute figures, i.e. in the intensive stage, labour-saving investment becomes necessary.

However, in the extensive development stage – rather, in its initial period – somewhat slower growth in productivity will be sufficient, while commodity production is to be increased more quickly. Therefore, *in agriculture itself* it is not greater capital investment that is needed but *the creation of circumstances in which agricultural producers are stimulated to increase production beyond their own needs and to ship the surplus to the market*. For that, considerable investment in infrastructure is needed (roads and general improvement of transportation) as well as the creation of supply in respect of both consumer goods and the simple tools and vehicles serving agricultural production, further to the bringing about of an adequate market organisation. *The substance of the matter is to utilise better the existing agricultural manpower*.

Later, still in the extensive stage of development, emphasis shifts to developing the methods of agricultural production in a non-capital-intensive way, improving agricultural technology, and providing improved techniques for increasing yields (fertilisers, plant-protecting agents). Therefore, an organisation is needed which is suitable for spreading and introducing the improved technology, and to this end a wide educational activity is also necessary, partly in close relationship with the agrotechniques and partly as general education to support the special training. This stage could be called the 'technical-intensive' stage of development, though the term is not sufficiently elegant or exact, since not only capital-intensive technology is meant. The later, intensive stage of development is obviously a labour-saving one, as it also requires capital-intensive investment, which now characterises the agriculture of the developed countries. Of course, most developing countries have not yet attained this stage.

Two remarks should be added. On the one hand, the means necessary for the development described (development of transportation, advanced agrotechniques, and specialised know-how) cannot be procured by an agriculture with subsistence economy by itself or with the aid of existing market relations; and the large-scale farms in the developing countries are not interested. This, therefore, is a task of society, or rather of government. In addition, the various measures are truly useful only if they are properly co-ordinated; this too is a problem for the society as a whole. Finally, at the beginning of development, industry and agriculture do not demand resources of the same character. Industry needs mainly capital, agriculture mainly agricultural techniques; therefore, development of the two sectors is of a complementary rather than of a competitive character. We will later revert to both viewpoints in detail.

EFFICIENCY OF LABOUR IN THE AGRICULTURE OF DEVELOPING COUNTRIES AND THE LABOUR-INTENSIVE DEVELOPMENT

In the above we have assumed that agricultural production can be considerably increased with the aid of labour-intensive methods, and without substantial investments – or, to be more exact, without substantial investment of fixed assets directly into agriculture, involving the purchase of machinery, etc.

Growth can be attained partly with a better utilisation of labour – both by improving current cultivation and by investment claiming only or mainly labour – and partly by improving technology in a way which promises quick returns (fertilisers, better species of seeds, etc.) – also, of course, by developing knowledge to the necesary extent. According to our assumption, it is under such conditions that the agricultural population, which decreases in relation to total population but increases in absolute terms, is able to supply the whole population with agricultural goods at least on an unchanged level. Obviously, the strategy of economic development greatly depends on whether this assumption holds or not. The problem must be examined in somewhat greater detail since the possibility of developing agriculture in a 'labour-intensive' way has by no means been unequivocally accepted.

According to several authors discussing the theoretical implications of economic growth in the developing countries, these countries are characterised by an 'unlimited supply of labour for the [capitalist] sector working with modern methods, and this can be traced back to the fact that in subsistence agriculture [but also in other, non-productive sectors] the efficiency [marginal productivity] of part of the labour force is zero, negligible, or even negative'.[29] In other words, neither does reduction of the agricultural labour force diminish output, nor does its increase raise it. This is, of course, also true if further growth of agricultural production is limited in absolute terms by other factors of production, notably by land. In this case part of the labour force is superfluous: its shadow price would be zero in a programming model.

With a less abstract reasoning, the argument denying the possibility of labour-intensive development in agriculture runs as follows. The application of labour-intensive technology, though feasible, has only a very limited scope. In the state where the preconditions are created for starting economic growth,[30] it may be sensible to utilise the possibilities still existing for raising productivity, by applying fertilisers, improving species, etc. But sustained growth necessitates a shift to labour-saving and more mechanised agriculture, which means that labour should be moved away from agriculture and capital drawn in instead. As long as a great part of the population remains in labour-intensive agriculture, cultivating small plots, the sector puts a brake on economic progress. Only a rapid shift to capital-intensive mechanised agriculture, and sufficient industrialisation to employ the labour released from agriculture, makes sustained economic growth possible. Thus, economic development is equal to transferring people from traditional agriculture into other sectors.[31]

Thus, according to this line of reasoning, the absolute decline in agricultural population and, in this context, mechanisation and capital-intensive development of agriculture (and the employment in industry of the population released) are indispensable conditions of economic growth.

But, as matters stand, there is hardly any possibility for such development in most of the developing countries. First of all, the necessary capital is lacking. We have already shown above how long the period of extensive agricultural development is (i.e. the growth of agricultural population) with various values of population increase and the rates of growth of the non-agricultural sector. If population grows at an annual 2 per cent and the non-agricultural population amounts to 20 per cent of the total at the start, then employment in the non-agricultural sector should be increased by about 10 per cent annually in order that the extensive period should end in twenty years. Growth as quick or even approximately as quick as this is, however, not characteristic of the developing countries. As can be seen from Table II/3, the growth of the adult male population in the non-agricultural sector was around 2–4 per cent annually according to the experience of the 1950s, and decline in agricultural population was exceptional, occurring only in small countries with a low population increase.

Table II/3

RATIO OF AGRICULTURAL EARNERS

	1950	1960	1965	1970
Developed capitalist countries	28·5	20·3	17·0	14·1
North America	13·0	7·2	5·4	4·4
Western Europe	31·0	23·5	20·1	17·2
Developing countries	75·9	71·3	68·4	65·2
Africa	84·7	80·5	78·1	75·5
Latin America	53·3	47·9	44·8	41·5
Near East	74·9	69·3	66·0	62·2
Asia and Far East	78·0	74·0	71·2	67·9
Other developing countries	84·2	80·4	77·6	73·8
Socialist countries	73·7	64·4	60·1	55·8
Asian Socialist countries	85·2	75·6	71·2	67·0
European Socialist countries	54·9	42·5	37·6	32·4

Source: W. Schulte, L. Naiken and A. Bruni, 'Projections of World Agricultural Population,' F.A.O., *Monthly Bulletin of Agricultural Economics and Statistics*, January 1972.

Otherwise, closer statistical investigation has not supported the thesis that labour supply would be unlimited in the developing countries, in the sense that the marginal productivity of labour was zero or very small. Relying on statistics covering about 3,000 small-scale farms, Indian surveys have established[32] that with growing farm sizes the yields per unit of area diminish, as do the labour used per unit of area and the 'utilisation' of land, the latter depending on the extent to which land is left idle and double harvests are customary.

Thus, in smaller farms specifically more labour is used, and with this labour greater agricultural production is achieved. In addition, wage labourers are employed not only on larger but also on smaller farms, though in smaller numbers. Thus, in the technical sense, even with the very high population density of India, and with its rather low agricultural level, the marginal productivity of labour cannot be zero or very low.

It may, however, be asked why, under such conditions, they do not employ more wage labourers, at least in the bigger farms? The answer is that under existing social conditions there is not a sufficient stimulus that would work in this direction; the answer is *not* that with existing technological conditions additional labour would not raise production.[33]

The approach which can conceive the development of agriculture only with a simultaneous reduction of agricultural population and substantial investment is probably also incorrect because it neglects the technological development which has taken place in agriculture in the last twenty or thirty years and forgets the non-technical but social circumstances that at present hinder the growth of production in the developing countries.

The question must be formulated in the following manner: can the efficiency of agricultural labour in the developing countries be raised in comparison to its present level for some time, while agricultural population is simultaneously growing, even without mechanisation and other capital-intensive investments which can be recovered only after a long time? Or, in other words, *can such industrialisation be carried on – for some time – where the total agricultural population is growing*? The problem has two closely interrelated bearings; one of them is technical, the other social, or rather political.

In technical relations, modern agricultural techniques have two main trends. Mechanisation is mainly of labour-saving character. The application of fertilisers and plant-protecting agents, the improvement of species and the introduction of complex cultivation methods require, on the one hand, additional labour input (if not always, as the application of plant-protecting materials may also save labour) and result in growing yields per unit of land. Of the two methods mechanisation is more capital-intensive and requires investment with returns over long periods. Yet, from the viewpoint of the developing countries, this can be more directly and easily applied. As a matter of fact, this technique emerged and got stabilised earlier, and, what is more important, it can be more easily transferred from one country to another, and adapted even under different conditions. A tractor, or some other machine produced in an industrially advanced country, can be applied without any greater difficulty even under the different climatic and other conditions of the developing countries, if the necessary skill to handle machines is present.

The 'biological' agricultural techniques, which serve mainly to raise yields, are relatively new even in the developed countries. It is important, however, that these can hardly be transferred without changes into different climatic and soil conditions, because under different climates and with different soil conditions, a quite different combination of cultivation methods, seeds and chemicals is needed. This can only retard, but it cannot exclude the successful application of yield-increasing methods, and the view which considers the *only* modern agricultural technique to be mechanisation cannot be called correct.

The emphasis, however, is on yield-increasing investments, with short pay-back periods – not on excluding mechanisation. There also exists mechanisation which satisfies these requirements. In Pakistan, for example, the ratio of production to agricultural population diminished from 1947/8 to 1957/8, since agricultural population increased by 2·4 per cent annually, while production only increased by less than 1 per cent. From 1958/9 to 1964/5 the tendency was reversed, and agricultural production increased by an annual 4 per cent. Three-quarters of the increase were due to the greater application of fertilisers and the spread of tube-well irrigation. Between 1961 and 1965, about 35,000 small tube-well units were put into operation. The success of this technology was quite unexpected, and no such development had been taken into account in the plans. For these irrigation works it was characteristic that with given price relations the cost of the pump and the diesel engine used was recovered very quickly, frequently in one year. Furthermore, the equipment was produced mostly in countryside workshops with primitive tools.[34]

Let us accept, for the time being, that the possibility exists – from the technical point of view – to develop agricultural production in a non-capital-intensive way. How, then, do we explain the well-known phenomenon that in a subsistence economy production is raised slowly, labour and the available technology not being properly utilised? There are authors who seek an answer in the sociological aspect. They believe that in developing countries people do not want to produce more – owing to the conditions of the African extended family, or to religious and other causes. They do not wish to change their way of living and their working conditions – an attitude which is 'non-rational'.

This explanation is hardly acceptable. It is, of course, obvious that backwardness, superstition and prejudices, and even more illiteracy and the low level of education that goes with it put a brake

on technological progress and on the application of modern production methods. However, the circumstance that in the developing
countries there is a general striving toward the cities and towards
the procurement of the industrial products characteristic of modern
life, and the eagerness to enrol children into schools, tend to refute
the thesis that these countries are underdeveloped mainly because of
the backward mentality of their population.

Growth of agricultural production is limited in the developing
countries by much more obvious social circumstances, mainly land
ownership. Again we are simplifying considerably by stating that
there are three dominant kinds of land tenure in the agriculture of
the developing countries: 1, lease (mainly in Asia); 2, the latifundia
(mainly in Latin America) and 3, the tribal (common) land (mainly
in Black Africa). Backward ownership relations hinder a proper
utilisation of the manpower which is relatively abundant. If the
lessee has to pay a high portion of his output for the use of the land,
precisely because of high population density, then stimulation to
harder work is smaller, and much too small to allow for the purchase of, for example, fertilisers. Under unfavourable conditions
he could even incur losses, since costs will exceed what remains after
payment to the landlord. The great latifundia, cultivated with extensive methods or even left idle, hinder even more the increase in
agricultural production, since on the one hand, land is not cultivated
properly, and on the other, labourers with no land of their own will
not work. The common land, too, is not without problems. In
Africa, some tribes own land which they do not use, but still do not
hand over to others for cultivation. Owing to common land ownership, the right of a family to the land cultivated by them is not stable
and this reduces the intensity of cultivation. Of course, there are
also progressive elements in the common ownership of land, insofar
as they promote or may promote the emergence of various co-operative forms of farming.

Therefore, the necessity of a land reform in the developing countries is generally acknowledged. The ownership relations are the
main, or one of the main, obstacles to developing agriculture in Asia
and Latin America, and on both continents laws have been passed
and other measures taken to implement land reform. However, as
far as can be established, development is slow in this respect, and not
very efficient. Especially little progress has been achieved in Latin
America (with the exception of Mexico) because the political influence of the landlords hindered the practical implementation of
reform.[35]

Thus in the majority of cases – according to generally accepted
opinion – a change in land ownership would help the growth of

agricultural production and productivity, and frequently it is an indispensable condition of any major step. This, most likely, would be promoted even with unchanged technology; the decisive problem is not technological, but the fact that change in ownership would promote precisely the application of modern agricultural techniques of the kind which do not require investment with a long recovery period. In order that this should come about, suitable prices and markets should also be created for the agricultural products, the consumer goods asked for by the agricultural population, and for the means of production. More exactly, this means that effective demand must emerge for agricultural products and a supply of industrial articles, and price relations must develop which promote the growth of production. This means a situation in which high prices have to be paid – in comparison to the prices of agricultural products – for the procurement of consumer goods, and it means that the growing agricultural utilisation of means of production of industrial origin (e.g. of fertilisers) should be profitable.

Logically, it should be obvious that the creation of such conditions (i.e. the development of agriculture) is possible initially with 'capital-extensive' methods. It is questionable, however, whether the actual experience of the agriculture of developing countries verifies this logical possibility. However, in my opinion this question can be answered in the affirmative. In the developing countries, agriculture – and within it food production – has regularly increased since the period before the First World War, and to a quite considerable extent. As can be seen from Annex IV (according to the data of F.A.O.), by 1964/5 the agricultural production of developing countries had increased by 70 per cent in comparison to the pre-war years, while against the average of 1948/53 the growth was 50 per cent. The trouble is that, owing to the great population increase, *per capita* agricultural production hardly increased, and that, owing to the deterioration in terms of trade, part of the advantages of growing production got lost for the developing countries in foreign trade.

This growth of production took place in such a way that in the meantime agricultural population also continued to grow – with some exceptions where the increase of total population was slow. In the last decade this growth rate varied; the rule was that in the developing countries agricultural population (more exactly, according to the available F.A.O. data, the adult male population) increased more slowly than total population, and the non-agricultural population more quickly.[36]

Again according to F.A.O. data, the average size of holdings increased only rarely in the developing countries; rather, in general it diminished–i.e., growing production was not the result of the spread of large-scale farms and concentration.[37]

It can also be stated unequivocally that the technological level of agricultural production in the developing countries has recently improved. According to Table II/4, fertiliser utilisation increased from 1952/7 to 1968/70 by 493 per cent, and the number of tractors increased by 84 per cent from 1960 to 1969. It is more difficult to establish unequivocally whether growth has taken place in the above outlined non-capital-intensive direction. True, fertiliser utilisation increased more quickly in percentage terms than the number of tractors, but the difference is not essential and even tractors more than doubled. Some conclusion may be drawn perhaps from the fact that in Asia, where population density is high, the amount of fertilisers used per unit of area has been four times that in Africa. In Africa, however, the number of tractors per hectare is one-and-a-half times that in Asia. If, again, the *growth* in the number of tractors from 1954 to 1963 is examined, this was much quicker in Asia than in Africa (though it started from a very low level).

4. *The Necessity of Rapid Industrialisation*

Thus, the increase of agricultural production and productivity is possible in the period when agricultural population is growing, with the capital-extensive methods outlined. It should be obvious that the food supply of the population must not decrease in this period either, thus ensuring that the productivity of agricultural labour must grow. According to what has been said above, this is possible without major direct agricultural investment, because it depends rather on social conditions, on market relations and on the growth of know-how.

In the long term, the key problem of economic growth is the change in the structure of employment. Let us assume that the growth in employment in the non-agricultural sector depends mainly on the growth of manufacturing and the latter mainly on investment. (The first assumption seems to be sufficiently realistic; the second is more doubtful, but may be accepted as a first approximation.) Let us assume that, at the start, the non-agricultural share of the population is 20 per cent, and the annual population increase is 3 per cent. In this case, according to the data presented earlier, and to Annex II/1, the extensive period will last thirty years if the growth rate of non-agricultural employment is 6 per cent annually. If, however – by our assumption, with a reduction in industrial invest-ment – this growth rate will be only 5 per cent on annual average, the extensive stage will last fifty-five years, and if the non-agricul-tural sector grows only at the annual rate of 4 per cent, the extensive period will last 132 years. This consideration alone *should put into the foreground a quick development of industry.*

Another argument seems to support this. It is easier to adopt and introduce modern technological methods in industry than in agriculture. In other words, the circumstances of industrial production are, on the whole, very similar in the developing countries to those in the industrialised ones – viewed, of course, only from a purely technical point of view and neglecting social conditions, infrastructure or training. Thus, apart from certain differences in raw materials, similar techniques can be employed in the developing countries as have been developed in the industrialised ones. The same equipment and the same methods can be used to produce synthetic fibres or steel in Africa and Asia as in Europe or North America.

Up-to-date agricultural technologies *appropriate to the endowments* of the developing countries are, however, not available, or they are only beginning to emerge. The most suitable species and agricultural techniques have been developed in the past in the conditions of the temperate zones and soils. Circumstances in the developing countries are mostly not very favourable for agricultural production. In the tropical areas the soil is generally poor. Successful application of fertilisers is a more complicated problem than in the temperate zone (for example, rain easily washes it away); the whole complex of agricultural techniques has not yet been worked out. Animal breeding is not sufficiently productive, green fodder contains little nutritive material, and the great heat is unfavourable for animal husbandry. Animals get sick more easily – a factor that does not only relate to animals, as the tropical monocultures are also sensitive to plant diseases.

All this does not mean that the conditions for agriculture in the developing countries are *permanently unfavourable* (it is well known that certain products grow only there, while others – e.g. oil seeds – have greater yields), but only that circumstances are *different*, and this raises doubts about belief that development in the agriculture of the developing countries is a simple task without technical problems. The agricultural techniques conforming to given circumstances cannot – as opposed to industrial technology – be directly taken over, but must be developed or adapted.

This obviously requires a longer time than the immediate takeover of industrial technology, if only because – owing to the biological character of the problem – a quite long time is needed for achieving results, and this needs well-trained specialists in the field in question – as it were, a special new discipline.

However, for as long as the proper agricultural technology has not been worked out, the technical efficiency (that is, efficiency indepen-

Table II/4

FERTILISER UTILISATION AND TRACTOR STOCKS

	Fertilisers in effective substance					Tractors			
	1945/6	Average of 1952/3 to 1956/7	Average of 1968/9 to 1969/70	Increase from 1952/3 to 1969/70	Utilisation per hectare of arable land 1969/70	1960	1969	Increase from 1969 to 1970	Number of tractors per 1,000 hectares of arable land in 1969
	million tons			per cent	kg.	thousands		per cent	units
Western Europe	3·2	7·5	16·0	213	162	3,093	5,206	168	51·4
European socialist countries	0·8	3·4	14·6	430	54	1,444	2,609	180	9·3
North America	2·7	5·9	25·0	254	70	5,265	5,415	103	24·6
Oceania	0·4	0·7	1·6	228	32	337	428	127	9·1
Japan	0·1	1·1	2·3	209	410	129e	396e	307e	21·9e
DEVELOPED COUNTRIES*a*	7·2	15·4	35·5	237	94	8,824	11,445	129	29·6
Latin America	0·2	0·5	2·5	500	21	355	625	176	4·9
Far East	—	0·6	4·2	700	13	56	129	230	0·5
Near East	—	0·2	1·0	500	25d	76	173	228	2·3
Africa*b*	0·1	0·1	0·6	600	3	84	122	145	0·7
DEVELOPING COUNTRIES	0·3	1·4	8·3	593	12	571	1,049	184	1·6
TOTAL*c*	7·5	20·2	61·3	303	44	10,891	15,208	139	10·6

Source: F.A.O., *The State of Food and Agriculture,* Rome, 1971.
a. Including Israel, South Africa and Kuwait; *b.* Excluding South Africa; *c.* Including China; *d.* In case of areas cultivated several times a year, calculated for the area reaped. Converted to arable land, this means 13 kg.; (*e*) Japan, South Africa, Israel.

dent of price relations) of the factors of production will be lower in the developing countries. A comparison has been made, for example, of the additional yield resulting from fertiliser utilisation in rice production in India and in the U.S.A. It has turned out that, even if calculated at identical Indian prices, in the U.S.A. three times as much fertiliser per hectare is economically efficiently used as in India (45 kg. per hectare in the U.S.A. and 17 kg. in India). The net gain from the application of fertilisers, that is the difference between the increment in the price of output and that of fertilisers used, is three to four times the Indian figure in the U.S.A. (both at identical prices). If the calculation is made at actual prices, further differences arise, since in the U.S.A. the price of fertilisers is lower and that of rice is higher. Under such conditions, the efficiency of the use of fertilisers grows in the U.S.A. to four times that of India, and the net gain to eight to ten times.[38]

It cannot be justified to assume, even from the point of view of the training of the labour force, that the development of agriculture would be an easy or simple task. From this viewpoint it is difficult to compare industry with agriculture and, for lack of sufficient and reliable data, it is hardly possible to compare in quantitative terms and show the costs and the benefits of training labour adequately in the one and in the other sector. Of course, in agriculture the labour is on the spot, well versed in traditional methods of cultivation, but its skill is certainly insufficient for a successful application of new intensive methods, which are necessary for development. The knowledge of traditional methods is not exclusively an advantage; those who possess it find more difficulty in abandoning the old methods and accepting the new ones. Industrial production is new for the majority of the labour to be trained, who have to become acquainted with and used to circumstances foreign to them and to the discipline required by industry, but here old-established methods do not hinder acceptance of the new technology. By its concentrated character, the industrial organisation aids training, it leads and checks by itself, as it were, particularly in the case of continuous production processes.

In the farms with less concentrated localisation, particularly in the small peasant farms, there is no such automatic leadership and control. Of course it is obvious, in the present and even in the fore-seeable future conditions of the developing countries, that *on average* greater skill is needed in industry than in agriculture, involving also longer training.

For the developing countries it is obviously general education and the overcoming of illiteracy that is the central task and not yet special industrial or agricultural education; this is equally necessary for both sectors. In addition, development of industry and training

C

for skills in industry is useful also for the labour supply of agriculture, because it helps to train manpower with some practice in the handling of modern techniques, particularly machinery, while the agricultural labourer applying more advanced agricultural methods (and knowing how to read and write) can be more easily re-trained for industrial jobs. Thus, also from the viewpoint of vocational training, industry and agriculture are not only competitive but complementary.

To sum up: *In economic development the individual branches mainly help, stimulate and promote development mutually,* and the competition for scarce resources is of only secondary importance. As regards the relation to each other of industry and agriculture in the developing countries, *such development may achieve success which results in maximum stimulation and minimum restriction.* From the viewpoint of agriculture this would mean a development which initially has, as far as possible, a labour-intensive and capital-saving character.

The key to sustained long-range development is a change in the structure of the economy which reduces the relative share of agriculture and increases that of industry. The growth of industry is necessary in order to supply the population and the other branches of the economy with industrial goods to diversify the economy and increase its independence (this does not of course, mean, autarky, but its reverse: the expansion of foreign trade). The high ratio of agricultural population is characteristic of the developing countries, together with a quick population increase. It follows that agricultural population continues to grow, even with rapid industrial development, for a considerable time.

An increase in agricultural productivity due to structural change is necessary even on an unchanged level of supply. This is possible also with labour-intensive and relatively capital-saving methods, if agricultural technology relies mainly on chemical and biological methods and if the agricultural population is provided with proper (material and other) incentives. A significant growth in agricultural productivity – i.e. the modernisation of agriculture – is possible also without labour-saving investment with long pay-off periods, though investment in infrastructure (e.g. for developing transportation) is necessary and this tends to be capital-intensive.

This kind of agricultural development is in many places hindered by the existing relations of tenure, partly because a considerable part of the agricultural population cannot obtain land, or it can do so at such a high rent as does not stimulate the raising of production sufficiently. In addition, strata with important economic and political power do not support the growth of peasant commodity production, since this would create competition for their own products, and would increase wages to be paid because of the increase of employment and standards of living on the land.

Even without detailed discussion, it can be established that for the development outlined, industry has to supply: (*a*) consumer goods, (*b*) simple and cheap agricultural implements, (*c*) vehicles (partly simple ones, drawn by animals), (*d*) chemicals (fertilisers, plant protective agents), and, as far as this can be considered as an industrial activity, (*e*) better species of seeds.

From the viewpoint of developing domestic industry, consumer goods, simple agricultural implements and simple vehicles can be considered first. The production of more complicated vehicles can presumably be reckoned with only in a later stage of development or in a bigger country, while the domestic production of fertilisers in bigger countries and the solution of the problem for smaller countries through some kind of international co-operation, is urgent for development of agriculture.

The development model described is obviously a simplified one and does not properly account for several circumstances. But to account for these is possible only in the case of a given country, on the one hand, and on the other, this would not change the substance of the interrelations. It is, for example, not sufficient to supply the population with agricultural products on the old level, but the level of nutrition must be raised in most of the developing countries, not only from the social point of view, but also in order to raise the productivity of labour. From this, however, it only follows that agricultural productivity must be raised more quickly than if an unchanged level of supply were assumed. There are also differences in respect of the land area that can be newly drawn into cultivation; this is small in Asia, but considerable in Africa and Latin America. What has been said is modified by this fact only in the latter case: namely, if new land is available, agricultural production can be increased in a labour-intensive way, not only by applying chemical and biological methods, but also by drawing new land into cultivation. Finally, foreign trade can change the picture to a certain extent since, in the case of favourably utilisable (and saleable) natural resources, this makes it possible to use more capital and imports. In certain countries it may even happen that – because of an unfavourable distribution of natural resources, and particularly because of the limited development potential of certain agricultural branches – a sizeable trade in agricultural products and even considerable food imports must be reckoned with. But not even these circumstances change the substance of the matter – namely, that agriculture must be first developed in a labour-intensive manner and with a corresponding development of industry, which is made possible partly by this type of agricultural growth.

*   *   *

It seems that the practical experience of recent years supports what has been explained above. Of course, it is not easy to recognise the new tendencies which have not yet established themselves finally and unequivocally, and – owing to the great number and diversity of the developing countries – examples could probably be quoted to support several views. From the viewpoint of agricultural growth, however, the case of India should be considered as particularly important. First, a considerable part of the total population of the developing countries of the world lives there, and secondly, the conditions for agricultural development are particularly difficult in India – among other reasons, because of the high population density. It may be stated without exaggeration that if the problem of agricultural development could be solved in India, it could also succeed in other countries.

The expected tendencies of Indian agriculture are not uniformly judged by specialists. Lately, however, several have expressed the opinion that, as against the 3 per cent average growth in the 1950s and the 2·5 per cent in the 1960s (not counting the drought years of 1964/5 and 1965/6), for the next ten to fifteen years a 3·5 per cent annual growth rate at least can be expected in Indian agriculture, in view of the technologies introduced and implemented, and relying on the resources certain to be available. The potential growth is related from the point of view of production technology mainly with the spread of the use of fertilisers and new seeds and their successful application.

In 1962–5 450,000 tons of fertilisers were used annually (calculated in effective substance), while by 1966–7 this had increased to almost 900,000 tons, and in 1967–8 it presumably amounted to 1,300,000 tons, while in the next years it is expected to grow by 1,000,000 tons each year.

Species of rice have been introduced and spread which yield an increase of 40–100 per cent with the same amount of fertilisers, such species make better use of the fertilisers that are applied in greater quantities. The irrigated area also increased, but development here is not on a scale comparable to that of fertilisers and seeds.

The annual 3·5 per cent growth is more than the increase of population and would ward off the danger of famine, but a growth rate of at least 4–4·5 per cent is necessary for India not to be compelled any more to import food in considerable quantities. It seems that the raising of the resources that can be made available would solve this without major difficulties. With a quicker increase in fertiliser supply, for example, agricultural production could still be considerably boosted. Under present conditions, peasants would gladly use more fertilisers, since this is profitable for them, and fertiliser utilisation in India per hectare is only 10 per cent of the U.S. level and only 1 per cent of the Japanese level![39]

REFERENCES

1. Colin Clark, *The Conditions of Economic Progress*, Macmillan, London; St. Martin's Press, New York, 1957 and Jean Fourastier, *Le grand espoir du XXᵉ siècle*, Presses Universitaires de France, Paris, 1952.
2. Albert J. Robinson, 'Can Economic Growth be Based on Agriculture?' *Indian Economic Journal*, 1966, No. 4, p. 553.
3. Op. cit., p. 548.
4. For details see Annex II/3.
5. Robinson, op. cit., p. 341.
6. *Yearbook of National Accounts Statistics, 1963*, U.N., New York.
7. *The Growth of World Industry, 1938–1961: National Tables*, U.N., New York, 1963.
8. B. F. Johnston and J. W. Mellor, 'The Role of Agriculture in Economic Development', *American Economic Review*, September 1961.
9. *Processes and Problems of Industrialization in Underdeveloped Countries*, U.N., 1954, p. 3.
10. Norman S. Buchanan and Howard S. Ellis, *Approaches to Economic Development*, New York, 1955.
11. Op. cit., p. 149. Italics are mine.—G. C.
12. *African Agricultural Development*, U.N.–F.A.O., New York, 1966, p. 73.
13. Buchanan and Ellis, op. cit., pp. 128 and 130.
14. Op. cit., p. 138.
15. Simon Kuznets, *Modern Economic Growth: Rate, Structure and Spread*, Yale University Press, 1966.
16. Op. cit., pp. 88–9.
17. Karl Marx, *Capital*, Vol. I. Foreign Languages Publishing House, Moscow, 1961, p. 18.
18. Ibid., p. 504.
19. Ibid., p. 762.
20. Ibid., p. 762.
21. Ibid., p. 745.
22. Ibid., p. 726–7.
23. Marx, op. cit., p. 748.
24. Béla Kádár, *A gazdasági növekedés és az importhelyettesitőr gazdaságpolitika a fejlett országokban* (Economic growth and import-substituting economic policy in the developing countries), Budapest, Közgazdasági Szemle, 1965.
25. See Chapter IV, Table IV/3.
26. According to the article by Béla Kádár, quoted above, agriculture requires smaller investments, but a longer gestation period.
27. F.A.O., *The State of Food and Agriculture*, 1963.

28. See M. Perkins and L. Witt, 'Capital Formation, Past and Present', *Journal of Farm Economics*, May 1961, p. 333.
29. See W. Arthur Lewis, *Economic Development with Unlimited Supply of Labour*, The Manchester School, May 1954.
30. When preparing the 'take-off' in the Rostowian sense.
31. For details see Benjamin Higgins, *Economic Development*, W. W. Norton, New York, 1959, p. 454.
32. Morton Paglin, ' "Surplus" Agricultural Labour and Development: Facts and Theories', *American Economic Review*, September 1965.
33. It should be observed that in the economic sense – and according to the analysis by W. A. Lewis – for an 'unlimited supply of labour' it is sufficient that labour supply should exceed demand for labour, with a very low and on the whole stable wage level. The zero marginal productivity in the technical sense, though assumed, is not a necessary condition.
34. Walter P. Falcon, 'Agricultural and Industrial Interrelationships in West Pakistan', *Journal of Farm Economics*, December 1967.
35. For details see F.A.O., *The State of Food and Agriculture*, Rome, 1965, pp. 168–77.
36. See Table II/3.
37. See Annex II/2.
38. R. W. Herdt and J. W. Mellor, 'The Contrasting Response of Rice to Nitrogen in India and the United States', *Journal of Farm Economics*, February 1964.
39. Nathan M. Koffsky, 'The Food Potential of Developing Nations', *Journal of Farm Economics*, December 1967.

III

SOME PROBLEMS OF INDUSTRIAL DEVELOPMENT STRATEGY IN DEVELOPING COUNTRIES

As regards the most expedient methods of industrialisation in the developing countries, both theoretical ideas and practical methods show a great deal of divergence. It will be worthwhile to note that practice, influenced by the complex reality, is in fact more uniform than are theoretical views, which frequently consider only a single aspect of reality. In this chapter, three key problems of industrialisation strategy will be dealt with. An answer will be sought concerning the priorities in the course of industrialisation in respect of the following three pairs of alternatives:

(*a*) small-scale industries (handicrafts, cottage-industries) *versus* factory-type industries, in other words small-scale *versus* large-scale plants;

(*b*) labour-intensive *versus* capital-intensive technologies;

(*c*) import substitution *versus* export promotion.

There are, of course, other problems of industrial development strategy under discussion. One of these problems, affecting all the rest, has been dealt with in the preceding chapter, namely the problem of 'industry or agriculture'. A familiar problem, that of the preference for light or heavy industry, the production of means of production or that of consumer goods, will not be dealt with here in detail. Chapter IV discusses some aspects of the matter, namely the tendencies that appear in the plans of the developing countries in respect of the priority given to light or heavy industries. Chapter V treats the interrelations in somewhat greater detail, namely from the point of view of the development of the branch structure of industry.

It could perhaps be mentioned here that a distinction between the light and heavy industries – in particular the preference given to heavy industry – was justified in the Soviet Union at the beginning of industrialisation. The opinion was held that, in view of the politically hostile environment, it was necessary to increase the defence potential quickly and to create the technical basis of independent economic growth even if this meant sacrifices. However, in the conditions of the developing countries the problem emerges differently. The world situation in which they find themselves is different, the existence of the socialist countries is a help to them, and economic co-operation with the capitalist countries is, for the most part, close also. Therefore, other circumstances can and should be taken into account. There is neither the need – nor in most cases the possibility – to create immediately a heavy industrial basis enabling autonomous development. The advantages of the international division of labour can be better used, and industry can be more easily developed acccording to internal needs and resources, and the internal and external markets. In spite of this, as will be shown, heavy industry increased faster in the developing countries than did light industry, and this tendency will continue in the future.

The importance of the relative weight of government-owned industry and that in private ownership, as well as the role of foreign capital in industrialisation, are also no doubt central problems, but a thorough treatment of these would transcend the framework of the present study. In addition, the present situation, as well as the development possibilities and restrictions in this respect, are so different in the various developing countries that little could be said about this problem in general that would hold for all developing countries and that would be supported by practical experience. We shall revert to the problem in Chapter IV in connection with the role of government in industrial development.

The complex problems to be dealt with here in detail are *real* problems of industrial strategy in the developing countries; they differ to a greater or lesser extent from the problems to be met with in the industrialisation of developed capitalist or of the socialist countries.

In practice, of course, matters emerge in a more complex form than is indicated by the above pairs of contrasts. First, it is true also in this case, as with the choice between industry and agriculture, that the real problem does not emerge in the form that one alternative or the other must be selected exclusively – whether industry or agriculture should be developed – since both must be developed. The real problem is how to develop them, at what speed and by observing what priorities. Obviously one cannot develop only light industry or only heavy industry, although it is conceivable that circumstances can arise under which it will be expedient to develop manufacturing industry at the expense of handicrafts, or to introduce capital-intensive technologies, not only in addition to labour-intensive ones, but instead of them.

The fundamental problems of development strategy can be traced back to the fact that it is impossible to develop everything simultaneously, and it is therefore necessary to establish *priorities*. To formulate a development strategy, i.e. to establish priorities, is thus indispensable – mainly for planning, but priorities will prevail even in the most liberal market economy under the selective effect of customs, taxation and credit policies. Of course, concrete economic decisions necessitate concrete investigations, but to approach the problems of principle in development strategy, as a first approximation, in the perspective of the above contrasted pairs of concepts, is justified precisely in order to recognise the most important moments.

It must be said in advance that this examination is made difficult by certain circumstances. Some elements of development strategy are not independent of each other or of the answer given to the problems of industry versus agriculture; they cannot be chosen freely. It would be difficult, for example, to develop heavy industry with labour-intensive technology and as a small-scale industry (though we know there have been experiments of this kind). Therefore, one of the decisions taken – namely the development of heavy industry – will in practice also decide that capital-intensive technology and large-scale production must be chosen. It would seem that the single major experiment deviating from this pattern – the Chinese trend of creating 'people's furnaces' – has not met with success.

1. *Small-scale* versus *Manufacturing Industries*

In the industrialised countries the *large-scale plant* is the characteristic, dominant but by no means exclusive form of industrial organisation. Industrial production existed even before the industrial revolution; however, it operated mainly in small workshops, was directly coupled with agriculture and was built upon handicraft methods: traditional techniques inherited from generation to generation, based on human or animal power, with the transformation of materials being carried out by simple tools. Larger plants, major shipyards, and the use of hydro-energy were exceptional in comparison with small-scale production and handicraft methods.

In the advanced countries, factory-type industry with larger plant sizes and scientifically based, continuously developing technology has almost entirely supplanted the small-scale forms in the production both of consumer goods and of materials and tools. Today's most dynamic, technologically sophisticated industries have not evolved at all from traditional small-scale technologies. Production of electrical energy, electronic equipment and plastics have developed under the conditions of large-scale production right from the

C*

start. Small-scale production is exceptional, and is maintained in order to secure the undisturbed supply of certain goods of artistic value (for example, needle-work and fancy leather goods).

However, small-scale industries have not entirely disappeared, but they have changed in character, or rather *a new small-scale industry has come about which is a product of, and depends on, large-scale industry. Its main functions are servicing and repairing* (of cars, radio, TV, buildings, etc.). To a smaller extent, it is performing special operations or turning out parts for the large-scale plants as a *sub-contractor.* This kind of *modern* small-scale industry is characteristic of a developed economy, but production of final products in this sector is not significant.

It is easier to state the above in general terms than to prove it statistically. The line dividing small-scale industries from factories is not rigid, nor can the limits be traced by a single exclusive criterion. One criterion is, naturally, the manpower employed. But the value produced and the technology applied must also be taken into account. With highly productive equipment a smaller staff can produce a great deal. In this case a plant employing fewer people can be more like a factory in character than another one where more people are employed but produce less with simpler equipment. Since it is difficult to measure and compare among various branches the value produced and, particularly, the capacity of equipment, the size of the plants is usually shown only on the basis of a single criterion, namely the staff employed, and the division between small-scale industry and factories is made on this basis. It is a usual though not an exclusive procedure to consider the plants employing at least ten people as factories and, consequently, those with 1–9 people as small-scale industry (in the U.S.A., beginning with the late 1950s, those employing 1–19 people). Statistical data are available for several countries in this form. If this classification is accepted, it may be stated that the share of small-scale industries is about 2–8 per cent of manufacturing in the developed countries but there is not very close relationship, within these margins, with industrial or economic development levels. In West Germany small-scale industries employed, in 1965, 2 per cent of the labour force in manufacturing, while in the U.S.A. (see Table III/1) the corresponding figures in 1954–67 were 7·7–5·6 per cent, while if similarly classified the West German figure would rise to 3 per cent.

It seems that in the developed countries the weight of small-scale industries within manufacturing is quite stable over the course of time, even if measured with the aid of various indicators.

The situation is somewhat different as regards the factory-type 'small' plants which, in a developed industrial environment, are not

Table III/1
WEIGHT OF SMALL-SCALE INDUSTRIES IN THE MANUFACTURING INDUSTRY OF THE U.S.A.
(*enterprises employing 1–9 persons*)

Year	Number of enterprises	Employment	Wages	Value added	Investment
1954	68·4	7·7	6·0	6·1	10·6
1963	67·6	7·3	6·0	5·9	10·7
1967	65·0	5·6	4·9	5·1	8·6

Source: Statistical Abstracts of the United States, 1971.

rigidly separated from small-scale industries. These small points employ up-to-date equipment and technology but do not reach large-scale dimensions in terms of employment, capital, or production value. We shall revert to their role and importance in both the developed and the developing countries.

In the developing countries the role of the traditional handicrafts, small-scale and cottage industries, is significantly greater (though gradually diminishing). The majority of those employed in the manufacturing industries are working in such plants. (In the developing countries we consider the plants employing less than twenty people to be 'small-scale'.) For detailed figures, see Table III/2.

In the small-scale industries of the developing countries, traditional handicraft technologies dominate. In India only 3 per cent of the plants employing less than twenty people used mechanical energy in 1954; in Taiwan this ratio was 34–38 per cent in plants with 1–9 people and 90 per cent in those with 10–19 people (1961). Between the two world wars many of these smaller plants were not power-operated, not even in comparatively advanced Japan. Two other dominant characteristics of the cottage industries are the employment of mainly family labour and the location of plants in the countryside. In 1955, some 70 per cent of about 16,000,000 people employed in Indian manufacturing were working in small-scale industries. (By small-scale industries we mean here power-operated plants employing less than ten people or hand-operated ones employing less than twenty.) Within the 70 per cent, 60 per cent were employed in plants based mainly on family labour; and 50 per cent of the total were employed in small-scale plants using mainly family labour and situated in the countryside. According to estimates in large-scale plants, the value of output exceeded that of the small-scale and cottage industries (but not their staff) only in 1958–9.[1]

Table III/2
SHARE OF SMALL-SCALE (COTTAGE) INDUSTRIES
IN MANUFACTURING EMPLOYMENT
IN SELECTED COUNTRIES

Country	Year	Percentage share
India	1950–1	79·5
	1954	78·1
	1955	76·8
Ceylon	1952	83·2
Philippines	1956	84·3
	1957	82·9
Taiwan	1961	47·1
Japan	1930	56·1
	1940	37·3
	1952	34·0
	1958	30·1

Source: Shigeru Ishikawa, 'Choice of Techniques and Choice of Industries', *Hitotsubashi Jornal of Economics*, Vol. 6, No. 2, February 1966, p. 16.

It is highly characteristic of South-East Asia that a great part of those employed in manufacturing are working in countryside plants of cottage industry character, not using any mechanical energy. More up-to-date, large-scale plants are probably of greater importance in the industrially more advanced Latin American countries, perhaps even in the industrially less developed African ones, but data on the latter are less accessible. In general, small-scale handicrafts play an important part in the developing countries, within the existing and rather backward manufacturing industries, in comparison with the industrial countries. The share of the small-scale industries shows a rather close correlation with the degree of economic development.

This interrelation is well illustrated by Table III/3 showing the distribution of employment by categories of plant size in fourteen countries of Latin America and in Central America as a group. The source used in this case considers the plants employing 1–4 persons as cottage industries and the others as factories. It can also be seen in this table that small-scale industry has relatively greater importance in the more backward than in the more developed countries. If we want to come closer to the classification employed in the foregoing and add up the categories employing 1–19 persons, it turns out that in the first (more developed) group, 50·7 per cent, in the second 54·5 per cent, and in the third (most backward) group 82·6 per cent of the total employed are working in plants with a staff of less than twenty.

Owing to its different functions, the distribution by branches of small-scale industries is also different in the developing countries from that in the developed ones. Considering the distribution of those employed in the small-scale industries, we find in the developing South-East Asian and Latin American countries (for which more detailed data are available) that mainly the food and clothing industries (including footwear) are predominant. The importance of the textile industry varies: it is highly important in India, Burma and South Korea, with a lower share in the other South-East Asian countries. In developed countries, small-scale industries are important in the sectors connected with construction and the equipment of homes (wood processing, glassware and ceramics industries). Their share in the food industry is also considerable (though lower than in the developing countries), and in the metal-working industries it is even higher. As against the developing countries, the significance of the clothing industry within small-scale industries is much smaller.

EFFICIENCY OF SMALL-SCALE AND LARGE-SCALE ORGANISATIONS
IN THE USE OF RESOURCES

The question now arises as to whether it is expedient to build upon the existing small-scale industries in the developing countries, develop them, and create new small-scale plants, or whether it is not more desirable to build large-scale plants; how, too, can these two approaches be expediently combined?

There are – or were in the past – both economists and practical experts who would emphasise the advantages of the small-scale plant over the large-scale one, explaining that these advantages more than outweighed the disadvantages of 'smallness' in several fields (e.g. their lower productivity). The alleged main advantages of the small-scale plant are the following:

(a) it is relatively less capital-intensive;
(b) it is more flexible and reacts more quickly and easily to special requirements, and can therefore operate side by side with

Table III/3

DISTRIBUTION OF EMPLOYMENT BY PLANT SIZE IN THE MANUFACTURING INDUSTRY OF LATIN AMERICAN COUNTRIES, 1960

| | Cottage industry | Factories | | | | | Total of manufacturing |
| | | Categories by staff employed | | | | | |
	1–4	5–19	20–49	50–99	100+	Factories total	
Group I:							
Argentina	42·0	9·2	7·6	7·6	33·7	58·0	100
Brazil	43·9	9·0	6·7	6·2	34·2	56·1	100
Mexico	35·7	10·3	7·7	7·7	38·6	64·3	100
TOTAL	41·3	9·4	7·2	7·0	35·2	58·7	100
Group II:							
Chile	46·3	8·1	8·1	6·4	31·1	53·7	100
Columbia	66·3	6·4	5·1	4·0	18·2	33·7	100
Peru	61·6	8·8	6·1	4·3	19·2	38·4	100
Uruguay	28·8	16·6	11·2	7·8	35·6	71·2	100
Venezuela	40·0	21·7	11·5	4·1	22·7	60·0	100
TOTAL	54·2	10·3	7·4	4·9	23·2	45·8	100
Group III:							
Bolivia	87·6	4·3	2·2	1·6	4·3	12·4	100
Central America	63·5	9·6	7·6	5·9	13·4	36·5	100
Ecuador	80·0	6·8	3·6	2·8	6·8	20·0	100
Haiti	82·2	5·9	3·0	3·0	5·9	17·8	100
Panama	42·3	19·2	11·6	7·7	19·2	57·7	100
Paraguay	78·0	9·8	3·7	2·4	6·1	22·0	100
TOTAL	74·8	7·8	4·9	3·7	8·8	25·2	100
LATIN AMERICA TOTAL	47·9	9·4	7·0	6·2	29·5	52·1	100

Source: Economic Bulletin for Latin America, U.N., New York, 1967, Vol. XII, No. 1, p. 89.

the large-scale plants as a subcontractor, complementing the latter;

(c) it is better suited to launching new products, starting on a small scale and expanding in case of success, whereby the risks involved are reduced;

(d) it can easily adapt itself to the local market and local sources of raw materials, and may thus achieve savings in transport costs; this promotes decentralisation and the desirable location of industry in rural areas;

(e) it helps to mobilise savings which would not be coming forward – or at least not in *industrial* capital formation in the case of large-scale plants;

(f) finally, it is more efficient than the large-scale plant in utilising and training certain skilled labour since, on the one hand, it does not need highly qualified labour, and, on the other hand, it can train a certain number of skilled workers as well as management personnel.

Earlier, some authors used these arguments indiscriminately as relating both to the handicrafts (cottage industries) based on traditional technology and to the mechanised small-scale and medium-sized plants. Buchanan and Ellis argue in detail in favour of the *continuous and gradual* advantages inherent in the development of industrial production, and do not distinguish the cottage industry from the small-scale industry employing modern technology. It will be worthwhile to quote in detail some ideas from their reasoning. According to them, the beginning of industrialisation is hardly distinguishable from the developing and modernising of agriculture. This kind of industrialisation frequently appears in the form of a plant serving the processing of agricultural products, with the aim of preventing deterioration of the products and making possible a more diversified cultivation of the land. In their opinion, human resources should be used where they 'naturally' occur, that is, in the countryside, avoiding the time-lag, social problems and investment requirements caused by the migration of population to the towns. Although the large-scale industry of the towns is a necesary *completion* (my italics – G.C.) of the dispersed small-scale production going on in villages and farms, there is a great contradiction between the step-by-step development carried on in many places and the concentrated investment in some major enterprises.[2] The authors quoted leave no doubt that they are adherents of the first method, that is, of step-by-step decentralised development.

This, however, is misleading, particularly if applied to the developing countries. The handicrafts based on traditional technologies must be distinguished from the small-scale plants employing mechanical techniques. The traditional handicrafts cannot survive amidst the up-to-date manufacturing industries and, as in the industrially developed countries, will also disappear in the developing ones. These industries are not competitive in respect of either productivity and costs or the quality of their products. In general, handicrafts cannot become the basis of industrialisation, they cannot be developed into up-to-date industries since they require different equipment, to a considerable extent different technical knowledge, and special production organisation. In the developing countries these sectors mainly employ techniques which, since the beginning of the century, have largely disappeared, even in the industrially less advanced countries of Europe (hand-spinning, small-scale dressing of hides, etc.). In the fields where they have survived for a relatively long time (production of shoes and clothes) they are thrust into the background in line with the progress of industrialisation. Some products – especially those of heavy industry – cannot be turned out at all with traditional techniques, and even where this is possible, it would not pay because of higher costs. The decisive question is, of course, not so much the size of the plant but the application of the methods of modern technology; however, these can be applied mainly in plants larger in size than the traditional small-scale plant. The reasons are well known, and are related partly to the relatively large size of basic equipment which can be efficiently operated – as in the chemical industries where production is continuous – and partly to organisational factors, as for example the light or metal-working industries.

At present, as far as can be judged, the maintenance or development of traditional handicrafts is less frequently proposed than in the past. The view now advocated is that the displacement of small-scale plants by the creation of modern larger-scale industry should be considered as a sociopolitical problem and judged from the viewpoint of employment possibilities for the labour released.

Industrial development practice differs in this respect from country to country. In India, for example, the attempt has been made to maintain the traditional cottage industries and even to expand them on the basis of improved special handicraft techniques, mainly for the production of consumer goods. The problem will be reverted to, when treating the capital- and labour-intensive technologies, in connection with the so-called 'intermediate' technology.

Japan is often referred to as an example of the viability of small-scale industry, of the compatibility of small-scale and large-scale production, and of the small-scale application of non-capital-intensive methods. This is no doubt true to the extent that the importance of smaller plants, and within them of small-scale plants, is greater in Japan than in other countries at a similar level of industrial development, though we have seen that the share of plants employing less than twenty people in Japan also declined rapidly in total employment from 56 per cent in 1930 to 30 per cent in 1958. But the Japanese small-scale plants no longer employ traditional handicraft technology – apart, of course, from ceramics or other handiwork having the character of industrial arts. As distinct from the other industrially developed countries, in Japan the small-scale and even the cottage-family form of industry is applied on a wide scale, in a framework organised by the large-scale plants, for supplying components and spare parts, and performing subcontracting co-operation activities. In this respect also the small-scale plants are the products of large-scale industry since this provides them with markets, and frequently also machinery, materials and credit. In addition, the survival of cottage industry is made possible also by the dense network of electricity and the good transportation system established as a consequence of industrialisation, but above all by the circumstance that in these small plants exploitation is greater, hours of work longer and earnings lower than in the large-scale plants.[3]

However, these small-scale plants in Japan are not by any means employing traditional, or even capital-saving technology. For example, in producing components for bicycles, they use every labour-saving device, partly because this results in better and larger production and lower costs, and partly because these operations are such that their mechanisation is indispensable.[4]

On grounds of available statistics it cannot even be accepted that these Japanese small-scale plants would be particularly suited for saving capital since their capital intensity relative to production is higher than in the case of large-scale plants (bigger staff). The problem will be taken up later.

It should be considered a rule that traditional handicraft techniques must be supplanted by factory-type industry relatively quickly. This is a basic condition of the whole process of economic development, a condition which makes it possible for industry to expand production on the basis of self-financing and to supply products of adequate quality to the population and the other industries. The situation is different with small-scale *plants* employing modern equipment and techniques. Even here, it is difficult to establish unequivocal criteria with the aid of which they can be delimited partly from small-scale industry and partly from the large-scale plants.

The experience of developed countries proves that the share of such small plants is considerable in manufacturing employment, though its extent varies by countries. It would seem that the share of plants of such size is relatively stable, and in places it may even grow with development. In Japan, for instance, the share of plants with an employment roll of 20–100 decreased in total employment from 44 to 30 per cent between 1909 and 1940, and then increased to 40 per cent by 1958.[5]

In United States manufacturing in 1947, units with 10 to 100 workers employed 21·7 per cent of the total labour force; for 1954 the corresponding percentage was 21·9 and for 1958 23·5. In the Federal Republic of Germany, in 1965 the share of plants with 10 to 100 workers in total employment was 2 per cent in mining, 15·9 per cent in basic material industries, 11·9 per cent in engineering, 29·9 per cent in the production of industrial consumer goods, 29·7 per cent in the food industry, 18·6 in total manufacturing and 17·7 per cent in industry as a whole.

These small-scale plants have thus proved to be viable in a developed industrial environment, competing (and co-operating) with the large-scale plants. *How should these small-scale plants applying modern techniques be regarded from the point of view of industrialisation in developing countries?*

As mentioned before, it is usually proposed to develop small-scale plants on the grounds that they are allegedly less capital-intensive than the large-scale ones. Looking at it in somewhat greater detail, the support given to small-scale plants is built upon the assumption that the relation between production Q, employment L and capital C changes with the size of plants in such a way that

    (*a*) capital-intensity, the capital per worker C/L grows,

    (*b*) productivity Q/L increases;

    (*c*) the capital/output ratio C/Q grows, i.e. production per unit of capital Q/C diminishes.

The logical explanation of the above assumptions seems to be that with a greater size of plants, from the technological point of view, there are greater possibilities for specialisation, and thus for labour-saving investment; also, more powerful equipment coming about in this way results in higher productivity. However, this is at the price of a diminishing return on capital, which can perhaps be explained by the fact that first the investments of greater efficiency and later those of smaller efficiency are realised.

It is also said (including now wages W and profits P) that with growing plant size

    (*a*) the wage per worker W/L grows and

    (*b*) the rate of profit P/C increases.

The logical explanation is that the higher productivity due to greater capital-intensity makes it possible to achieve greater specific yields, that is, makes it possible also to pay higher wages and to attain higher profits per unit of capital.

It is rather difficult to put these assumptions to practical test; particularly as regards the developing countries, hardly any investigation of the subject has been conducted or published so far. Reliable comparisons have been made mainly in the case of continuous technologies and homogeneous products, as for example in metallurgy and the chemical industry in respect of the technical and economic parameters of plants of different size. From these comparisons it does not appear that capital efficiency has diminished with the growing size of plants, but rather the contrary. In planning chemical plants, it is for example a fairly widespread practice to calculate capital requirements growing with plant size at an exponential rate, with an exponent of 0·6.

The statistical information available does not yield unequivocal results. The most detailed data we have relate to Japanese industry. The Japanese ministry for foreign trade and industry published, for eleven categories of size, the data on production per unit of capital, on the capital per worker (capital-intensity), on labour productivity and on wages. (See Table III/4.)

These data corroborate the assumption that with growing plant size capital-intensity, productivity and wages per worker increase, but they contradict the assumption that production per unit of capital would diminish with growing plant size along the whole scale. According to the data, this indicator first grows, reaches its highest point with a plant size of 30–49 employees, and then diminishes. Table III/5, though using other data, also shows that the capital/output ratio is most favourable in relatively small, but not the smallest plants. The situation is similar in respect of the rate of profit.

Of course, the reliability of the data is weakened since they relate to the whole of industry and thus, in fact, to groups comprising plants that produce different products: strictly speaking, these are noncomparable. There are also, however, more recent data on Japanese industry, covering nineteen industries and relating to nine groups, from those employing 1–9 persons up to plants with staffs of 1,000–2,000. Bigger plants have not been taken into account for lack of data. This detailed analysis also confirms that with smaller plants productivity, capital-intensity (per worker) and average wages are lower than in bigger ones. The correlation between the capital/output ratio and the plant size is not strong, but on the whole it seems that with growing size the capital/output ratio also increases, though the relation is different at the beginning and the end of the scale, i.e. with the smallest and biggest plants.[6]

Table III/4
CAPITAL-INTENSITY, WAGES AND PROFITS IN JAPANESE INDUSTRY BY SIZE OF PLANTS, 1957
Compared to the average of industry

Plant size by employment	Capital/ output ratio	Fixed assets	Output	Rate of profits as percentage of fixed assets	Profit per worker	Average wages
		per worker (1,000 yen)				
1	2	3	4	5	6	7
1–3	104·5	28·7	30·2	51·8	14·8	56·3
4–9	139·8	29·9	41·9	98·7	29·6	62·5
10–19	192·5	27·8	53·5	160·1	44·4	68·8
20–29	202·2	29·9	60·5	173·4	51·8	75·0
30–49	213·5	31·5	67·4	201·1	63·0	75·0
50–99	194·0	42·0	81·4	195·0	81·5	81·3
100–199	166·1	57·4	95·3	174·6	99·9	87·5
200–299	151·9	71·9	109·3	160·1	114·8	100·0
300–499	126·3	106·5	134·9	143·3	151·8	106·3
500–999	109·8	137·9	151·1	124·0	170·3	118·8
above 1,000	75·2	237·3	179·0	81·9	192·6	156·3
Average of industry	100	100	100	100	100	100

Source: Industrialisation and Productivity 4, U.N., New York, 1961, p. 27.

Detailed correlation analyses can be found in literature relating to Indian industry, covering six years from 1953–8, using ten industrial groups and nine groups of plant size. The ten industries were: the beer and spirits industry, leather manufacturing, soap manufacturing, the glass industry, the sugar industry, the building materials industry, the paper industry, the cotton industry, and steelmaking. The size groups were:

under 20 employees	500– 999
20– 49	1000–1999
50– 99	2000–4999
100–249	above 5000
250–499	

The source quoted does not publish the basic data, but only the final result of the analysis and the correlation coefficients. According to the results of the analysis, with growing plant size productivity, average wages and the rate of profits increase; *so does output per*

Table III/5
PRODUCTIVE CAPACITY, DEGREE OF MECHANISATION,
LABOUR PRODUCTIVITY, CAPITAL-INTENSITY AND
MARKET SHARE, BY SIZE OF PLANTS, IN THE JAPANESE
ENGINEERING INDUSTRY AND TOTAL MANUFACTURING

Plant size by employment 1	Productive Capacity (output) 1,000 yen 2	Mechanisa-tion (fixed assets per employee) 1,000 yen 3	Output per worker 1,000 yen 4	Capital per unit of output 5	Market share of the group in total sales, % 6
Engineering:					
1–9	2,400	60	479	0·125	11·1
10–50	22,000	60	915	0·066	37·1
50–500	182,000	180	1,412	0·127	41·6
500–1,000	1,800,000	350	2,400	0·146	10·2
Manufacturing total:					
1–9	2,700	70	541	0·129	8·1
10–50	22,100	80	938	0·085	20·0
50–500	194,500	180	1,653	0·109	25·6
500–1,000	5,336,800	408	2,330	0·175	46·3

Source: Policies and Programmes for the Development of Small Scale Industry, U.N.I.D.O., ID/Conf. 1/6, April 1967.

unit of capital. This latter item is the only deviation from the Japanese data reviewed above, which first showed a rise and then, above a certain size, the diminishing of this indicator. It must be observed that the analysis relating to Indian industry used rank correlation coefficients, that is, it had to show unequivocally growth or reduction, and it was not sensitive to changes in tendency.[7]

The above data given as examples are related *not to total* but only to fixed capital, i.e. they do not comprise working assets (raw materials, intermediary and finished products). Thus, they cannot give a full picture of capital-intensity, since working capital is a considerable part of capital engaged. However, we have no unequivocal information on the ratio of fixed and working capital as a function of plant size. According to Indian data, the ratio of working capital is considerably higher in small plants. This is logically quite conceivable, particularly if we think of very small plants, because – owing to transportation and procurement difficulties – they have to keep in stock relatively greater quantities in comparison to their production, in spite of the small quantities they can procure or deliver on any single occasion. There are also contradictory Japanese data, according to which in larger plants – larger not by size but by total capital employed – the return on capital is slower, meaning that smaller plants are more mobile and can rest satisfied with smaller stocks.[8] It is worthwhile to note that the source now quoted confirms the fact already mentioned, namely that wages are considerably lower in the smaller Japanese plants. Comparing Japan in this respect with the U.S.A., it becomes clear from our source that while with decreasing plant sizes wages in Japan keep steadily diminishing, this relationship varies in the U.S.A. by branches: in some cases we find a decline, in others an increase. But in the case of a decline with smaller plant size, the reduction is always bigger in Japan than in the U.S.A.

Thus, from a technological viewpoint in the strict sense, the greater plant is more advantageous, meaning that the assumption, according to which capital-intensity regularly grows with growing plant size, does not hold. Since, however, it is proved by empirical facts that in the industrially developed countries the structure of industry by plant size (as measured by employment) is relatively stable, it is justified to assume that the smaller plants are able to counterbalance this disadvantage in other respects. The relative advantages of the small-scale plants may be summed up as follows:

(*a*) *The extent of the market*, i.e. the volume of demand (and of resources) and the rapid changes in requirements and possibilities, secure in some cases an advantage to the small-scale plants which are more flexible and hence better suited to meet limited and changing needs;

(*b*) *Due to technological progress*, requirements and possibilities are rapidly changing (this is related to the former problem). In small plants, however, it is less risky to start the production of new articles or to introduce new processes and further develop them in the case of success. Small-scale plants can also co-operate to meet such needs of several bigger plants for which the latter would not care to make arrangements themselves.

(*c*) *Decentralisation of industry* or, rather, industrialisation of backward areas, will be easier to carry out by setting up small plants, since this requires lower initial investment.

These points are undoubtedly valid for the industrially developed countries, and give some – if not a complete – explanation of the stability of the industrial pattern by plant size. It is, however, justified to ask the question, *to what extent do these points hold for the developing countries?*

The first point, i.e. the effect of the extent of the market on plant size, does in fact probably hold good to an increased extent. Low domestic demand (and, of course, various difficulties hindering industrial exports) are a central problem in the industrialisation of developing countries. Thus, if it is desirable to start domestic production and the market is not big enough, the setting up of small-scale plants is justified. The other viewpoints mentioned seem, however, to be less essential in the developing countries than in the advanced ones. *Autonomous* technical development is slow in these countries, where products or techniques untested elsewhere are introduced less frequently. The pattern of demand changes less rapidly, since, owing to the lower level of technical development, domestic production can satisfy efficiently only the more stable needs. The production of products that quickly become obsolete with technological progress, such as instruments, electronic equipment or chemicals, is obviously not typical now in the developing countries. Also the large-scale plants, by the meeting of whose needs some of the specialised small plants would find a market, are missing.

The situation is likely to be similar with respect to decentralisation. It is desirable in the developing countries for industrialisation to start, as far as is practicable, at several places. Subsidising small plants separately will, however, hinder rather than facilitate this, since – if, apart from direct investment, the necessary infrastructure is also taken into account – the small-scale plant is more capital-intensive. As a matter of fact, transport, electrical energy, water supply, and other expenses related to urbanisation will in any case consume huge amounts, and it would clearly be unreasonable to bring all this into being exclusively for single small plants. This can be helped if – as has already been proposed – several small plants are concentrated in one place. In this case, however, we will no longer be dealing with small-scale plants from the point of view of the decentralisation of industry.

Thus, if there exists a realistic possibility for choice between the *domestic* small- and large-scale plant, then it will be expedient more often than not to choose the latter. Setting up a small-scale plant will be suitable when the size of the domestic market or, owing to transport problems, that of the regional market within the country does not allow the establishment of a large-scale plant. Under such conditions there may be two different situations: (*a*) It is justified to expect that domestic needs – and, with proper experience, exports too – will enable large-scale production within a foreseeable time. In this case the creation of a small plant may be considered as a phase preparatory to that of a big plant. (*b*) If there is no such possibility, it should be examined which is the more expedient: to create a domestic small plant, or to resort to imports. In the first case it is fully justified to protect the small plant from foreign competition with customs duties or other measures in the period of transition; in the second case this can be justified economically only under rather special circumstances.

It is usual to argue in favour of the small-scale plants by saying that *they utilise labour resources better*, that is, they claim fewer qualified people than the large-scale plants and are also more suited to train qualified labour. Apart from the fact that the two statements are somewhat contradictory, it seems rather that in the present stage of technological development, the reverse is true as regards the proportion between qualified and less qualified labour: it is in large-scale plants where relatively more unqualified labour can be employed. Since, however – as has been mentioned – the large-scale plant is more productive, the employment needed to produce the same output is greater in the small-scale plant. But now we have to deal not with productivity but with the ratio of scarce qualified labour to the abundantly available unskilled labour.

From the point of view of qualification, the main categories are: *unskilled* workers, to be trained for some weeks; *semi-skilled* workers with a training time of a few months; *skilled* workers who are trained for some years and *highly qualified experts* (engineers and technicians), whose training time, inclusive of the secondary school, takes 6–10 years. The unskilled and partly also the semi-skilled worker may become manpower of full value in a short time on completion of this basic training. However, the skilled worker, and much more the engineer, will be a fully qualified specialist only after several years of practice. Now, since the beginning of industrialisation, technological development has been such that the ratio of highly qualified people has increased within the total labour force. This tendency has perhaps lately become even stronger. But in respect of the three worker categories, the tendency has changed. Earlier, the ratio of skilled workers had grown, since more and more operations could and had to be performed with machines, and the machines required individual control, setting and handling – that is, skilled labour. Recently, however, with mechanisation and partly due to automation, matters have changed. Machines and operations are specialised to the extent that the immediate handling of machines does not require greater knowledge, but can be done by semi-skilled workers, and qualified labour performs maintenance work or the setting which becomes necessary from time to time. The situation is similar with manual operations to be performed on the assembly line; a single worker does not perform the whole process of assembly, but only an element of it, and this operation can be quickly taught. Now, a technology which makes it possible for more unskilled and semi-skilled workers to work with a relatively small number of skilled workers (also thereby promoting, among other things, intra-factory training, i.e. that the unskilled should acquire skills during work) is obviously favourable for the developing countries. This kind of technology, however, can be employed much better in large-scale plants than the small ones.

There is allegedly a further argument in favour of small plants as against large ones in the developing countries; namely, that small plants *enable the mobilisation of capital and savings for productive purposes* which would otherwise remain in intermediary trade (excessive in any case), or would not serve productive purposes at all. This viewpoint should be taken seriously and if, under given conditions, the small plants were really suited to attract otherwise unavailable savings into industrialisation, their development should be considered favourably.

The proposals relating to the development of small-scale industry put great emphasis on the *tasks of the government* in this respect. These tasks spread from the examination of the technical and econo-mic possibilities of bringing small-scale plants into being to the creation of an organisation that would promote and support small-scale plants, not only by giving advice to those who ask for it, but by organising whole campaigns; a group of technicians may go from place to place with trucks giving demonstrations; they can convene meetings and discussions and formulate plans which will later be supported by technical, administrative and financial means.[9] Technical aid would cover the choice of materials, machinery and tools, their most efficient utilisation, advice on the equipment of plants, their operation and maintenance, production technology, the training of personnel, etc. Aid in the field of administration would cover every problem of organisation, including book-keeping and selling. As regards financial aid, owing to relatively high risks, the high costs of loans and the low profits of the banks, it is difficult for small plants to obtain credit, and they need special help. This can be provided mainly by government, and financing can be taken over by commercial banks only if the small-scale plants have been pro-perly developed and even then only with the guarantee of the state and with insurance cover. In addition, special tax reductions and customs preferences are advocated for small-scale plants – beyond those provided for large-scale plants – also priorities in allocating scarce raw materials, favourable rates of transportation and public services, and special export subsidies.[10]

If the small-scale plants really need all the help listed above, it should at least be examined whether – with the financial, technical and administrative efforts necessary for creating and maintaining the small-scale plant – it is not simpler and more efficient to create state-owned or mixed-property large-scale plants, since at any rate the government is expected to make the greatest efforts. The preference for small-scale plants may also have secret and less secret political reasons. One reason, which will hardly be openly admitted by the western advocates of the small plant, is that a small-scale plant offers less dangerous competition for foreign capital operating in the country or exporting from there than the large-scale plant. The second consideration – openly admitted – is the following:

> Finally, there are also political and social advantages of promoting the creation of small-scale plants. Such policy may contribute to bringing about a middle class consisting of small entrepreneurs, a necessary element of a democratic society.[11]

If, however, we do not consider the creation of small plants as an end desirable in itself, we have to apply to them criteria of economic efficiency, taking these for longer periods and not for one single enterprise, but for the economy as a whole, as we are investigating the rationality of government priorities. Once such criteria are applied, under the conditions prevailing at present in the majority of developing countries, the special government subsidies used for developing small plants instead of large ones are probably justified – not as a rule, but rather as an exception – and large-scale plants remain the main method of industrialisation.

2. *Labour-intensive and Capital-intensive Types of Technology*

Economic decisions on the development of production are often concerned with the question whether production should be based on *labour-intensive or capital-intensive techniques.*

Apart from a few exceptional cases, in the developing countries the problem is not whether to operate or liquidate existing equipment nor, even from the point of view of development, what to produce with existing equipment. It should be decided *what* kind of new equipment shall be created *where*; thus decisions relate mainly to investment serving development purposes.

The first problem – *what* to produce – involves the *sectoral allocation* of investments, that is, in which main branch of the economy and, within that, in which narrower sector development should be carried out, and what should be the range of the new products. If the development decision is not simultaneously a decision also on utilisation – that is, if utilisation is, for some reason, given – the decision will relate at the same time to exports and imports; namely, the part of domestic needs not covered by production must be imported and what exceeds domestic production (plus imports) must be exported.

The other decision – *how* to produce – may also have several aspects. It may relate to the territorial location of productive equipment or the materials to be used, on the size of the plant and the choice of *technology*, or in most general terms on whether development should be carried out with *labour-intensive or capital-intensive technology*.

The choice between labour-intensive and capital-intensive technologies has been discussed in the last decade in several books and articles. In this formulation the problem has emerged mainly in connection with the economic growth of the developing countries. In the literature discussing the problem of advanced capitalist countries, this problem did not present itself earlier as a macro-economic one affecting economic growth. The investment decisions were conceived of partly as decentralised decisions dictated by the profit motives of entrepreneurs, which cannot and need not be influenced from outside, since demand and supply develop market conditions and prices which will by themselves generate the optimum decisions. On the other hand, insofar as macro-economic problems emerged, these related to the elimination or mitigation of cyclical fluctuations, and to maintaining the level of employment – in general, to short-term equilibrium and not to long-term growth.

The various 'criteria' recently advanced in connection with the developing countries, however, amount to a critique of the market and acknowledgement of the fact that – at least in the conditions of the developing countries – the market in itself is not suited for an optimum allocation of resources from the viewpoint of the economy as a whole.

In this general form – as a choice between labour-intensive or capital-intensive technology – the problem has not emerged in the literature of the socialist countries either, at least not up to recent times. The problem 'what to produce' has been conceived of as one to be decided in the framework of the plan and not one to be answered by individual investment efficiency calculations. Although a vast literature on – and considerable practice in – investment efficiency calculations exist, decision on some investment project is, most often, not made primarily on the basis of efficiency calculations, even in our day. In decisions on 'how to produce', the efficiency calculations have a greater role, and a long discussion has taken place on the most suitable calculation method, but discussion has been related mainly to the choice of the formula and, within it, to the factors of selection – i.e. to the length of the pay-off period and the rate of interest to be applied. The latter, both the form of the formula and the factors of selection, of course have a far-reaching influence on whether the calculation finally shows the labour-intensive or the capital-intensive technology to be more efficient. Several of the arguments in the debate esssentially stressed that the formulae comprising shorter pay-off periods or higher rates of interests are not suited since they exclude the application of modern (i.e. capital-intensive) technology; but the discussion did not immediately relate to the choice between labour- or capital-intensive technologies.

Developing countries are characterised by an abundance of unskilled labour, scarcity of capital, a low rate of accumulation and a low level of production. The long-range aim of development is to increase living standards, i.e *per capita* output. In the short run, however, a choice must be made with respect to the allocation of resources between two alternatives. The first involves, in the short run, a faster growth of consumption and a slower one of savings which, other things being equal, means a slower increase of production for the long run. The second results, in the short run, in lower consumption and higher saving rates, but makes possible in the long run, a faster growth of production as well as of consumption. The same type of choice is to be made between consumption and savings, or more correctly, between present (lower) and future (higher) consumption in the case of labour- and capital-intensive types of technology. Since in the developing countries labour is abundant and capital is scarce, in the first approach it would seem as if it were with the scarce resources that there should be economies and more labour-intensive solutions chosen. Therefore, according to some distinguished economists – who either explicitly state it or let it be inferred from their reasoning – production should be maximised with the given amount of capital, which entails choosing labour-intensive techniques and maximising employment. According to the opinion of W. A. Lewis, in the countries where there is a great surplus of unskilled labour, money wages do not reflect the real social cost of labour input.

> In these circumstances capital is not productive if it is used to do what labour could do equally well. Given the level of wages such investments may be highly profitable to capitalists, but they are unprofitable to the community as a whole since they add to unemployment but not to output. . . . [12]

Other authors also propose – if investment possibilities are scarce – *to maximise the output per unit of capital.*

The objection to this general opinion was that it would consider capital as the only scarce factor. As an improved criterion for decision, the so-called Social Marginal Productivity Criterion has been proposed.[13]

According to this S.M.P. criterion in investment decisions, one should start from the capital/output ratio, and the value of output should be maximised in a way that the 'opportunity cost' of labour used, i.e. the cost of its substitution, should be deducted from the value of the actual output. Opportunity cost is equal to the (net) output the same labour would have produced elsewhere.[14] If this criterion is applied under the conditions of developing countries, assuming a labour surplus, that is the 'substitution cost' of additional labour drawn into production being zero, the application of the S.M.P. criterion will lead to the maximisation of the capital/output ratio.

The Western proposals relating to efficiency calculations on the micro-economic level, i.e. firm level, start from the position that under the conditions of developing countries, market prices do not reflect the real scarcity of resources. Actual wages are higher than would be justified in the case of surplus labour, either because the minimum wages are fixed by government or because the trade unions have been able to secure higher wages. Interest on capital is lower than it would be in a free capital market, either because of cheap government credits or because foreign credits are granted at a lower interest rate, or because aid is forthcoming.[15] In the calculations, therefore, *shadow prices* should be used – i.e. lower wages and higher interest rates than those actually prevailing – in order to arrive at economically correct decisions. Obviously, this correction works towards labour-intensive investment; the intensity of the effect depends on the extent of the corrections applied.

The investment efficiency formula of M. Turánszky, a Hungarian author, shows an interesting similarity to the S.M.P. criterion.[16] The formula is the following:

$$E = \frac{\text{yields}}{\text{costs}} = \frac{O}{I + M.I_M + L.I_L + M.I_L}$$

where O = output;

I = basic (direct) investment and indirect investment computed by individual analysis;

$M.I_M$ = the average investment requirement of materials used plus the sum of indirect investment due to the material requirements;

$L.I_L + M.I_L$ = the sum of labour-saving investments necessary to release the manpower necessary for the project – the first item relating to the basic project and the second to the indirect investments.

In his formula Turánszky expresses the opportunity cost not with the output created by labour elsewhere, as does the S.M.P. criterion, but by the investment necessary to release labour, and accordingly it is not deducted from the result in the numerator but added to the cost – the investment – in the denominator. Obviously, Turánszky started from conditions not of abundant labour but of full employment, i.e. from the fact that in the case of new investment, not only must the productive equipment be created but also the labour to be employed must be saved with the aid of labour-saving investment. If, however, the formula is interpreted under conditions of labour surplus, the third and fourth term in the denominator will be zero, since no investment is needed to release labour. Then as in the preceding cases, the maximum output per unit of capital would be optimum.

The S.M.P. criterion – i.e. the social marginal productivity criterion related to capital – allows, like any quotient of productivity or yield, for various interpretations, depending on the figures in the numerator of the quotient as yields and on those in its denominator as inputs. This criterion may be conceived of as a correction of market prices.[17] It may, however, also be conceived of that, with the aid of this criterion, the various effects of the investment are expressed in a common unit of measurement – both the direct implications, like the growth of production, and the indirect ones, i.e. the positive or negative effect on other sectors, as well as the effect on the trade balance.

If the latter is neglected because decision is needed only in respect of the choice of technology, and the effect of the various technologies on the balance of trade is identical, then the criterion suggests a technology giving the maximum capital/output ratio; this entails a solution where the labour/capital ratio is also the maximum. Thus, in the short term, both production and employment would be maximum.

The critics of the S.M.P. criterion point out precisely that labour-intensive investment will result in low productivity; as a result, both accumulation and the growth of the economy will be slow, i.e. in the long run the levels of both production and employment will be lower than in the case of more capital-intensive solutions. Therefore, according to Galenson and Leibenstein,[18] the investment criterion should be maximum economic growth instead of maximum capital/output ratio. This would come about with a *maximum reinvestment ratio and maximum growth in the quality of labour*, since from the point of view of economic development these are the most serious bottlenecks in the developing countries. However, to achieve this, not labour-intensive but capital-intensive techniques are necessary; labour-intensive techniques lead to stabilisation of the low level of productivity.

Galenson and Leibenstein also argue that the choice of a more productive technology – or, more exactly, of a *greater reinvestment – will result after some time also in higher employment*. This is illustrated by an example where they assume that the total profits (the difference between the net production value and wages) is used for expanding the production process *with the same technology*, machines are bought and new labour is employed. With some simplification, their reasoning may be presented as follows:

the number of machines $= N$
net production per machine $= p$
price of a machine $= c$
wage cost of operating a machine $= v$
wages of a worker $= w$
number of workers serving a machine $= e$
total number of workers $= E = e.N$;

Then the growth in the number of machines in a period will be:

$$\Delta N = \frac{N(p-ew)}{c} = \frac{\Delta E}{e}, \text{ because } \Delta E = e\Delta N$$

$$\Delta E = \frac{e(Np-ew)}{c} = \frac{E(p-v)}{c}$$

of which we get:

$$E_{t+1} = E_1\left(1+\frac{p-v}{c}\right)^t$$

Employment at the date $t+1$ increases in comparison to initial employment with the growing difference between output per machine and wage cost per machine, and diminishes with growing machine prices. Even without numerical proof it can be seen that – unless the more productive machine is not excessively expensive – after a certain lapse of time, more capital-intensive technology results in greater employment and, of course, in greater output.

As regards the necessity of capital-intensive technology, Charles Bettelheim arrives at a similar conclusion to that of the authors mentioned. He has dealt in detail with the two alternatives, labour- and capital-intensive technologies.[19] Bettelheim raises the problem in a more general form, not from the point of view of a given operation, machine or factory, as did Galenson and Leibenstein, but, like Dobb,[20] from that of the whole process of economic growth.

Bettelheim refers in his works both to Dobb's book and to the article by Galenson and Leibenstein.[21] His reasoning is particularly interesting because of his Marxist approach and because it is based on experience of Indian economic growth and Indian practical planning.

Since Bettelheim analyses the entire economic growth process – that is, as a problem incomparably more complex than the choice of adequate technology in the case of a definite operation, machine or factory – his answer to the question is complex. The substance of his standpoint is, however, that if – in the interest of short-term increase in employment – labour-intensive technology is used, the consequence in the long run will, precisely, be lower employment; thus, precisely to be able to increase employment in the long run, up-to-date technology must be employed. It follows that, in his opinion,

> to say that the rate of investment is low amounts at the present level of consumption to saying that the technology employed in production is so little efficient that output is just sufficient to cover the minimum needs of those working, and only a very small surplus remains for investment.
>
> In such a situation it is obvious that to increase the rate and volume of investments it is necessary to apply more efficient technologies and not to insist on the existing non-efficient technologies, nor to look for even less efficient ones to solve the problem of unemployment.[22]

Bettelheim also mentions that, contrary to quite widespread opinion, the labour-intensive (i.e. low-productivity) technical solutions are not necessarily capital-saving; modern technology, however, frequently yields simultaneously savings in labour and capital. His statement is supported by examples taken from Indian practice.[23]

It is justified to add a complement to the above statement. The problem of choosing between labour- and capital-intensive technologies is less general than one would conclude from many theoretical papers on the subject. For one thing, it should be considered self-explanatory that once some production process is more costly from the viewpoint of both labour and capital inputs than some other solution (the other inputs, of materials for example, being the same), it must be considered inefficient. Furthermore, certain technical solutions should be considered as necessary, even independently of capital and labour intensity – as, for example, because they are more economical from the viewpoint of material consumption than any other procedure, or because they are necessary to secure adequate

quality in the product. In some industries, therefore – e.g. in metallurgy, many branches of the chemical industry, etc. – labour- *versus*
capital-intensive technology does not even emerge as a real alternative, at least not in respect of fundamental productive processes;
other circumstances are the decisive ones. There are, of course, other
industries, such as the textile industry, where the alternative in question is entirely realistic.

At any rate, a general application of labour-intensive technologies
can by no means become the general method of industrialisation in
the developing countries, nor one able to solve their employment
problems. Obviously, the problem must be examined separately
in every case. In certain cases the application of more labour-intensive technologies than in the advanced countries may be fully justified.

3. *Intermediate Technology*

From the point of view of the techniques to be applied in developing
countries, the proposals aimed at choosing and elaborating what is
called intermediate technology deserve special attention.[24] The
arguments of those advocating this solution seem at first convincing.
In their opinion, the production methods employed in the advanced
countries were unsuited to the poor countries, since they had been
developed under conditions characterised by an abundance of capital
and scarcity of labour, whereas in the developing countries the reverse situation was true. The introduction of capital-intensive techniques in poor countries may even be socially dangerous, since they
would destroy the usual framework of production, and cause mass
unemployment. The solution would thus consist of expanding production on the basis of full employment, in such a way that the necessary
consumer goods would be produced in the developing countries
themselves, instead of being imported – without the labour-saving
devices and sophisticated techniques applied in the rich countries,
but with the aid of some intermediate technology, still to be worked
out. The difficulty is that for this type of development project the
less developed countries are not receiving any help.

From the relevant proposals it is, however, rather difficult to establish what is being meant by intermediate technology. Yet it seems
justified to understand it as something between traditional (labour-
intensive) and modern (capital-intensive) types of technology, probably nearer to the former as regards capital requirements but superior
to them in respect of efficiency and productivity. Also various U.N.
publications mention the intermediate technology in connection
with industrialisation, but do not elaborate on the problem either
theoretically or in practical terms.[25]

D

Let us examine the possibility of applying such technology, with the aid of two simple models. (*a*) Let Q denote the volume of production and K that of capital. Production per unit of capital will be:

$$(1) \qquad \alpha = \frac{Q}{K}$$

The amount invested out of profits will be I, and the reinvestment ratio:

$$(2) \qquad \beta = \frac{I}{K}$$

The purpose of investment K is twofold: on the one hand, production (Q) must be increased, since this is the means to increased consumption, and on the other hand, subsequent further growth in production must be secured, which requires the highest possible rate of saving (I) and reinvestment. To express this relationship in mathematical form, we may say that objective function

$$(3) \qquad V = Q + \lambda . I$$

must be maximised.[26] The magnitude of parameter λ depends here on the weight attributed to future growth (proportional to reinvestment) as against present production. If $\lambda = O$ or is very small, the value of the objective function depends only on production, while if it is great, mainly on investment.

On the basis of the above relationships

$$(4) \qquad V = K(\alpha + \lambda . \beta)$$

The magnitude of and possible interrelations between quotients α and β are shown in Figure 1, on page 87.

Let (1) be the traditional and (2) the modern technology. In this case it may be assumed that $\alpha_1 > \alpha_2$ and $\beta_1 < \beta_2$; that is, with traditional techniques the output per unit of capital is higher and the amount of reinvested profits lower than with modern techniques. Let us further assume that the value of the intermediate technology or techniques satisfies the requirements

$$(5) \qquad \begin{matrix} \alpha_1 > \alpha_0 > \alpha_2 \\ \beta_1 < \beta_0 < \beta_2 \end{matrix}$$

In the opposite case – with the given model – the technology will be more advantageous where both coefficients α and β are higher, and there is therefore no problem of choice between them.

With the above conditions prevailing, V will be maximum when ($\alpha = \beta$) is maximum, since we are looking for the best utilisation of

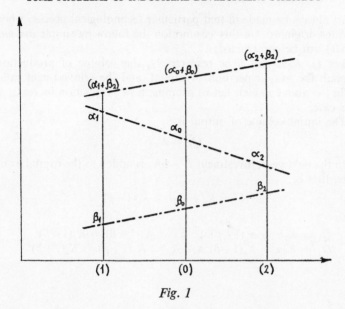

Fig. 1

the same investment K. The maximum value depends on the magnitude of parameter λ; since, however, the changes in the latter only change the direction of the line connecting the points $(\alpha + \beta)$, the value belonging to (0) may at most be equal to the value belonging to either (1) or (2) but cannot be higher than both.

The result may be interpreted as meaning that
– if the technological possibilities fall between the two extremes – the traditional and the modern – in a way that reinvestment (β) is a linear function of capital per unit of output; and
– if there is full liberty in respect of reinvestment – i.e. it is not necessary to use the accumulation originating from some given technological process for the expansion of the same process, then in principle, it is not possible to find a better intermediate technology than either the traditional or the capital-intensive one: in the best case, a technology of equal value can be found.

This model is, in a certain sense, *static* since it remains unaffected by the purpose for which reinvestment is used, expressing simply that a choice is to be made between the process resulting in the highest production/capital ratio and that resulting in the highest rate of reinvestment. Which of the two should be chosen will, of course, depend on the value of λ, i.e. on the importance attributed to future growth as against the present-day level of output.

(*b*) The situation will be different if we assume that reinvestment must always be made in that particular technological process where savings originate. On this assumption the following simple *dynamic* model can be constructed:

Let Q, K, α and β be respectively, the volume of production, capital, the output per unit of capital, and the reinvestment ratio, as in the above model. Let us examine how production increases in this case.

The initial volume of output is

(6) $$Q_o = K_o \alpha$$

In the next year, investment $I = \beta K_o$ is added to the capital available, that is

(7) $$K_1 = K_o + K_o \beta = K_o(1+\beta)$$

and

(8) $$Q_1 = K_1 \alpha = K_o(1+\beta)\alpha; \quad K_2 = K_1(1+\beta) = K_o(1+\beta)^2$$
$$Q_2 = K_2 \alpha = K_o(1+\beta)^2 \alpha; \quad K_3 = K_2(1+\beta) = K_o(1+\beta)^3$$

.
.
.

$$Q_n = K_{(n-1)}\alpha = K_o(1+\beta)^n \; \alpha \text{ with the lapse of } n \text{ years}$$
$$Q_n = K_o \alpha (1+\beta)^n.$$

According to the assumptions of this model, the traditional technology, due to its lower capital-intensity, yields a higher output in the initial stage. With modern technology, however, production volume grows faster because of more reinvestment, and will, with the lapse of N years, reach and then surpass the level of output yielded by the traditional technology.

Which of the two types of technology proves more advantageous will obviously depend on the value of N and on the time preference, that is, the length of the period one is prepared to wait for increased investment to yield a higher output.

The two types of technology would yield an identical production volume (with the lapse of N years) in the case of the same *initial* capital, if

(9) $$\alpha_1(1+\beta_1)^N = \alpha_2(1+\beta_2)^N$$

$$ln\alpha_1 + Nln(1+\beta_1) = ln\alpha_2 + Nln(1+\beta_2)$$

$$N = \frac{ln\alpha_1 - ln\alpha_2}{ln(1+\beta_2) - ln(1+\beta_1)} = \frac{ln\dfrac{\alpha_1}{\alpha_2}}{ln\dfrac{1+\beta_2}{1+\beta_1}}$$

The growth in production with the two types of technology is shown in Figure 2.

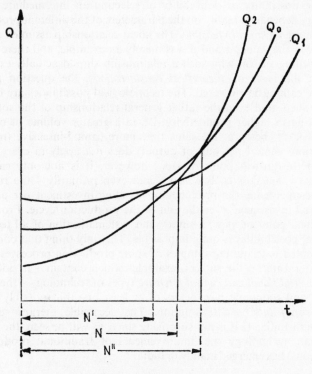

Fig. 2

Figure 2 leads to the conclusion that if the above assumptions (that is, a linear relationship between α and β) are valid, an intermediate technology can in principle be found which has a higher rate of re-investment than the traditional technology, together with a higher output per unit of capital than the modern technology. The $Q^{(0)}$ curve of production growth of this intermediate technology reaches curve $Q^{(1)}$ of the traditional technology in a shorter period (N years) than does the curve of modern technology $Q^{(2)}$. The latter, however, reaches the curve $Q^{(2)}$ in N'' years and then surpasses it.

Whether it is desirable to choose the intermediate technology or not will depend on the time within which the capital-intensive technology catches up in production with the former. If this period is short, i.e. if ($N''-N'$) is not long, the application of modern technology is preferable. In the opposite case, choice must be made between the traditional and the intermediate technologies on the basis of an identical criterion.

The possibility or desirability of selecting an intermediate technology depends in reality on the parameters of the different processes which are *technically feasible*. The linear relationship assumed above between the values α and β was merely an example, and there is no compelling reason why such a relationship should actually exist.

On the basis of *theoretical considerations*, the question posed above cannot be answered. The technological possibilities are highly diversified, and even the rather general relationship of the solution resulting in higher productivity (i.e. in a greater volume of output per worker) being at the same time more capital-intensive (requiring more capital per unit of output) does not apply in every case. From the growth point of view, however, it is not only capital-intensity that counts, but also – and even primarily – the rate of reinvestment, i.e. the production-expanding investment per unit of original investment after the end of the production cycle. From the practical point of view, a survey and systematisation of all technological possibilities is quite impossible. The only thing that could be attempted is to quote examples of some production processes from the literature on the subject, examples which contain – in addition to the *traditional and capital-intensive* types of technology – the technical and economic parameters of at least one (but possibly more than one) *intermediate* solution. The accessible literary sources relate to India. This is not surprising since, as will be seen, the intermediate technology (i.e. improvements of traditional production methods) has emerged mainly in India.

VARIOUS METHODS OF MACHINE-MILLING OF RICE[27]

In this study, eight different methods of rice-hulling (three mechanical and five manual) are surveyed and characterised with the proper technical and economic parameters. If the output/capital ratio is calculated for the whole capital employed (that is including liquid capital), the choice between the mechanical and traditional techniques on the one hand and the improved manual (intermediate) ones on the other is entirely possible, since the *mechanical techniques are more advantageous from the point of view both of reinvestment and the output/capital ratio* than the manual techniques. Even among the mechanical techniques, the highest output/capital ratio can be found with the most productive one, which at the same time ensures also the highest rate of reinvestment, i.e. not only the fastest growth but also the highest production level with the given initial capital. The relationship between parameters α and β is such that – with the exception of two cases out of eight – a higher value of α involves a higher value of β too, meaning *that in the given case the technology securing faster growth is also more economical from the point of view of capital engagement.*

HAND SPINNING, MECHANICAL SPINNING AND INTERMEDIATE (IMPROVED HAND) SPINNING[28]

The output/capital ratio of manual technology is higher and its reinvestment ratio is lower than that of mechanical technology. The parameters of improved manual technology are, however, less favourable in both respects, i.e. both the output/capital ratio and the reinvestment ratio are lower than with traditional technology. *The intermediate technology brings no advantages whatsoever as against the traditional one.* In the short run it is the traditional, in the long run the mechanical technology which ensures higher production. The coefficients are the following:

	Technology	α	β
(10)	I. Traditional—manual	0·34	0·03
	II. Intermediate—manual	0·445	0·01
	III. Mechanical	0·43	0·13

VARIOUS TYPES OF COTTON WEAVING TECHNOLOGY[29]

	Technology	α	β
	I. Hand weaving (traditional)	0·97	0·32
	II. Improved (intermediate) hand weaving	0·97	0·39
(11)	III. Mechanical weaving in factories	0·68	0·51
	IV. Mechanical cottage-industry weaving	0·66	0·40
	V. Automatic mechanical weaving	0·41	0·40

As can be seen from the table, increasing β values are accompanied only to a limited extent by decreasing values of α. Thus, types III and V drop out since, in comparison with the others, lower α values are accompanied by lower and not higher values of β. Similarly, technology I drops out against II. Choice must be made between the technology II working with higher production/capital ratio and technology IV securing faster growth. Using the formula derived previously

$$(12) \quad n = \frac{ln\alpha_1 - ln\alpha_2}{ln(1+\beta_2) - ln(1+\beta_1)} = \frac{ln\,0·97 - ln\,0·26}{ln\,1·51 - ln\,1·39} = 2·64$$

4. *Import Substitution and Export Promotion*

Industrialisation of developing countries is generally characterised by *import substitution*, that is development of the domestic production of industrial, mainly manufactured, goods previously imported from abroad. This process and the underlying economic policy have been much criticised in recent years; it is to this that several authors would attribute the difficulties of economic growth, equating import substitution with some autarkic inward orientation. Since imports (import substitution) and exports (export promotion), i.e. participation in the international division of labour, really belong to the cardinal problems of economic growth in general and industrialisation in particular, it is worthwhile to discuss this problem in greater detail from the point of view of the developing countries.

First a few quite simple and obvious notions and interrelations should be clarified, which are given insufficient consideration and frequently overlooked altogether, in the criticism of import substitution. Obviously, the phenomena of import substitution and export promotion can be interpreted only dynamically, as compared to some previous state. In this respect, the term import substitution may be used in two senses:

(a) *Import Substitution in the narrower sense.* This is the case when domestic production is substituted for imports in a way that the volume of imports decreases also in absolute terms. Let us call this case autarkic or absolute import substitution, since it is accompanied by shrinking foreign trade, or rather imports.

(b) *Import Substitution in a wider sense.* This is the case when the volume of imports continues to increase, though at a lower rate than domestic production; i.e., *the share of imports* in meeting domestic needs is decreasing. In this second case, we can hardly speak simply of autarky, since the process is accompanied by growing foreign trade (imports), though certain autarkic tendencies may appear. Let us call this case relative import substitution.

The only cases where relative import substitution, i.e. diminishing of the share of imports in satisfying domestic needs, will not take place are when

(a) the growth rate of domestic industrial production is equal to or lower than that of industrial imports, or

(b) the growth rate of industrial exports is at least equal to that of industrial production.

In the first case the capacity of the world market (mainly of the more advanced countries) to absorb the traditional export goods of the developing countries would restrict domestic consumption as well as the growth rate of industry and of the whole economy.

Changes in the pattern of consumption, decreasing material input per unit of output and the advance of synthetic materials all tend to reduce the growth in the material exports of the developing countries, particularly if we disregard one of the major export goods of the developing countries, namely crude oil. The latter, however, yields foreign exchange revenue only to some of the developing countries. The critics of the economic policy of import substitution are actually proposing, in most cases, increased orientation towards traditional export goods. However, in view of the somewhat limited market, which is not likely to expand exceptionally fast in the future, this will hardly lead to growth.

The second possibility is a *dynamic* increase in exports originating in the newly developed industries, and then specialisation in some groups of products, while others can be imported. This alternative, though desirable, is hardly practicable under present conditions in the majority of developing countries. The problem will be reverted to later.

The process taking place in the developing countries is an import substitution in the second, wider sense only. In the last ten to fifteen years, industrial production has increased at an annual average of 6 to 8 per cent, industrial imports at 3 to 4 per cent. A 4 per cent compound annual growth rate means in ten years nearly 50 per cent, and in fifteen years 80 per cent growth; i.e. there is no import reduction at all in an absolute sense. Autarkic industrialisation in the first sense has always been exceptional, and in the developing countries at least, the consequence of some external compulsion factor rather than of deliberate economic policies. It took place whenever the developed countries were unable to supply industrial goods, as in war time, or when – as during the depression – they restricted their raw material purchases to such an extent that the developing countries were unable to earn the foreign currency necessary for imports. True, these conditions lent a strong impetus to industrialisation, particularly in Latin America.

Relative import substituion in the second sense is *quite general and natural* in a 'late industrialising' country. This is what happened in earlier periods of their economic history in countries now advanced industrially such as the U.S.A., Germany and Japan. In some particular industries, something similar is now happening in the developed countries when some new branch of production – e.g. in electronics or in the chemical industry – develops earlier in one or two of the most advanced countries. In these cases, the domestic market is first supplied with imports, and only later will the domestic production of a new electronic or chemical product be started. Of course, there is a considerable difference here between the developed and

D*

the developing countries; *in the countries with a developed industry, the transition period from production for the domestic market only to that for exports is a short one.*

If the criticism of import substitution is interpreted as meaning that it would not be right to reduce the share of industrial imports in satisfying domestic needs, i.e. (on the basis of a static interpretation of comparative advantages) that it would be wrong to raise industrial production at a quicker rate than imports, the logical conclusion would be to dismiss the possibility or the expediency of industrialisation. We need not deal here in detail with this problem. This does not, of course, mean that all import substitution was right in principle; the practice of the developing countries shows that the criticism is not altogether unfounded. But, before proceeding any further on this subject, let us clarify some problems of orders of magnitude in connection with industrial growth and import substitution.

In the mid-1960s, taking into account all developing countries, 20 per cent of all home supplies – i.e. domestic industrial output plus imports – was covered by imports. This average conceals, of course, a wide variety in the individual countries, ranging from 9–10 per cent (Argentina, India) to 40–50 per cent (Panama, Ceylon).[30] In some small African countries this ratio may have even been higher. Considering this 20 per cent average and the 6 to 7 per cent annual growth in industrial output, it should be obvious that it is *a priori* impossible to raise production by means of import substitution in the narrower sense. This possibility of expansion, or more exactly the market due to import substitution, would be exhausted within two to three years. The primary source of growth must thus be the expansion of the domestic utilisation of industrial products. For this reason alone, absolute import substitution cannot be the main road to industrialisation.

Why is import substitution in the wider sense the only road to industrialisation in the developing countries? The viability of a manufacturing industry requires a certain minimum scale of production, varying by branches. The domestic market of the developing countries is limited. In such a limited market the demand for a completely new, hitherto unknown product can only grow rather slowly, hence domestic production can only build on already existing consumption, i.e. *on substitution.* Either the products of domestic small-scale and cottage industry or the imported products can be substituted. The substitution possibilities of the products turned out by small-scale industry are limited. These small plants would not turn out all varieties of products, but are confined mainly to consumer goods, and small-scale industry does not have an equally important place in every country (its significance is highest in Asia). Moreover, a too rapid elimination of the small plants would give rise to employment problems. Finally, from the point of view of the balance of trade, it is generally more desirable in the conditions of the developing countries to launch the production of something which hitherto had to be paid for in foreign currency than of a product which can be turned out domestically, even though less modern methods are used.

Import substitution requires – at least in the industrially backward countries which we are discussing – *drastic interference* with accustomed economic processes, and a readiness to make certain sacrifices in the short run in the interest of advantages in the long run. This does not conform to the short-term interpretation of comparative advantages or to the free play of market forces. Apart from special cases (e.g. high transport costs) recently started industrial production is usually more expensive in the developing countries than possible imports (provided, of course, that imports are possible at all from foreign-exchange and other points of view). This is related to the generally smaller scale of production and the lower productivity due to the untrained labour force. Not infrequently, greater material inputs and the more rapid deterioration of mechanical equipment also play a part. True, with the passing of time this *comparative disadvantage* tends to diminish, or ceases to exist. The production of textile goods, steel or machinery may require greater input, more capital, material and labour, and even higher wages in the young industry of the developing country than of the traditional producers. But the products of the domestic industry have a market, satisfy real needs, and are a dynamic element of development, while the agricultural produce turned out with comparable advantage may be unsaleable or can be sold only at steadily decreasing relative prices. *The first solution stimulates economic growth, diversification of production and thereby stabilisation of the whole economy, while the other leads to stagnation and works towards the maintenance of monoculture and economic instability.* Obviously, every realistic and economic possibility must be utilised to increase both production and exports of traditional export articles.

In the case of import-substituting industrialisation, however, help must be secured in some form of state support given to overcome the comparative disadvantages. This may assume the form of protective customs duties, tax reductions, state investment or credits, restriction of competitive imports by managing foreign exchange or imports, or some combination of these measures.

Thus, import-substituting industrialisation in the *wider* sense is one of the principal alternatives to industrial development policy in the developing countries; its importance is greatest where the level of industrial production – or, more exactly, the export potential of domestic industry – is lowest. Therefore, as regards all the developing countries, we will, in general, find industrialisation of an *import-substituting character*, in so far as industrial output grows quicker than industrial imports and the share of domestic production in meeting domestic demand is growing.

This happened in the periods 1955/9 – 1960/4, when the share of complementary imports (i.e. the ratio of imports to the sum of domestic production and imports) in the developing world fell from about 24·5 per cent to 21·9 per cent.[31] This ratio in the developing countries may even, as a matter of fact, seem low in view of the low development level of their industries. It should, however, be taken into account that it is not only the level of industrial production that is low, but also the consumption of industrial products, which is also related to the underdevelopment of the economy. In Hungary, in the corresponding period, import substitution no longer prevailed, but the share of imports was increasing i.e. industrial imports (and, indeed, also exports) were rising at a faster rate than industrial production. This is the general tendency in the industrially more advanced countries, whether socialist or capitalist. The industrial exports and imports of the latter have more than doubled between 1955 and 1965, i.e. both have grown at an annual rate of more than 7 per cent, while industrial production increased only at the rate of about 5 per cent per year.

Economic development based on import substitution implies that development takes place in the short run under conditions not of comparative advantages but of disadvantages; primarily it is not the production of raw materials for exports which is developed, but that of industrial products for domestic use. In the present circumstance, it is in respect of raw materials, mainly some agricultural products, that the developing countries have comparative advantages, and the production of manufacturing products is comparatively disadvantageous. The question emerges as to whether this method of economic development – the domestic production of goods that can be more cheaply bought from abroad – is possible in the long run, whether this is a rational, practicable way of development and of promoting the international division of labour.

It does not require more detailed proof that the developing countries are at an *absolute disadvantage* as regards industrial production. This disadvantage is expressed most characteristically by the low level of productivity. As a consequence, the costs of industrial production and the prices of manufactured goods are higher in the developing countries than in the advanced countries. This fact is well known, although it is difficult to prove numerically. Owing to differences in price and cost relations, it is rather difficult to compare production costs internationally, even in the case of countries with more or less similar structures, like the European socialist countries or the developed capitalist countries. The comparison is even more difficult between developing countries on the one hand and industrially developed countries on the other; therefore, reliable comparisons of this type are even fewer in number. Perhaps the final results of a comparison of this kind may be illustrative:

The U.N. commissioned at the end of the 1950s a comparison of the costs of nitrogenous fertiliser production and beer bottle production as between the U.S.A. and Central America, for various scales of production. The data, appropriately converted and grouped, can be found in Table III/6.

Table III/6

COST AND PRODUCTIVITY LEVEL IN
CENTRAL AMERICA

(*U.S. corresponding levels = 100*)

	Fertiliser production	Bottle production
Raw material	200	150
Capital	145	135
Wages	25	20
Productivity	60–65	60–65
Unit costs	40	32

Source: 'Problems of Size of Plant in Industry
in Underdeveloped Countries', *Industrialisation and Productivity*, No. 2,
1959.

It appears from the comparison of cost elements that wage costs in developing countries are much lower, and since in this case this difference is greater than the difference in productivity (though productivity is also lower), unit costs are much lower. But capital costs are higher, which may be traced back partly to higher rates of interest and partly to the lower qualification of the workers, and to a quicker depreciation of equipment owing to worse supply of spare parts, etc. Higher costs of materials also reflect the generally lower level of productivity.

The final cost proportions depend on the labour-intensity of production. This again depends partly on the character of production (on technology, on the branch of industry), and partly on the scale of production. With a larger scale of production, labour-intensity relatively decreases. This is unfavourable for the developing countries.

A comparison of production costs in the case of the two kinds of production and for various scales of plant can be found in Table III/7.

Table III/7

RELATIVE COSTS OF PRODUCTION IN CENTRAL AMERICA

FERTILISER PRODUCTION:					
Ton/Day	50	100	150	300	
U.S. cost level = 100	126	134	137	142	
PRODUCTION OF BEER BOTTLES:					
Machines installed for bottle					
production, units	1	2	4	6	12
U.S. cost level = 100	102	106	109	110	111

Source: 'Problems of Size of Plant in Industry in Underdeveloped Countries', *Industrialisation and Productivity*, No. 2, 1959.

Insofar as this example reflects realistic cost proportions (and proportions are probably realistic, since the analysis commissioned by the U.N. was most detailed and thorough), it may be stated that the disadvantage of the developing country is much greater in fertiliser production than in producing bottles (since the latter is more labour-intensive) and that the effect of plant size on the relative cost level is similarly greater in the first case, at least after having reached a certain size. In addition, costs of glass transportation are also relatively higher (including damage owing to broken glass), thus increasing the potential advantage of import substitution. The question now emerges in the following way: import-substituting industrialisation can undoubtedly take place if, in spite of initial costs in the newly created industry being higher than import prices, the difference can in a short time be equalised or at least essentially reduced, and if in the mean time the industry receives a subsidy borne by the whole economy. However, what will happen if there is no hope of the difference in productivity being eliminated or reduced within a foreseeable time? This is usually the problem in the case of developing countries.

According to historical experience, even a considerably protracted period with a lower productivity level is no obstacle to economic development (not even to increasing trade among countries with different levels of productivity) or to becoming a considerable exporter of industrial products. Let us compare, on the basis of *per capita* G.N.P., i.e. the overall (not only industrial) productivity, Japan with the U.S.A., and Italy with Germany. (We accept here *per capita* G.N.P. as an approximation of the relative productivity levels.)[32]

Table III/8

COMPARATIVE *PER CAPITA* G.N.P. LEVELS

	1870	1913	1938	1965	1970
Japan as percentage of U.S.A.	36	30	48	45	50
Italy as percentage of Germany (1965: only West)	78	63	61	61	67

Source: Angus Maddison, *Comparative Productivity Levels in the Developed Countries*, Banca Nazionale del Lavoro, Rome, 1967, for 1870–1965; the figures for 1970 calculated from *La Croissance de la Production 1960–1980.*

International comparisons of productivity covering a long period are not particularly reliable. It is probable, however, that over about a century the ratio of Japan's productivity to that of the U.S.A. has increased only slightly, with the productivity level in Japan attaining half that in the U.S.A. only by the end of the 1960s; it is also probable that productivity in Italy as related to that in Germany has diminished rather than increased over the same period. However, both Japan and Italy have in that period rapidly raised their industrial output, particularly since the Second World War, and have been competitive also in exports. Already today, the greater part of the exports of both countries is of industrial origin; in the case of Japan 92 per cent and in that of Italy 78 per cent (according to 1965 data).[33] Japan's main trading partner is the U.S.A. and Italy's is West Germany. In 1961, 27 per cent of Japanese exports were directed to the U.S.A. and 18 per cent of Italian exports to Western Germany; for 1965, the corresponding percentages were respectively 30 and 21.

Of course, the two examples prove only that both the development of industry and substantial industrial exports are possible at a much lower productivity level than that of some of the partners. Japanese and Italian industrialisation has – at least in recent times – obviously not been of an import-substituting character, but export-promoting, and the example seems to indicate that this path should be followed by the developing countries as well.

According to one argument against import-substituting industrialisation, this process had already come to an end, since where such substitution was possible at all, as for example in the textile industry, the possibilities have been exhausted. However, in industries which require a higher technological level or a wider market (a case in point is engineering), the possibilities of the developing countries are, according to the opponents of import-substitution, extremely limited on account of technical difficulties.

The possibility of further import substitution in some industries can be approximately characterised by confronting the complementary imports of the industry in question with the total import of industry, relating it to the share of the industry in question in total industrial output. The greater this 'coefficient of potential import substitution', i.e. the quotient of the two shares, the greater the possibility of import substitution – depending, of course, on technical possibilities, qualification, capital supply, etc. In 1963, 7 per cent of total industrial imports and 11 per cent of total industrial output were textiles, thus the coefficient was 0·635. The coefficients of other important branches are as follows:

Food industry	0·415
Chemical industry	1·000
Metallurgy	1·280
Engineering	2·820

Thus, if only the proportions are considered, after the food industry it is the textile industry where import substitution has already taken place to the greatest extent, while reserves for further import substitution are biggest in the chemical industry, metallurgy and particularly in engineering. But this is only the most general aspect of the problem. The problems of developing the textile industry, and within that, those of exports and imports, will be dealt with in detail in Chapter V.

It is a fact that in textiles the developing countries, taken together, are already net exporters. According to U.N. data, in 1965 the textile exports of these countries amounted to $1,572,000,000, whereas the value of imports was only $1,400,000,000. But exports and imports are very unevenly distributed by main areas and countries. The bulk of textiles exported from developing countries come from a small number of countries, several of which – especially in Africa – are still in the import-substitution phase. In addition, the pattern of textile exports differs from that of textile imports insofar as imports consist mainly of highly finished goods, whereas exports are composed overwhelmingly of goods that have undergone a low degree of processing. Thus, in the case of trade volumes of identical value, the developing countries are buying more industrial *work* (value added) and selling less. (The situation is quite similar with respect to other industries.) Accordingly, the process of import substitution is to continue in individual countries and areas, with a shift in both production and export patterns towards a higher degree of processing; but as interpreted purely in global value terms and for the developing countries as a whole, it has – or is about to – come to an end, with exports having begun to grow at a rate as high as or higher than production.

As regards machinery, it is erroneous to deny the possibility of import substitution. It is precisely the metal-working industries where some kind of development is possible in every country, even the industrially most backward. This is sufficiently proved by the fact that in the developing countries the engineering industries – which are still rather underdeveloped – are growing at a rate far exceeding the average growth in industry. Of course, the possibilities of starting and expanding domestic production are related – because of the narrow domestic market and the wide range of products – also to exports. The main basis of development, however, is for the time being the domestic market, as will be explained below. Thus the further possibilities of import substitution exist for the entirety of the developing countries, even in the industries requiring greater technical skills, and also in those where the process is most advanced. This does not imply that the possibility exists for every industry of every country.

To what extent then is the criticism aimed at import substitution in the developing countries justified? The new industries have come about under the effect of protectionism, i.e. protected by high import duties and under conditions of foreign exchange controls. Exaggerated protectionism or protection lasting too long will, however, lead to stagnation, both from the technical point of view and as regards quality and costs. The profit possibilities afforded by protectionism, the lack (or deficiency) of planning and the stagnation or even absence of exports due to high costs or low quality have in some places led to idle capacities.

The problem is, of course, not insoluble. Protection of the new industry and seclusion of the domestic market from foreign competition should be gradually abolished, even according to the relevant theories; foreign goods should be allowed to compete with the domestic products on the home market, even in order to maintain the ability of the domestic industry to compete and to make it gradually better capable of exporting. This circumstance (namely export capability) may be one of the main criteria of industrial development.

Another, often justified, criticism is that import substitution will increase rather than reduce imports. The problem is essentially this. Industrial development requires the importation of materials which cannot be produced in every country because of natural conditions, e.g. non-ferrous metals, rubber, etc. It is also a widespread phenomenon that a full vertical structure of industry cannot be built from below with a higher phase of processing established only when the lower phases are already operating. Accordingly, materials must be imported for further processing. But even if the raw material processing phase – or one nearer to raw-material processing – is established, it cannot be complete and all-embracing. Therefore, certain materials, especially those more difficult from the technical point of view (e.g. alloyed and stainless materials in metallurgy, or special synthetic materials, etc.), will be imported. All that does not cause any particular problem if we are dealing only with import substitution in the narrower sense, i.e. if something that was previously imported is being produced, because in that case, even with an import-intensive domestic production, less will have to be imported. But if development involves also a growing utilisation of domestic industrial products, which is desirable in several respects and in certain cases indispensable, the final result might be increasing imports instead of import substitution.

THE POSSIBILITY OF DYNAMIC INDUSTRIAL EXPORTS

There is no doubt that the development of industrial exports is desirable, and in the course of industrialisation even indispensable. The problem is to what extent and at what rate it is possible.

It is desirable to increase exports since the equilibrium of the trade balance requires foreign exchange earnings; increasing specialisation is economically advantageous, and in many respects indispensable for industrial growth; also technical progress, the raising of productivity and the reduction of production costs require participation in competition. In the period surveyed here, the manufacturing exports of the developing countries have, of course, increased to a considerable extent. From 1955–9 to 1960–4, according to U.N. (U.N.I.D.O.) data, the annual average growth rate was 8 per cent, according to S.I.T.C. 5–8, or with the usual interpretation of manufacturing, according to I.S.I.C. 2–3 it was 5·5 per cent.[34] Whichever growth rate is considered, it will be obvious that industrial exports have substantially increased. But the growth rate was lower than that of production (which was 7 per cent per annum according to I.S.I.C. statistics), a fact indicating that exports were *not yet a dynamic element* of industrial growth in the developing countries in this period.

To prevent further deterioration of the negative balance of trade in industrial goods, with the present development of domestic production and home consumption of industrial goods, exports should be doubled in about ten years. The rate of this increase is merely the past rate of growth in production; such an increase in exports, or even a greater one, can hardly be considered as being limited by the production capacities available in the developing countries. Thus, a faster growth in exports than hitherto is essentially a problem of markets.

This is why *it is not realistic* to expect that dynamic industrial exports, growing at a faster rate than industrial production, can be achieved in the near future by the developing countries as a whole. The main reasons can be summed up as follows. The actual industrial exports of the developing countries are highly concentrated in product groups representing a lower degree of processing, the demand for and total consumption and imports of which grow at a relatively slow rate.[35] Though the production and exports of chemical and engineering products are growing faster, their share in total industrial exports is low (only 10 to 15 per cent in 1960–4). A radical change in export patterns cannot be expected within a short time, and the present pattern of exports – a direct consequence of the backwardness of industry in the developing countries – does not make any particularly rapid development of exports possible in global terms in comparison to production.

The principal markets for the industrial exports of developing countries are the developed capitalist countries; the share of other developing countries and of socialist countries is much lower. In 1960–4, about two-thirds of industrial exports and more than 70 per cent of total exports were directed to the first group. From the point of view of the developed capitalist countries, it can be stated that the developing countries play an important role in their raw material imports with a share of 50 per cent, whereas in total imports of industrial goods – or rather manufactured goods – this share is only 14 per cent (22·5 per cent in light-industrial imports and 12 per cent in the imports of heavy-industrial products). Food imports are of the highest importance: the share of developing countries is here 35 per cent, while in textile imports it is 24 per cent. It should be mentioned that in the machinery imports of developed capitalist countries, the share of developing countries is below 1 per cent.

From the above it should be clear that, unless some extremely rapid structural changes come about, the growth in the industrial exports of developing countries will be determined by the imports of the advanced capitalist countries. It has been proposed that the developed countries should unilaterally reduce the customs duties on industrial products and open their markets to them. The argument is that this would be easy for the developed countries, since in the early 1970s the total of possible industrial exports from developing countries would not amount to more than 1 per cent of G.N.P. in developed capitalist countries.

However, this argument is misleading. The industrial exports of developing countries should be compared not with the total national income of developed capitalist countries but with domestic production and with imports originating from other countries. As regards the latter, a fast rise in imports from developing countries may hurt powerful economic interests. Therefore, although the first U.N.C.T.A.D. conference has already passed a resolution on the reduction of customs duties,[36] hardly anything has been done so far to implement it in the developed capitalist countries. Although something is bound to be done in the interest of preferential treatment of industrial exports from developing countries, and also a change in the attitutude of developed capitalist countries can be expected, only the future can show whether this will enable a continuous gradual expansion of exports rather than a radical growth in comparison to that experienced so far, and to what extent concrete measures are taken in view of general political commitments and to what extent under the influence of the particular interests concerned.

The system of customs duties in developed capitalist countries does not impose an equal burden on industrial products, the rates being higher for products representing a higher level of processing. This is shown by the pattern of the industrial exports from developing countries by degrees of processing. According to U.N.I.D.O. estimates, the pattern, by degrees of processing, of exports of manufactured goods from developed and developing countries is the following. (Same source in footnote 34.)

Table III/9
PATTERN OF EXPORTS IN DEVELOPED AND
DEVELOPING COUNTRIES
(*per cent*)

	Materials	Semi-finished products	Finished products	Total
Developed capitalist countries	2	33	65	100
Developing countries	32	33	35	100

The interpretation of the above categories is as follows: materials are agricultural or mineral products which have undergone only minimum processing; semi-finished products are manufactures which require further processing or must be built into some other product to be taken into use as investment or consumer goods;

finished products are suited for immediate consumption or use as means of production. Developed countries usually levy higher duties on highly processed goods.

The structural differences depend, however, *not only on tariffs but also on the technical level of industry*. There are industries whose products generally represent a higher degree of processing. For example, 90 per cent of the machinery exports of developed capitalist countries belong to the third category, while this percentage is 94 in the developing countries. The point, however, is that machinery exports constitute a substantial part of total exports from the developed capitalist countries, whereas they are negligible in the exports from the developing countries. In the latter, however, it is probably not protective customs duties that are decisive but the export capacity based on industrial potential and the established trading organisation. As mentioned before, in textile exports the share of products with a high degree of processing is much higher in the developed than the developing countries. This too is more than simply a problem of customs duties, and a change in tariffs alone will not result in radical changes; the raising of the technical level of production will need a considerable time.

Two different types of proposal have been put forward to solve the problem of the technical development level and of export potential. According to the first view, special *export industries* should be developed in the developing countries at a high technical level, irrespective of whether the domestic market can absorb a substantial part of their products or not. This export sector should differ from the domestic economy also from the point of view that 'it must be more developed than the rest of the economy . . . more capital-intensive and consisting of the non-traditional industries employing more advanced techniques.'[37]

Apparently, this kind of reasoning does not take into account the importance of marketing possibilities in the domestic market and disregards also the fact that to control the quality and to follow up the problems of utilisation requires close co-operation between producers and users, particularly in the case of new enterprises or new products. Apart from the rather special case of Hong Kong (and, to some extent, Israel) no example can be found of such special export industries.

According to other proposals connected with the marketing of industrial exports, trade among the developing countries should be increased mainly in the framework of regional co-operation, enabling them to export to less exigent markets and to set up larger and more efficient plants, taking into consideration the full demand of the other countries or the entire region.

Undoubtedly, such co-operation is desirable, but as regards its future possibilities and results, it would be mistaken to cherish great illusions.

As mentioned before, the main market of industrial exports from developing countries is to be found in the developed capitalist countries. In 1965, only about 29 per cent of the exports of manufactured goods from developing countries were directed to other developing countries. This percentage is rather low, particularly if we consider the fact that in the two other major regions of the world – the developed capitalist countries and the socialist countries – this 'internal ratio' is much higher: 73 per cent in the trade among the developed capitalist countries and 70 per cent among the socialist countries.

Nor is it quite correct to compare in this respect the totality of developing countries to either the developed capitalist or the socialist countries. The European socialist countries are situated geographically near to each other, and the case is similar with the developed capitalist countries where the major part of foreign trade is transacted among the West European and North American countries (the U.S.A. and Canada), which can be reached by cheap waterways transport. Thus, from the point of view of transport, these countries are in a reciprocally favourable position.

As regards the main regions (continents) of developing countries, the present export volume is even smaller. Intra-regional trade amounts to only 25 per cent of the exports of manufactured goods in Latin America, 27 per cent in Asia and a mere 11 per cent in Africa. It should be added that although these countries are situated geographically nearer to each other, the primitive transport facilities result in this advantage not necessarily being reflected in transport costs. In particular some African countries can trade at lower cost – and, what is even more important, with less difficulties – with the developed countries than with each other. Thus, the development of intra-regional trade can start only from a rather low level and under not particularly favourable circumstances.

Furthermore, it should be taken into account that, in general, the developing countries are poor in resources necessary for the development of industry, and lack both capital and specialists. They cannot, therefore, provide much help to each other in this respect, but only insofar as the scarce resources can be better utilised by joint and co-ordinated exploitation and – what is of greater importance – insofar as the countries concerned can produce for a wider market. This, of course, is a considerable objective advantage – the rapid implementation of which is, however, hindered by a number of circumstances.

The larger countries are less interested than the small ones in the co-operation that consists mainly in the utilisation of the advantages of a wider market. However, from the point of view of the world economy, the industrialisation of the developing countries will be decided precisely by the large countries among them: India, Pakistan, Indonesia, Brazil, etc. In addition, there are substantial differerences in development level among the individual countries. For example, in Latin America, the industrialisation of Peru, Ecuador, Columbia or Bolivia could be impaired by a customs union with Mexico or Brazil and the opening of their markets to the products of these countries. Although this danger could be reduced by drawing up detailed joint plans and by regulating the process of integration, such detailed planning is hardly conceivable under the present conditions; even if it were realised, it would certainly slow down the development of reciprocal deliveries.

The intensification of regional co-operation requires special measures, some type of a common market, common protective customs regulations and the reduction of customs duties in reciprocal trade, or a system of special import quotas. Measures of this type would, however, hurt quite important vested interests. Consumers would hardly rejoice at the fact that, whereas in the past they had been in a position to import from any advanced country, in the future they should be restricted (at least to a greater extent than before) to the industrial products of other developing countries. Moreover, in the case of reduced duty rates, the customs authorities would find themselves with a reduced revenue compared with the past. Under these conditions it should obviously not be difficult to find objective arguments in favour of breaking or preventing the measures aimed at co-operation.

When organising regional co-operation, a distinction should be made between existing industries (or production) and industries which must be newly established. In the first case, it is probable that the industry in question has attained some development level in all the countries concerned. Whether or not, in this case, the advantage of a wider market potentially offered by integration outweighs the disadvantage that competition will grow in future on the domestic market is a serious problem. In the case of new industries, however, it is rather difficult to distribute proportionately and justly among the countries concerned the burden involved in their creation, namely investment, the loss of earlier customs revenue and of the advantages of increased employment, higher taxes, etc.

Thus the development of regional co-operation will need decisions at government level that subordinate short-term interests to long-term ones and, what is even more difficult, a consistent political and government activity to implement in practice the theoretical decision taken on principles of co-operation. The governments of the developing countries frequently emphasise their mutual solidarity in the arena of world politics; a certain solidarity really does exist and some common steps are taken (particularly in respect of economic demands on the developed countries and on the remaining centres of colonialism). There are, nevertheless, numerous old or new tensions between neighbouring developing countries, where the political attitudes of governments are often opposed to each other: all of which hinders co-operation on urgent economic problems.

Taking all these facts into consideration, it seems that in the near future we can hardly expect a radical change in the area of industrial co-operation among developing countries. A favourable development is more likely to take place in the smallest and industrially least developed countries of Central America, West Africa and East Africa, where development is taking place on a sub-regional rather than regional level. Although this may have a beneficial influence on the development of the countries concerned, it will not greatly affect the industrialisation of the developing world as a whole.

REFERENCES

1. L. I. Revizner and G. K. Sirokov, 'Industrial transformation in contemporary India', *Narody Azii i Afriki*, 1967, No. 2 (in Russian).
2. N. S. Buchanan and H. S. Ellis, *Approaches to Economic Development*, New York, 1955, pp. 267, 268, 269.
3. See in detail 'Organisation and Operation of Cottage and Small Industries' (Recommendations of a group of experts based on a survey of cottage and small-scale industries in Japan), *Industrialisation and Productivity*, New York, 1959, p. 2.
4. Ibid., p. 39.
5. See Ishikawa, op. cit., p. 16.
6. *Policies and Programmes for the Development of Small Scale Industry*, United Nations Industrial Development Organisation, I.D./Conf. 1/6, April 1967.
7. J. C. Sandesara, 'Scale and Technology in Indian Industry', *Bulletin of the Oxford University Institute of Economics and Statistics*, 1966, No. 3. For definition see James and James, *Mathematics Dictionary*, Princeton, N.J., 1968, p. 84.
8. Konosuke Odaka, 'On Employment and Wage-Differential Structure in Japan: a Survey', *Hitotsubashi Journal of Economics*, June 1967, Vol. 8, No. 1.
9. *Policies and Programmes for the Development of Small Scale Industry*, International Symposium on Industrial Development, I.D./Conf. 1/6.
10. Op. cit., pp. 17–20.
11. Eugene Staley, *Les programmes de développement des 'micro-industries': Méthodes de Développement Industriel et leur application aux pays en voie de développement*, O.C.D.E., 1962.
12. W. A. Lewis, *The Theory of Economic Growth*, London, 1955, p. 386.
13. A. E. Kahn, 'Investment Criteria in Development Programs', *Quarterly Journal of Economics*, February 1951.

14. See Annex III/1.
15. For details see *Manual on economic development projects*, United Nations, 1958.
16. *Beruházások gazdasági hatékonysága* (Economic efficiency of investments) Közgazdasági és Jogi Könyvkiadó, Budapest, 1959, p. 38.
17. Chenery ('The application of investment criteria', *The Quarterly Journal of Economics*, February 1953) says that the effect on national income can be worked out on the basis of the profit calculations of businessmen, applying certain corrections.
18. W. Galenson and H. Leibenstein, 'Investment Criteria, Productivity and Economic Development', *Quarterly Journal of Economics*, August 1955.
19. Charles Bettelheim, *Studies in the Theory of Planning*, Asia Publishing House, Bombay, 1959.
20. M. Dobb, *On Economic Theory and Socialism*, London, 1955.
21. Bettelheim, op. cit. p. 343.
22. Op. cit., p. 297.
23. Op. cit., pp. 338–40.
24. E. F. Schumacher, 'Phoney War on Poverty: Aid on the Crossroads', *Statist*, 24 Dec. 1965.
25. Economic Commission for Latin America, *The Process of Industrial Development in Latin America*, U.N., New York, 1966, pp. 43–4; Economic Commission for Asia and the Far East, *Industrial Development: Asia and the Far East*, New York, 1966, p. 43.
26. This relationship is the formula presented by A. K. Sen, but used in a different context and to investigate different problems. See A. K. Sen, 'Choice of technology, a critical survey of a class of debates', *Planning for advanced skills and technologies*, U.N., New York, 1969.
27. A. S. Bhalla, 'Choosing Techniques: Handpounding v. Machine-milling of Rice: An Indian Case', *Oxford Economic Papers*, March 1965.
28. A. S. Bhalla, 'Investment Allocation and technological choice', *The Economic Journal*, Sept. 1964.
29. A. K. Sen, *Choice of Techniques*, Oxford, 1960, Appendix C.
30. *Industrial Development Survey*, U.N.I.D.O., I.D/Conf. 1/46, 1967.
31. Op. cit., p. 118.
32. In a more exact calculation this should, of course, be corrected for the level of employment.
33. *International Trade Yearbook*, U.N., 1965.
34. *Industrial Development Survey*, Vienna, 1967, U.N.I.D.O. I.D./Conf. 1, 1/46. According to the second, wider (I.S.I.C.) interpretation, the foodstuffs and tobacco in categories 0–1 of S.I.T.C., as well as vegetable fats and oils (S.I.T.C. 2 and 4) come under 20–22 of I.S.I.C. and the oil derivatives in S.I.T.C. 3 under 32 of I.S.I.C., that is, they are classified as manufactures.
35. S.I.T.C. 0 and 1, that is food, beverages and tobacco largely unprocessed, S.I.T.C. 3 (mineral fuels and related materials) in manufacturing proper. S.I.T.C. 6, that is mainly materials and semi-finished goods and within S.I.T.C. 8 (miscellaneous manufacturing), clothing and footwear, having slow growth rates compared to chemicals (S.I.T.C. 5), or engineering products (S.I.T.C. 7 and 86).
36. U.N.C.T.A.D./T.D./82 Add. 1–4.
37. U.N.C.T.A.D./E./Conf., 46/11.

IV

ECONOMIC PLANNING AND THE ROLE OF GOVERNMENT IN THE INDUSTRIALISATION OF DEVELOPING COUNTRIES

Fifteen or twenty years ago, economic planning and socialist economy were considered as essentially identical concepts. Economic plans were drawn up only in the Soviet Union and, relying on the example of the Soviet Union, in the socialist countries born after the Second World War. This situation had radically changed by the beginning of the 1960s. Plans are worked out in several developed Western countries, though planning has not yet achieved an accepted status everywhere in this area. In the developing countries, however, that is in the Latin American, African and in the Asian (non-socialist) countries, *the necessity of planning has been generally accepted.* Since the early 1960s, medium-term economic plans (covering 3–5–7 years) are being drawn up in almost every developing country. The planning thus emerged or emerging in the individual developing countries shows certain similarities – at least if confronted with the planning in the socialist and the advanced capitalist countries – at least as far as similarity can be mentioned at all in respect of countries of such different size, development level and economic potentials as, say, India, Ghana or Mexico. Economic planning in the developing countries obtains special emphasis since it is closely related to the increased economic role of the state; it asserts itself on this basis and as its most important tool, in fact, in certain countries it provides a framework, as it were, for the entire economic activity of the government.

The surprisingly quick spread of economic planning in the developing countries has several closely interrelated causes. (These causes may, of course, be of varying importance in different countries and regions.) For a better understanding of these interrelations it will be worthwhile to outline them briefly.

1. *Causes of the Rapid Spread of Economic Planning*

In the developing countries, particularly in Africa and Asia, one of the most important objectives of the countries which became independent after the Second World War was to liquidate their economic backwardness by fast economic growth. The emphasis was not merely on development but on *fast* development. This is necessary not only because of their poverty, but also because of the fast increase of their population. This is why the example of the Soviet Union, which from being a relatively backward country, became a big industrial power after the First World War, and the economic growth of the other socialist countries impressed them so much. Understandably, they attribute the results achieved – at least partly – to the planning of the economy. This approach makes economic planning desirable for them.[1]

In some countries, though by no means in the majority of the developing countries, the official policy of governments or governing parties was also that the means of production should be in social ownership in some branches.[2] Already in the 1930s, the Congress Party in India took a stand, if not quite unequivocally, for the state ownership or state control of key industries, mines and transport, and already in 1938 created a commission to study the problems of economic planning. It is, however, worthwhile to note already at this point that in several developing countries economic plans are drawn up, though official policy stands firmly on the basis of private ownership. Even in these countries the state may create industrial enterprises, but this is regarded rather as a transitory solution – as for example in Pakistan – and as soon as it becomes possible they are handed over to private capital.

In some countries which today are independent, a few of the ruling powers, mainly Britain and France, began after the Second World War, and partly already during the war, to work out programmes which tried to take stock of the possibilities and needs of the area in question, and drew up estimates for the various resources and mainly for government investment in the framework of a co-ordinated and coherent programme. In the earlier British and French African colonies and the British West Indies, the economic plans mostly emerged as a continuation of these programmes.

The quick spread of drawing up economic plans is also related to the circumstance that *in the economy of the developing countries the state plays a greater role than it did in the now developed capitalist countries at the start of their economic growth.* From the political point of view it is a determinant circumstance that economic growth is considered in the developing countries not only a condition of growing public welfare but as one of political-national independence as well. Therefore, it is the task of the government to take the initiative and to control economic growth; this is also expected by public opinion.

Beyond this political factor, the controlling role of the state has become necessary also because of economic circumstances, largely owing to the following causes:

Domestic capital formation is low, and in particular the capital which would serve investment with long pay-off periods and requiring a substantial sum is scarce. In these sectors, therefore, government investment or foreign aid must be resorted to. Even in respect of the latter the participation of the government or some of its bodies or their initiative is in many cases unavoidable.

Owing to the weakness of the business community there is also a scarcity of suitable entrepreneurs and qualified high-level specialists. A great part of the few domestic specialists (engineers, economists) are employed by various government offices. Thus, if they do not want to allow foreigners to keep their leading role in the economy, the state has to fulfil many entrepreneurial functions which, in the now developed capitalist countries, were and are still played by private capital.

Foreign trade is of particular importance in the economy of the developing countries. The ratio of foreign trade is high in comparison to national income, and a considerable part of government revenue, not infrequently more than half of it, derives from taxes levied on foreign trade. In the modern sector of the economy, either agriculture or industry, the importance of foreign trade is even greater. Industrialisation, particularly in its initial stages, is in most developing countries closely interrelated with import substitution, i.e. with the introduction of the domestic production of articles previously imported. Therefore, industrialisation, and through it the whole of economic development, is influenced by government handling of import duties, import licences and subsidies.

The foreign capital operating in the country, and foreign aid and loans also necessitate government interference in order to regulate foreign capital, or, conversely, to offer a guarantee to foreign capital.

It is a widespread experience in the developing countries that financial, taxation and budgetary, as well as other economic decisions, have been taken for the short run, in an unco-ordinated manner, neglecting the perspectives of economic development. The means serving investment and other economic development purposes are distributed among the individual ministries or other offices. These means are then used without consideration for the indirect effects, or the interests or needs of the economy as a whole. In addition, in the developing countries the representatives of various local and group interests – for all their good intentions – can exert great pressure on a department entrusted with taking some measure, or taking a decision on some particular investment. The foreign loans and aids also frequently contributed to the resulting chaos. Owing to the budgetary system of the country granting the loan, or to other reasons, the sums offered must often be spent fast, neglecting the necessary analyses and consideration. Such a situation, of course, does not favour a rational and efficient utilisation of resources, and it is understandable that it should usually generate dissatisfaction. Thus, the necessity has arisen to co-ordinate the many-sided economic activity of the state in some way or other. The requirement that this co-ordination should be realised by drawing up economic plans for several years has therefore been pushed to the foreground.

The developed countries granting loans, and particularly the United States, were outspoken against plans up to the 1960s. They emphasised that a plan does not properly allow the market forces and private enterprise to assert themselves; according to their standpoint, these are the factors which best promote development. The standpoint of the U.S.A. radically changed in the early 1960s with the coming to power of the Kennedy administration. From being enemies of planning, the Americans become its most fervent advocates. The Alliance for Progress of the American countries, well known as being backed mainly by the U.S.A., expressly recommended for its members the drawing up of economic development plans, and made it into a condition for obtaining foreign loans. We cannot, of course, treat here in detail the causes of the change in behaviour of the American government. Some part was presumably played by the favourable experience in Western Europe – namely that this West European kind of planning can be reconciled with private ownership of means of production and does not endanger its existence. French planning even contributed to strengthening the French capitalist economy. The most important circumstance, however, was probably the experience that the aid and loans obtained are used in the developing countries very inefficiently. The Americans also expected that planning would contribute to the strengthening of the economy in developing countries – of their capitalist economy, of course – and with this, to expanding the possibilities for American capital exports to earn profits. Besides the various international organisations, the Latin American and Asian Economic Commission of the U.N. in particular had already been dealing earlier with the methods of economic planning, which they tried to work out in conformity with the circumstances of the developing countries and make them known and popular in those countries.

It was no easy task for economic theory in the leading Western countries to justify the acceptance of the necessity of planning. According to the school which had ascendancy in the past, it is the market and the price mechanisms that most perfectly secure the rational and most efficient allocation of resources and, simultaneously, the fastest economic growth; planning was considered not only superfluous – because economic development cannot be foreseen with sufficient accuracy – but harmful as well, since it distorted the free play of market forces. More conservative economists maintain this standpoint for the advanced capitalist countries. But in respect of the developing countries, the view now prevails that the 'imperfection' of the market mechanism there does not allow prices properly to guide economic decisions. They advocate planning as a way to eliminate this deficiency, as a tool which promotes rational choice among the various investment or other development objectives.

Since, owing to these reasons, most governments in developing countries desire to have an economic plan, in most cases some document is drawn up and called a plan. Understandably, however, these plans may differ greatly in their details, their degree of realism, their connection with actual economic development and with the economic policy of the government, and finally in respect of their efficiency.

2. Efficiency of Economic Planning in the Developing Countries

It is not easy to give a balanced account of the results of economic planning in the developing countries, of their actual effects on the economy. This is difficult also because very different things can be called 'results'. In a broader sense, and looking at the problem from a more general aspect, the result of planning is a rapid or accelerated growth of the economy, and the attainment of desired structural changes, e.g. reduction of income differences between regions or between individual strata of the population, or fast growth of particularly important economic sectors. But we know that growth of the economy may be affected by several other factors besides planning, and it would not be justified to ascribe to planning the consequences of some natural calamity or bad harvest, just as a particularly good harvest or a rise in the world market price of some export article could not be attributed to planning. The actual effect of planning could be measured rather by the extent to which the potentialities of the country have been used in the interest of developing the economy.

The answer is not easy. It is hardly possible to establish what would have happened if no economic plan had been drawn up.

Similarly, it is difficult to separate the effect of the plan from that of plan implementation. The problem does not become easier if one compares countries which do or do not prepare economic plans, or those with more and less detailed plans, since the circumstances of the individual countries, particularly developing ones, may differ from each other to a great extent.

The efficiency of planning, interpreted in a narrower sense as a method, is characterised also by the extent to which planning techniques have been developed, in other words: (*a*) to what extent is the *planning* method suited for a realistic assessment of possibilities, for the calculation of the best utilisation and allocation of the resources? and (*b*) to what extent is the method of *implementation* suited for the control and management of the economy in the desired direction, relying on the plans drawn up and adopted?

Insofar as we examine the efficiency of planning in the broader sense, i.e. from the viewpoint of economic growth in the developing countries, we have to establish that since there has been a wider spread of planning, economic growth has not accelerated.

Table IV/1

AVERAGE RATE OF GROWTH OF PRODUCTION AND FOREIGN TRADE IN THE DEVELOPING COUNTRIES, 1950–70 (*per cent*)

	1950–5	1955–60	1960–5	1965–70
G.N.P.	4·9	4·5	4·7	5·6
per capita G.N.P.	2·8	2·1	2·0	2·8
Industrial output	—	8·1	7·0	7·2
Agricultural output:	—	—	—	1·0
Africa	—	1·9	2·1	2·5
Latin America	—	3·9	3·7	2·0
Far East	—	2·8	2·1	3·6
Near East	—	4·5	3·4	2·5
Exports	2·6	4·4	5·9	8·5
Imports	5·1	4·1	4·7	8·3

Source: 'Development Plans: Appraisal of Targets and Progress in Developing Countries', *World Economic Survey 1964*, Part I, U.N., New York, 1965; *World Economic Survey 1966* Part II, U.N., New York, for 1950–60 and U.N. *Statistical, Yearbook 1971* for 1965–70.

It appears from Table IV/1 that the growth rate of gross national product has hardly increased in the last 20 years. In the first half of the 1950s, the growth rate was, on annual average, 4·9 per cent, while in the sixties it was 4·7–5·6 per cent. The growth of *per capita* income shows first a declining and then a stagnating trend. As regards the two major components of national income, the situation is that industrial output increased satisfactorily, by 7–8 per cent annually, while agricultural production grew only slowly, by 2–3 per cent annually. Since in the national product of developing countries agriculture still has a preponderant role, its effect appears also in the growth rate of the total G.N.P.

Taking the individual countries separately, very different growth rates can, of course, be found. In the decade 1953–63, for example, there were developing countries whose G.N.P. increased very quickly, by about 10–11 per cent in a year (e.g. Israel, Trinidad and Tobago), while the economies of other developing countries stagnated (e.g. Uruguay, Morocco); in the other developing countries we can find any growth rate between 2 per cent and 8–9 per cent.[3]

A comparison of the planned and actual rates of growth reflects partly the efficiency of planning and plan implementation, but partly also the effect of external factors:

Table IV/2

PLANNED AND ACTUAL GROWTH RATES OF G.N.P.
IN SOME DEVELOPING COUNTRIES

	G.N.P.		*Per capita G.N.P.*	
	Planned	*Actual*	*Planned*	*Actual*
Taiwan (1961–3)	8·0	7·0	5·0	3·5
U.A.R. (1960–3)	7·0	6·1	4·5	3·5
Burma (1962–3)	6·0	5·9	4·0	3·7
Ceylon 1960–3)	6·0	3·5	3·0	0·8
Morocco (1960–3)	6·0	4·4	4·0	1·7
South Korea (1962–3)	6·0	5·2	3·0	2·3
Tunisia (1962–3)	6·0	3·9	4·5	1·7
Chile (1961–3)	5·5	3·9	3·0	1·6
Colombia (1961–3)	5·5	4·6	3·0	2·3
India (1961–3)	5·5	3·2	3·0	1·1
Sudan (1961–3)	5·0	7·5	2·0	4·4
Pakistan (1960–3)	4·5	5·3	2·5	3·1
Malaysian Federation (1961–3)	4·0	5·9	1·0	2·5

Source: 'Development Plans: Appraisal of Targets and Progress in Developing Countries', *World Economic Survey 1964*, Part I, U.N., New York, 1965.

Thus we obtain a mixed picture even in this respect. Among the thirteen countries in the table, three have exceeded the planned growth rate of G.N.P., and ten have lagged behind. From another aspect: in seven cases the deviation exceeded 1 per cent, in the others the planned and actual figures essentially coincided. If planning is analysed from some abstract point of view, these results do not reflect great exactness or reliability as regards forecasting and plan implementation. If, however, we consider that in the first half of the 1960s the fulfilment of the medium-term plans of the European socialist countries shows an essentially similar picture in respect of the accuracy of planning and plan implementation; and furthermore take into account that these countries have greater experience in planning than the developing countries, and that, in socialist countries, both the attained level of economic development and social relations create better conditions for planning than those under which the developing countries have to draw up their plans, we must draw the conclusion that in the developing countries economic planning was not altogether unsuccessful in the period reviewed.[4]

More detailed data on plans and plan fulfilment, broken down by major branches of the economy, are available only for eleven countries. Among these, the targets in three were met in both industry and agriculture, in a further three only those set for industry and in four none. From this the conclusion can be drawn that in agriculture it is more difficult to draw up realistic plans and implement them than it is in industry. (It must, of course, be added that the experience of socialist countries is similar.)

There are many indications that the general *increase in the working out of economic plans among the developing countries does not mean that if the plans comprised well-considered and well-founded economic objectives, to implement which the necessary means are available, they can also put these means to purposeful use.* This is also indicated by the fact that one can obtain some information on the plans, but hardly any on their implementation. A U.N. publication of 1965, 'Development Plans: Appraisal of Targets and Progress in Developing Countries',[5] gives the data on the growth of G.N.P. from the plans of thirty-eight Afro-Asian and Latin American countries (division by regions: Africa 18, Asia 13, Latin America 7). But *even the U.N. Secretariat* succeeded in collecting the plan fulfilment data on the growth of G.N.P. for only thirteen countries. In a breakdown by branches, the planned and actual growth of G.N.P. could be shown for only eleven countries, and the planned and actual investments for only five. On the basis of the lack of data on plan fulfilment, it seems that, although the plan is drawn up, the realisation of the plan somehow gets lost, or is not taken too seriously.

E

Among specialists engaged in economic planning, there is a general opinion that among the developing countries it is India where planning is best, and which has accumulated the most experience.[6] Yet in India there is great dissatisfaction with planning. (Of course, this dissatisfaction is only a reflection and a part of the dissatisfaction with Indian economic growth.) This is well illustrated by the statement voiced in the presidential address to the 48th annual conference of Indian economists in December 1965: 'Planning and planners are on the defensive in India today. . . . Planning has not, on the whole, delivered the goods.'[7]

The critique related to the plans' lack of reality, to the over-centralised and bureaucratic planning apparatus, but mainly to bad implementation; for the deficiencies it put the blame not so much on planners and planning as on the general political and social conditions, and advocated not less but more and, at the same time, better planning.

3. *Special Problems of Planning in the Developing Countries*

As has been mentioned, there is a fairly general consensus that planning is necessary in the developing countries. There is also a view, particularly in some developing countries, that planning is more efficient in the backward than in the developed industrial economy.[8] This view is supported by the following arguments:

(*a*) In the developed countries it is more difficult to bring the existing institutions under the control of the plan or of the state than the newly established ones in the developing countries (for example, if the industrial enterprise is created by the state and remains under its control and, depending on circumstances, in its ownership).

(*b*) The new investment in the developing countries, if properly co-ordinated, can be more efficient than similar investment in the advanced countries.

(*c*) Attainment of the national goals – national independence and defence – is better secured by the economic plan than by a market economy operating without a plan.

(*d*) In a developing country the development of heavy industry is of greater importance than that of light industry, while private capital prefers rather the light industrial investment that is quickly paid off.

We shall revert to the comparison of planning in the capitalist and the developing countries. It must be noted, however, that ideas (*c*) and (*d*) support the *necessity* of planning rather than its greater efficiency in the developing countries. In reality, the introduction of economic planning is indeed necessary, but its efficient implementation is rather more difficult and certainly not easier than in the advanced countries.

As is known, the economy of the developing countries is a so-called 'mixed economy' where we find side by side the pre-capitalist subsistence economy (the majority of agriculture with the related cottage industry), the state (social) ownership of the means of production and, in addition, the (domestic and foreign) capitalist sectors. *Per capita* national income and capital formation are low, the share of industry and transportation in the national income are also low, and the economy is heavily dependent on foreign trade and overwhelmingly also on foreign credit and aid. Owing to backwardness, the statistical service necessary for planning (mainly the economic and demographical statistics), is underdeveloped and there are few specialists who understand planning.

Let us examine the problems that are created by these circumstances for the drawing up and implementation of economic plans; we shall divide planning, for the sake of an easier survey, into the following three, closely interrelated parts:

(*a*) the drawing up of long-term (medium-term) aggregate economic plans, and plans broken down by sectors;

(*b*) the drawing up of more detailed plans, not like the annual plans of the socialist countries, but concrete measures, mainly from the viewpoint of planning the investment to develop the economy;

(*c*) the implementation of the plans and the realisation of the necessary measures.

The basis of *long-term planning* is the definition of main objectives of economic policy and determination of the means available for their implementation. In this broadest context the development policies of the countries in question have taken shape. In general, it is usual to set as main economic objective the quickest possible growth of the economy (in terms of the growth of national income globally and *per capita*), the development of backward regions, the reduction of income inequalities, the raising of employment, and the diversification of the production and/or export pattern of the country. In the long run there is usually no contradiction between economic growth and the other goals mentioned, but in the short run this may occur. In the economic policy of developed market economies (or their economic plans) it is not infrequent that price stability or the stability of the balance of payments is really considered as more important than economic growth. In the developing countries, however – and probably correctly – economic growth is considered to be the main goal, and it enjoys priority over other goals.

This circumstance is reflected also in the plans of the developing countries, since they plan a fast growth rate of economic development. The annual average growth rate in those plans which are actually valid is – according to a survey of the plans of about forty countries – about 5–8 per cent, against the actually experienced 4–4·5 per cent of the last decade. Only in exceptional cases do we find a decreasing growth rate in the plan against the preceding period and only when the earlier growth rate was so outstanding that there is no hope of maintaining it.[9] Not infrequently, a considerable growth in national income is planned, 4 per cent or even more against the earlier period. In order to accelerate growth, the plans of the developing countries increase both the absolute volume of investment and their share in national income; i.e. the ratio of consumption is decreased. Only a few countries provide for a decreasing dependence on foreign aid, several countries count on increasing aid.

When *more detailed plans are drawn up*, greater difficulties emerge. The plan comprises the development of the most important economic indicators (production, consumption, foreign trade, etc.), as well as the allocation of resources among the various economic sectors. The necessary methods – i.e. the various methods of prognostication, and the balance-methods suited for checking the consistency (equilibrium) of resource allocation – are well known; these are applied in the developing countries, or at least they are applicable in principle. But the *efficient* use of the methods has quite a few obstacles. As mentioned, proper statistics are lacking, even the most important comprehensive economic and demographic data. In several developing countries only approximate data are available even on population. Similarly, the data on national income are frequently lacking or are available only with a considerable time lag.[10] The data on industrial or agricultural output, transport, or the production of individual articles are lacking or deficient. Even if the statistical data are available, the special circumstances of the developing countries (fast changes in structure, etc.) make planning very difficult.

Planners expect the improvement of resource allocation – at least to a significant degree – from various aggregate or detailed econometic models. The construction of such models was attempted in the developing countries, and in their efforts they obtained help from the most distinguished experts (e.g. Ragnar Frisch worked in the U.A.R., and Tinbergen in the framework of the Asian Economic Commission of the U.N.), but for the time being without any outstanding success. One of the reasons is that even the most complicated, most detailed model is too simple in comparison to reality.[11] And since the prognostication of the basic data is particularly uncertain in the economies of the developing countries, the use of the models does not diminish the role of subjective judgements, of intuition in planning. This is why the models and the more sophisticated planning methods have not yet obtained a significant role in the economic plans of the developing countries. (Of course, there is also the lack of experts, but this, in my opinion, is not the heart of the matter. In several developing countries, e.g. India or some Latin American countries, the recruiting of domestic or foreign experts versed in programming does not cause any trouble.) Thus, the developing countries are at a disadvantage as against the economically advanced countries in respect of perspective planning, owing to the smaller accuracy of prognoses, and the weaker scientific foundation of resource allocation, which may be traced back to the lack or unreliability of basic data, and to quicker changes in the economic structure.

In spite of all this, the drawing up of plans has some advantages. It is a serious practical advantage that under present circumstances it is easier to obtain foreign loans with than without plans.[12] In addition, planning promotes the acquisition of data and other knowledge necessary not only for planning but for the control and influencing of the whole economy. In many developing countries the development of economic and demographic statistics, geological and several other surveys are closely related to the drawing up of plans. The planning process itself – quite apart from the realisation of plans – contributes to the diagnosis, discussion and wider knowledge of the country's development problems.

The perspective plan, comprising the expected or desirable growth rate and the structural changes of the economy and the main sectors, is in itself obviously not sufficient for measures to be taken on the strength of it in order to implement the objectives outlined in the plan. For that purpose more detailed planning is needed. The contents of the more detailed plans are, in view of the conditions of the developing countries, mainly the *investment* projects. In this field the difficulties of the developing countries are substantially greater than in perspective planning. The problem emerges in a rather different manner with respect to government and private investment.

Government investment comprises resources available through the budget, inclusive of the credits granted to private enterpreneurs as well as the foreign loans and aid given to or through the government. The volume of government investment in the developing countries is rather high – though it shows wide dispersion – amounting to about 40–50 per cent of total investment; in certain branches, particularly in agriculture, transport and energy production, it is even higher. With direct government investment the problem is the best allocation of the available resources in conformity with the social objectives laid down in the plan and with other decisions on economic development, i.e. the calculation of investment efficiency.[13] The difficulties are thus related to the correct choice of the magnitude of the time-factor (rate of interest), the formula to be used, the commensurability of results and inputs of different dimensions (e.g. the increase of employment or the development of some backward area or an industry), the correct evaluation of inter-industry relations and indirect effects, the comparison of domestic currency with foreign exchange, etc. The problem seemed important enough for an international symposium to be convened in Prague in 1965 by the Secretariat of the U.N. to discuss and study the related, mainly methodological problems[14] and, relying on the lessons of the Prague symposium to organise local seminars in several places in the developing countries (up to now in Mexico, Ceylon, India and Iran).

In my opinion, the *methodological* problems related to the economic calculations necessary for 'filling in' the framework of the plan, though they must not be underestimated, can be solved relatively easily. The *procuring and proper evaluation of the technological and economic data constituting the basis of the calculations causes more trouble*. It should be taken into account that trained experts are scarce in the developing countries. If they avail themselves of foreign specialists from developed capitalist countries, not infrequently a certain lack of objective approach must be reckoned with, namely that – even if not in a dishonest way – they make efforts to propagate in the course of their expert activities the products of a certain country or enterprise. A further difficulty is that under the conditions of the developing countries the plants or technological processes regarding which there exists no domestic experience at all are not rare. This causes difficulties even for trained experts who know the technology in question, since it cannot be transplanted without any change into the different conditions of another country. (The U.N. wishes to help overcome such difficulties by collecting the characteristic technological and economic parameters of various industries and factories and making them available to the developing countries.)[15]

The greater part of state investment – which in the developing countries generally amounts to more than 50 per cent – serves the development of infrastructure in the broader sense, i.e. it is not an immediately productive investment but it creates, or improves, the conditions for production (energy, transport and, in agriculture, irrigation, amelioration of soil, etc.). Owing to their nature, such investment is paid off slowly, its immediate economic effect cannot be assessed in a reliable way, and what has to be calculated is rather the choice of the variant most suited for the realisation of given objectives. However, as regards the directly productive, mainly manu-facturing investment – particularly where the plans reckon mainly with private investments – the situation is different: here the profit motive has primary importance. According to the experience of past years, and particularly according to the opinion of international financial institutions granting credits to the developing countries, the obstacle to a greater increase in such investment and to the opera-tive 'filling out' of the frameworks of the plans is not lack of capital, but the fact that there are not enough investment proposals that would be sufficiently attractive. This circumstance may be traced back to several causes. The concrete circumstances of individual countries have not been satisfactorily disclosed, from the point of view of either the perspectives of economic development or from that of natural conditions. This disclosure is served by the economic plans themselves, but the details of such work – e.g. in the case of geological prospecting – are costly matters, and they may also re-quire a quantity of specialists such as are not available in the develop-ing countries. Thus, the number of investment proposals could be increased – which may seem favourable for the foreign creditor (or domestic investor). But this is not the whole story, since under the conditions of the developing countries it is not always easy to find adequately profitable possibilities for private capital owing to the lack of specialists, the frequently narrow market, transportation difficulties and other causes.

In the course of *implementing* the plans of the developing coun-tries difficulties are caused by the circumstances already mentioned in connection with drawing up the plan, i.e. the lack of properly trained and qualified specialists, the great influence of particular – foreign and domestic – interests, the lack of uniform government apparatus, etc. Beyond all these circumstances, however, the im-plementation of the plans is made difficult in these countries by their extremely strong dependence on foreign trade. This dependence appears not only in the fact that a considerable portion of the national income of developing countries is realised through foreign trade (in this the smaller socialist and capitalist countries are in a similar situation), but in that their foreign trade position is particularly unstable because the overwhelming part of their exports is made up from a small number of raw materials, and a great part of their volume of foreign trade is not infrequently directed towards one or two developed countries. Monoculture and the resulting lack of diversified exports puts the foreign trade situation of these countries into a particularly vulnerable position. Since the machinery and equipment needed for development – and often a considerable part of the raw materials or spare parts necessary for the operation of newly established industries – also originate from imports (in recent years, the importation of foodstuffs has been growing too), the maintenance of exports and their constant augmentation is of pivotal importance for the developing countries.

The above circumstances are well known. It is less well known that in a great part of the developing countries often half or even two-thirds of government revenue originates from taxes levied on foreign trade.[16] A decline in exports or even non-realisation of expected development holds back economic development in the developing countries, as a rule either because of narrowing markets or owing to falling prices. Such disturbances, however, have been frequently felt in every developing country. It is not unjustified to assume that the efforts characterising the economic plans of the developing countries – namely industrialisation mostly through import substitution and the diversification of exports – can be traced back much more to such past experiences than to theoretical considerations in respect of industrial policies.

4. *Particular Features of Planning and the Economic Role of the Government in the Developing and the Developed Capitalist Countries; 'Global' and 'Selective' Measures*

The planning introduced in individual non-socialist countries is far from uniform as regards general conditions, results or methods. A clear survey of the matter is also hindered by the circumstance that the information available in writing is not too authentic, or, even if it is, prepared from different aspects, which would make a comparison misleading.[17]

It is instructive to compare the planning of the developing countries and of the developed capitalist countries. In comparing planning in the two groups with respect to methods, general conditions and expected effects, several similarities and, at the same time, substantial differences will be found. In quite general terms, the main difference is related to the fact that, while in the advanced capitalist countries planning is the *result* of economic growth, in the developing countries it is the *precondition* of development.[18] In the first case, the main function of planning is rather the rational use of existing resources: their development is, as it were, a by-product of proper utilisation. In the second case, its main function is to develop productive forces for which, of course, also rational use of existing productive forces is necessary.

The spread of economic planning is related in both groups of countries to the economic role of the government. The opinion is rather uniform that in the developing countries, the 'traditional' methods of industrial capitalism – when the influence of the government on the economy is restricted to creating some general rules and to taking over such social tasks as, for example, education or road building – are not suited to modernising the economy and accelerating growth. Thus the government necessarily plays an important role in the economy, and this role is bound to grow in the future owing to political, technological and economic factors. As has been mentioned, this role is already greater than it was in the now developed capitalist countries in the nineteenth century or at the beginning of the twentieth, though these countries were even then more developed than the developing countries are now, and in spite of the fact that it can be proved that the economic role of the state or, more exactly, *one of the characteristics* of this economic role, i.e. the ratio of government expenditure to national income is growing in the capitalist countries with economic growth. In the Western European countries in the 1870s, the budget amounted to about 4–5 per cent of national income; it remained below 10 per cent even at the beginning of this century, while it is now around 14–16 per cent.[19] The same ratio in the developing countries – though depending heavily on development level and on the relative magnitude of foreign trade – remains only in exceptional cases below 10 per cent (in the less developed countries which, at the same time, transact the smallest amount of foreign trade) and is frequently higher than 20 per cent.[20]

There are important differences in respect of *the views on, and interests related to*, planning. The views emerging in the developing countries, particularly the Afro-Asian countries, in their most influential circles, regarding the economic role and tasks of the government, differ from the views dominant in the same circles in the now developed capitalist countries and particularly from those prevailing at the start of their economic development. Economic growth in the latter group began in a period when the belief in the blessings of free-competition capitalism was widespread; hence, growth – the unfolding of the economic forces of society – was expected to follow precisely from abolishing the coercive rules applied by the central power and the authorities to the greatest extent possible, thereby promoting the freedom of capitalist enterprise. In this concept, the role of the government would be restricted (with some exageration) to maintaining public safety, and development would come about only through the activities of individual capitalist entrepreneurs co-ordinated by the market and price movements. In the developed capitalist countries, free-competition capitalism – where government was, as a matter of fact, never really 'neutral' from the economic point of view – actually brought about economic growth, although burdened with crises and linked with exploitation

E*

and mass poverty. Today the role of the government in the economy is already considerable, and it is growing. Efforts are made, however, to present this role as temporary, as a necessary evil. The reason is that, although in its entirety government activity corresponds on the whole to the interests of the entrepreneurs, there is a stratum of capitalists which is against interference or at least against some forms of it. At any rate, it is in the interests of the whole capitalist class not to acknowledge the necessity and general spread of government interference, since this would provide an argument for the increased restriction of capital and even for its nationalisation in the public interest.

In the developing countries there is no such tradition that free-competition capitalism – as far as it prevailed in these countries – would have brought economic growth; in fact, their lagging behind is strongly linked with the period when this concept was dominant in the developed world. There is no capitalist class strong enough to counter government action; in fact, there is no influential capitalist stratum whose interest would be to reduce the economic role of the state. Obviously, government interference hinders the activity of capitalists. There are frequent complaints that government measures are cumbersome and bureaucratic, and a great part of the complaints is certainly justified. Yet the governmental measures serve the interests of 'those in possession', and in practice frequently create monopolistic situations, thereby promoting the emergence of higher profits and the concentration of economic power. The state allocates raw materials or foreign exchange, issues import licences, grants permits to open certain factories or to start production of certain goods, secures favourable terms of credit, etc. and thus provides resources for some while keeping them away from others, since it is always the scarce resources that must be managed. All these benefits can be acquired more easily by an already existing capitalist enterprise than by one that wishes to start something new, and more easily by the larger than the smaller enterprise, and even more easily by the one which has good (mainly political) connections. It cannot even be assumed that the creation of state enterprises would be detrimental for capitalists. Owing to the general scarcity of capital, it should hardly be feared that the existing capital cannot be fruitfully employed. The state enterprises put up competition to private enterprises; rather they supply something which the latter could otherwise only get with difficulty (e.g. raw materials or machinery), and to keep their prices low is a general tendency which again increases the profit-earning possibilities of private capital. The taxation system of the developing countries offers enough possibility for profits to be kept high in spite of the theoretically high taxes.

In the developed capitalist countries, the main aim of government measures is to *counter business fluctuations, to maintain short-term equilibrium*, mainly from the point of view of employment, prices and foreign trade. The methods are mainly *global*, (i.e. they do not discriminate among sectors, enterprises or products), having a *financial* and budgetary character. The success of such measures is assured by economic development, the high share of the state budget, the developed market relationships and the close interdependence of the whole economy. Here production reacts quickly and vividly to such impulses as cheaper or more expensive, more or less credit restriction or expansion of government expenses, raising or lowering of taxes, and not only in the immediately affected branches but, because of the intertwining of individual sectors, in the whole economy. In the developed capitalist economies, economic planning has become most efficient and an organic part of government economic policy where it has been based closely on financial and budgetary institutions. Even where it did not start in this manner, as in France, the relation is becoming closer and closer, and global financial methods are increasingly used for the implementation of the plan. (This does not mean, of course, that in the capitalist countries *long-term plan objectives* do not exist, together with the most different measures of implementation.)

In developing countries, however, the fundamental objectives of government economic policy are *long-term and structural ones*, since in the interests of development, it is necessary to change the whole economic structure (for example, to industrialise – i.e. to increase the share of industry considerably; to diversify agricultural production and increase commodity production, etc.) Nor can the measures of government interference be mostly global (financial and budgetary), since the economy reacts to such impulses much less; the reasons for this are the great weight of the traditional (subsistence) sector, the looser relations among sectors and the usually less developed market. With such measures the state can influence the economy less than in the advanced countries. The government measures must therefore be much more *selective* (i.e. relate to definite sectors, products and enterprises), state investment or subsidies must be directed towards a definite aim, export and import licences must be applied, etc.

In the developed countries planning is mainly 'financial' in character. It has been examined above how in these countries employment influences demand and demand influences the prices, how the development of the domestic and foreign price levels act on exports, how demand changes under the effect of taxes, rates of interest, and the growth or restriction of government investment. The structure of the economy is stable, it is not exposed to the danger of a sudden scarcity emerging in some sector; owing to the integrated character of the economy and to various reserves, supply adjusts to changes in demand relatively smoothly.

In developing countries planning very often strengthens the non-capitalist more than the capitalist aspects of the economy. In these countries the main obstacle to accelerating development is the lack of savings, of foreign exchange receipts and of properly trained experts. The starting of some new productive activity (or the introduction of a new technology) may cause radical structural changes in the economy. If such needs (for example, the demand for materials or energy) are not foreseen, this may quickly create bottlenecks in some places. This circumstance makes central planning necessary, not only with the aid of aggregate financial indicators, but also in *physical terms, with the aid of indicators expressed in physical units of measurement*, in order properly to assess the implications of planned developments.

Physical planning – i.e. the assessment, in mutual confrontation, of needs and resources mainly in physical units of measurement – makes it possible not only to disclose the bottlenecks that immediately threaten, but also to account for indirect relations and thereby to mark out the strategic points where the means available can be most efficiently used – considering also the long-term and not directly material factors (e.g. training). Physical planning can, of course, be more efficient and a better reflection of reality in the backward than in the more advanced industrial countries; the range of products is much narrower in the developing countries. This can be felt at home, owing to the low standard of living and to the subsistence economy, but it shows particularly in exports. Though efforts are made to reduce dependence on the export of two or three materials, this process is bound to be slow, even if aided by planning.

Development necessitates the concentration of means available (at first mainly capital) in several respects. Means must be concentrated in fields where their use promises the greatest results under the conditions of the country (initially mainly the greatest growth of savings); they should be concentrated – at least to a certain extent – on major projects instead of fragmenting them to many tiny ones, since investment costs do not generally grow proportionately with output and this may result in more efficient use of capital, often also increasing the possibility for saving.[21] Finally, means should be better concentrated regionally, since this results in a better utilisation of the necessary infrastructure. All these elements bring government investment and the increase of government savings to the fore. A more concentrated use of other scarce resources, promoting better use of the plans, is also apparent. This may necessitate government control in respect of foreign exchange and scarce resources, such as for example certain basic materials or sources of energy. This government control, together with state investment results – or may result – in a certain restriction of the capitalist elements of the economy, without their expropriation. It is, of course, another question to what extent the government can make effective use of this possibility, or wants to do so.

The above considerations relate mainly to the development of industry. Development of agriculture belongs to a large extent to the subsistence sector, and is at least equal in importance to industrial development but, according to experience gained up till now, it is a much more difficult problem. Development of agriculture involves the emergence of commodity production, and is naturally accompanied by the strengthening of capitalistic tendencies. Economic planning works against these tendencies insofar as it promotes co-operation – with the use of government means and institutions and in the interest of a more concentrated use of resources in production as well as in marketing.

Strengthening of the non-capitalist elements is not, of course, the only possible and necessary consequence of economic planning. As mentioned, it can happen that a factory is built with government funds and is later handed over to private capital. It can also happen that the plan is conceived of as if its main task were to create profitable possibilities for foreign capital, which is considered indispensable for the development of the country.

5. *The Role of Plans in Industrialisation*

Economic development in the Afro-Asian and Latin American countries has taken place since the Second World War under the influence of industrialisation, at least insofar as industrial development was the most dynamic element of the economy.

As has been mentioned, there is general agreement on the question whether industrialisation is necessary. Accordingly, the plans of the developing countries are *at the same time plans for industrialisation* as, practically without exception, they provide for faster growth in industry than in agriculture. (Of course, the situation is different in respect of the part of available resources destined for the development of industry and for that of other sectors.)

Before we analyse the plans more closely, it must be mentioned that the plan is no prognosis, i.e. it is not an elaboration of the most likely trend and rate of development, nor is it something considered as most desirable. It is rather an economic development that seems still possible under given conditions, i.e. considering domestic savings, foreign aid and loans, markets and other conditions, as well as the experience of the given country in planning. In practice the investment necessary (mainly government investment) is assessed from the aspect of needs and financial possibilities, together with their best allocation, though on the whole only for the major branches and not in greater detail. The possibilities of plan implementation from the aspect of concrete realisation and operation of the investment, labour (particularly qualified labour) requirements and availabilities are hardly examined in the light of experience.

It is a very common feature of the economic plans of developing countries that they provide for a growth in domestic savings but without planning the reduction of foreign assistance. In the period 1962–4, net investment (exclusive of amortisation) in the developing countries amounted to about 11 per cent of their national income, and about 3 per cent of national income – i.e. more than a quarter of the total – was foreign assistance and credit.[22]

With such proportions it is understandable that the continuation of assistance and credits is of vital importance for the developing countries, at least under present conditions. (Of course, in profits, interest, repayment of loans and other forms, a considerable part of the national income of developing countries is transferred to the advanced capitalist countries.)

Relying on a growing rate of saving, the developing countries made forecasts for a substantial growth of industrial production and for a more moderate growth of agricultural production. In this respect, Table IV/3 is quite unequivocal. The growth rate of industrial production is higher in every country except the Sudan – and sometimes much higher, than that of agriculture, and it seems as if a higher industrial – or, more precisely, a higher (planned) manufacturing – rate of growth were accompanied by higher agricultural growth. The distribution of investment presents a much more mixed picture. As regards total investment, manufacturing investment is higher in the table in the majority of countries, than agricultural investment. But the objectives and priorities of the economic policy of governments are better reflected by government investment. Here agricultural investment has a substantial weight. In the majority of the countries figuring in the table, a greater – and in many cases much greater – part of government investment serves the development of agriculture. The efforts at developing agriculture emerge even more clearly if we investigate what part of agricultural and manufacturing investment is financed by governments. Here the share of agriculture is higher without exception, and in most of the countries investigated it attains 60–80 per cent of total investment in the branch. The higher industrial growth rate in the plan thus can-

INVESTMENT IN THE ECONOMIC PLANS OF THE DEVELOPING COUNTRIES

Country	Plan period	Annual growth rate of G.N.P.				Of total investment		Of government investment		Share of branches in government investment	
		Total	of which: Agriculture	Manufacturing	Construction	Agriculture	Manufacturing	Agriculture	Manufacturing	Agriculture	Manufacturing
						per cent					
Algeria	1969–73	9·5	3·0	13·8	21·6	—	—	—	—	—	—
Taiwan	1968–72	7·1	4·4	9·3	9·5	12	36	—	—	—	—
El Salvador	1967–72	6·0	2·9	9·8	9·5	—	—	—	—	—	—
Ethiopia	1967–8	6·0	2·9	13·8	9·1	—	—	—	—	—	—
	1972–3		3·5	4·5	9·0	—	—	—	—	—	—
Fiji	1970–5	6·7	3·5	4·5	9·0	11	20	66	56	14	21
India	1968–9	5·7	5·0	7·7	8·6	—	—	—	—	—	—
Kenya	1973–4	6·7	4·6	8·9	8·8	—	—	—	—	—	—
	1967–74					23	29ᵇ	67	58ᵇ	23	26ᵇ
Marcoo	1968–73	4·3	2·1	4·3	8·5	12	15	11	5	4	2
Pakistan	1969–70–	6·5	5·5	10·2ᵃ		22	13	94	54	31	10
	1974–5					—	23ᵇ	78	31ᵇ	28	10
South Korea	1965–71	7·0	5·0	10·7ᵃ		16	29	59	4	23	3
Senegal	1967–6–	5·6	5·9	7·6	2·3	—	—	—	—	—	—
	1972–3					—	—	—	—	—	—
Sudan	1969–70–	8·1	11·2	9·5	2·7	—	—	—	—	—	—
	1974–5					29	14ᵇ	100	25ᵇ	33	4ᵇ
Trinidad and Tobago	1968–73	4·3	5·0	5·0	6·0	28	14ᵇ	74	52ᵇ	38	13ᵇ
Tanzania	1968–9	6·5	5·1	13·0	10·0	—	—	—	—	—	—
	1973–4					—	—	—	—	—	—

ᵃ. Manufacturing and construction. ᵇ. Including mining.
Source: *Journal of Development Planning*, No. 3, U.N., New York, 1971.

not be traced back to the fact that it has been better supplied with the government funds necessary for development, but rather that, relying on earlier experience, a faster growth rate is assumed, and private as well as foreign investment is reckoned with to a greater extent than is the case in agriculture. (It must be observed that investment serving the infrastructure, mainly in transportation, which in the developing countries is mostly made by governments, presumably helps the development of agriculture more than it does that of industry; and a part of industrial investment – e.g. in fertiliser production – helps precisely to develop agriculture.) As regards growth rates, it must also take into account that high growth rates in industry are related in many cases to extremely low levels. Owing to a low starting level, what is a small growth in absolute terms may be high if expressed in percentages. The high growth rates is partly related to this fact. Thus, for example in the Sudan the contribution of industry to national income was only 2 per cent and the planned annual growth rate of industry was 21 per cent. The corresponding figures for Tanzania are 4 and 14·5 per cent, for Ethiopia 5 and 13·5 per cent, and for Ceylon 8 and 12 per cent.

It is a further characteristic feature of the development plans that they provide for a faster rate of growth in manufacturing than in total industry (see Table IV/3). As can be seen from Table IV/4, relating to the preceding plan period, the development of total manufacturing is always faster than that of light industry, owing to the higher growth rate of heavy industry. Certain branches and certain products of heavy industry are to develop particularly quickly, according to the plans. (All this is, of course, also related to the underdevelopment of the existing heavy industry.) At any rate, it is characteristic that in metallurgy, the engineering and chemical industries, as well as in steel and fertiliser production, growth rates under 10 per cent can hardly be found. In the case of fertiliser production, the forecast annual growth rates range between 20 and 50 per cent.

On the basis of statistical and plan figures and other information available, it seems that in the industrial development plans practical considerations dominate over principles. By this it is meant that although in a part of the developing countries it has been voiced that in certain industries only government enterprises will be created or at least the government has to obtain a dominating role, in other countries industrial development is left in principle to private capital. What mostly happens in practice is that, in addition to investment serving development of the infrastructure, investment in heavy industry is also financed by official sources, since private capital does not undertake such big investment with the related risks. Heavy

Table IV/4

ANNUAL GROWTH RATES OF MANUFACTURING INDUSTRY AND SOME
INDUSTRIAL BRANCHES OR GROUPS OF PRODUCTS IN THE ECONOMIC
PLANS OF THE DEVELOPING COUNTRIES IN THE FIRST HALF OF THE 1960s

Country	Manufacturing industry	Consumer goods produced by light industry	Mining	Electrical energy	Metallurgy	Engineering	Chemical industry	Steel	Cement	Fertilisers
Sudan	21·0	—	25·0	13·5	—	—	—	—	9	(a)
Tanzania	14·5	—	4·0	12·5	—	—	—	—	—	—
Venezuela	13·5	11·0	4·5	18·0	55·0	26	13	—	—	—
U.A.R.	13·5	7·5	27·5	11·5	46·9	19	22	—	—	—
Ethiopia	13·5	—	52·5	19·5	—	—	106	(a)	8	33
Taiwan	12·5	8·5	—	14·0	20·0	41	19	13	17	(a)
Ceylon	12·0	—	—	17·5	—	—	—	—	26	(a)
South Korea	11·5	9·5	—	—	18·0	20	15	10	21	51
India	11·0	—	—	—	—	19	20	22	9	—
Morocco	9·0	—	4·5	7·0	—	—	—	—	—	—
Bolivia	8·5	7·5	8·5	6·5	—	—	—	—	7	56
Colombia	8·5	6·0	—	—	14·0	14	11	16	7	—
Ecuador	8·5	6·5	7·0	7·5	—	15	—	—	23	52
Pakistan	8·5	—	—	—	—	—	13	—	5	20
Tunisia	8·0	7·0	2·0	4·5	—	7	13	8	—	—
Trinidad and Tobago	7·5	—	3·0	8·5	—	—	—	(a)	5	21
Jamaica	7·5	—	2·0	10·0	—	6	—	—	—	—
Chile	6·5	4·5	6·0	—	8·0	9	8	—	—	—
Kenya	5·5	—	3·0	8·5	—	—	—	—	32	—
Burma	—	—	—	—	—	—	—	—	—	—

(a) = Production just starting.

Source: 'Development Plans: Appraisal of Targets and Progress in Developing Countries', *World Economic Survey, 1964 – Part I,* U.N., New York, 1965, pp. 59–60.

industrial products are needed, however. As will be seen, similar practical viewpoints prevail in respect of whether orientation should be towards heavy or light industry in industrial development, and whether towards large-scale or small-scale industry.

The above statements rely mainly on the data provided in Tables IV/3 and IV/4. I had the opportunity to analyse the main trends of industrialisation efforts in the developing countries also with the aid of more detailed data,[23] looking more closely at the extent to which they bring the growth of manufacturing in general and, within that, heavy industry or light and small-scale industry, to the fore-front.

The information derived mostly from the development plans of the countries in question, for various periods, and partly from answers to a special inquiry and from reports of the U.N. technical assistance missions. The material used originally served quite different purposes. Even so, information could be obtained only for a part of the developing countries (mainly for the Afro-Asian ones, hardly any for Latin America); also the periods covered by the plans and other reports varied from country to country. Therefore, the statements and conclusions of the following survey should be taken with certain reservation.

In the survey in question, the original problem would have been to establish how the various developing countries answered in their own development concepts to the question 'how to industrialise'. But those contained in the available material only answered the question as to what emphasis has been put on the development of manufacturing in general, and within that, on heavy industry, light industry and small-scale industry, respectively. Though the scope of this problem is more modest than the previous one, an unequivocal answer, if such can be obtained, will reflect a clear standpoint in respect of industrialisation. For example, the standpoint which does not emphasise industrialisation in general, or emphasises *only* small-scale industry, reflects essentially the primacy of agricultural development.

It must be noted that in the survey not only were the official plans approved by government used, but also various studies on economic development and other documents reflecting ideas about the subject, if official plans were not available. In addition, plans for earlier periods were in some cases also used if the plans for current or future periods were missing. In the majority of cases the plans and other documents used gave rather unequivocal answer to the question asked. Thus, for example, the economic development plan of the U.A.R. provides for faster growth in industry than in agriculture and, within industry, for faster growth in heavy than light industry; thus the intention of the plan is to develop mainly industry, and within it, heavy industry. The 1962–7 economic development plan of the Philippines allocated about one-third of all investment to industry and about 56 per cent of that to the production of ferrous and non-ferrous metals, and to the engineering and the chemical industries – i.e. to heavy industry. In other cases the idea was reflected by the *text* of the plans, thus, for example, the plan of the Ivory Coast put emphasis mainly on agriculture, and in the second place on energy production and mining, while manufacturing was to be developed only insofar as this could be considered as complementing agricultural development. The situation was similar in the case of Nigeria, where the development of only such industrial fields was considered justified as promoted either the supply of industrial goods for agriculture, or the industrial processing of agricultural products. In some cases, however, it was not so easy to establish the exact objectives of the countries. In spite of this fact, Table IV/5 probably correctly reflects the aims of these countries, at least to the extent that they are reflected by the available plans.

In the table, thirty-three developing countries are ranked by the G.N.P. of the countries in terms of U.S. dollars, in decreasing order. This figure (the product of *per capita* G.N.P. by the number of population) more or less correctly reflects the 'economic size' of the countries in question. In the table the sign x indicates the emphasis on manufacturing, heavy, light and small-scale industry. For certain countries there is no sign at all in columns 3–6, which does not mean that the plan is *against* industrialisation, but that no special emphasis has been put on these.

The table indicates that *an unequivocal relationship exists between the size of the economy in a developing country and its industrial development policy*, in the sense that countries of greater economic size emphasise industrialisation and particularly the development of heavy industry. With diminishing size, light and heavy industries obtain equal weight, while, at the end of the list, industrialisation is not emphasised separately. The tendencies mentioned can be seen more clearly with the largest and smallest countries in respect of 'economic size' and less so towards the middle. But – at least until surveys of greater detail are performed – it seems that with diminishing size emphasis shifts from heavy industry to light industry and then to small-scale industry.

Two interesting statements can be made on the basis of the table: first, that the importance attributed to industrialisation or to the development of heavy industry is not strongly related to the relative economic development level of the country in question (as characterised by *per capita* national income); the second statement is that the role of heavy industry or of industrialisation (at least as reflected

Table IV/5

NATIONAL INCOME AND THE PREFERRED
INDUSTRIAL SECTOR IN THE ECONOMIC
DEVELOPMENT PLANS OF DEVELOPING COUNTRIES

Country	National income (G.N.P.) in 1958		Manu-fac-turing	Heavy industry	Light industry	Small-scale industry
	Total 1	Per capita 2	3	4	5	6
India	27,577	70	x	x		
Turkey	6,672	254	x	x	x	
Indonesia	6,518	73	x	x		
Pakistan	5,706	64	x	x		
U.A.R.	3,823	155	x	x		
Nigeria	3,215	95	x	x	x	
Philippines	2,908	113	x	x		
Algeria	2,159	208	x	x	x	
Morocco	1,654	151	x	x	x	
Malaysia	1,211	186	x			
Ceylon	1,143	122	x	x	x	
Burma	1,115	55	x			
Ghana	1,093	170	x		x	
Ethiopia	915	46	x	x	x	
Sudan	731	66	x		x	
Afghanistan	699	54	x	x	x	
Kenya	640	84				
Jamaica	614	398			x	x
Tunisia	586	154	x	x	x	
Tanganyika	567	57				
Senegal	458	178	x	x	x	
Nepal	448	50			x	x
Uganda	411	65	x			x
Ivory Coast	400	129				
Trin./Tobago	383	486	x			
Madagascar	383	74	x		x	
Cambodia	306	65			x	
Nigeria	170	64				
Upper Volta	146	42				
Somalia	95	48	x			x
Gabon	76	182				
Congo (Brazz.)	72	92				
Barbados	60	264				

Source: Columns 1 and 2: U.N. Yearbook of National Accounts, 1963,
Part D, Table 3A. Columns 3–6: Economic plans, special inquiries
and reports of U.N. technical assistance missions.

by the plans) seems to be independent also of the importance in the given country of state ownership of the means of production or, in general, of central planning. As is known, in India the state sector and economic development plans are of high importance, while in the Philippines private enterprise is preponderant, without plans of an obligatory character. Yet the plan of the Philippines reveals that greater importance is attributed to the development of heavy industry.

This characteristic feature of the plans and of economic policy is understandable. The size of the home market is a particularly important factor of economic and industrial growth. Since, in the early stage of industrialisation especially, export possibilities are restricted, there is a close relationship between the industries that function efficiently and the size of the domestic market. In heavy industry the minimum plant scale which can be operated profitably is greater than in light industry, and thus it is understandable that the (economically) smaller countries, or the countries at a lower stage of economic development, are able to make less effort towards developing heavy industry. In economically bigger countries, however, light industry has already attained a certain level, consumer goods are produced (and not infrequently even exported), and their further economic development depends on heavy industry to a greater extent.

Obviously, the role of governments in the developing countries in influencing the economy and thus industrialisation is not exhausted by planning; they must and do use other well-known instruments and also new ones for influencing the economy.

Let us first mention some 'classical' tools of control (without aiming at preparing a complete catalogue of these tools), which can be used either as global or as selective means of control. (It should be noted, of course, that the use of the measures in question is mostly independent of whether there is an economic plan or not, but planning is a progressive element of government control in the developing countries and is suited to harmonise and co-ordinate various tools of control in the interest of main economic objectives.)

Taxation not only serves to provide funds for government expenses, but it results also in promoting or hindering the development of various branches of the economy. It will be obvious without any detailed explanation that the various systems and types of taxes influence the costs of industrial and other activities and thereby influence their competitiveness. (The system of taxation may prefer or retard small-scale industry, etc.)

A general raising or reduction of taxes is a tool for promoting or braking economic activities – used to some extent in the developed countries. It is, however, a selective measure if new industrial activities or enterprises are granted *tax exemptions* of varying degree and for varying duration; this measure was frequently resorted to in the now developed countries in the period of their industrialisation and is also widely used in the developing countries.

In the field of foreign trade, the most general measure is the customs duty, which is not only a tool for managing and directing the economy, but an important source of government revenue as well. This source of revenue is even more important in the developing than in the advanced countries, owing to deficiencies in administration and the tax system as well as poor tax collection. This is why in the developing countries we find export duties employed widely, while in the developed countries this hardly occurs now.

Protective duties have always been an important tool of industrialisation in the 'late industrialising' countries. They played such a role even in countries that are now developed, such as Germany or the U.S.A. In the developing countries, domestic industry was not protected by customs duties in the colonial period, not even in the politically independent states.[24] In the present practice of the developing countries the protection of industry with tariffs is quite general. The duties are used not only as a global tool of control or to stimulate industry, but also as a selective measure. In order to stimulate production, the competent government agencies first apply higher (and then, in certain cases, diminishing) duties when the production of such articles as they consider desirable is started.

The system of *import* (and partly export) *licences* is also widely applied in the developing countries. It needs no detailed explanation that with import licences certain industries can be preferred, since major investment or a better supply of materials is made possible in this way.

The system of import licences is a tool similar to customs duties but much more rigid. Customs duties make imports more expensive and thus restrict them, but they do not exclude them entirely. The import licence, however, excludes the importing of products for which no import licence was granted by the competent authorities.

As is known, government *credits* belong among the important tools of control and may be used both globally and selectively. The granting of cheaper or more expensive credits (by changing the discount rate) may be used, together with changing their volume with the aid of state measures, to put a brake on boom or to promote economic activity. In practice, these measures can be used more effectively in the developed countries. The developing countries use much more, in creating or expanding adequately selected and useful projects, the selective measure of direct credits. As regards their purpose and the functions of the transaction, credits may differ widely. Direct credits may be granted by government agencies (from the budget), or through some government-owned bank. The credit may serve for the creation of a state enterprise (which may eventually be handed over to private capital), or of a mixed enterprise with the participation of either domestic or foreign private capital; it may also contribute to creating mixed enterprises with the participation of domestic or foreign capitalists, etc. It is worth noting that in several developing countries, one of the truly important organisations for industrialisation is precisely some government bank. In Iran, for example, one of these banks not only grants credit to the domestic entrepreneurs intending to invest, but provides them with economic and technological advice and even has a special department for searching for adequate investment possibilities.

As is equally well known, the role of the budget in influencing the economy manifests itself not only in taxes but also through expenditure. The volume and distribution of government expenditure (investment and other) raises direct and indirect demand for, among other things, industrial goods. The *financial sphere proper* is closely related to all the fields mentioned. Owing to the disproportion between government revenue and expenditure, the developing countries are apt to have inflation, and the disproportion between exports and imports leads to a decline in the foreign purchasing power of their currency. Thus, their financial policies have far-reaching effects on industrialisation. Accordingly, in a great part of the developing countries foreign exchange is not freely available; hence imports, and the use of foreign exchange necessary for imports (in some cases also exports), are subject to licensing. It is clear that in the granting of licenses preferences are asserted, which is an important tool of selective control over industrialisation.

In the organisation and transaction of *technical aid* (without reimbursement), the government apparatus of the developing countries also has a central role. The aid may be multilateral or bilateral, and it may serve the sending of experts, training, the creation of pilot plants, etc. Though this type of aid, consisting of the transfer of knowledge and resources, is smaller – considering the number of experts sent and, particularly, the sums involved – than the credits or the 'aid' provided in the form of capital exports, it is nevertheless important since the latter come about mostly in the case of objectives that are acknowledged as profitable to private capital, while technical aid is widely used precisely for investigating profitability (as well as for education and training) and other goals set by the governments of the developing countries.

The survey of these problems – and several related ones not even mentioned here – far exceeds the scope of this book (and their detailed investigation would exceed that of a single investigation).

Therefore – although very important questions are undoubtedly involved which influence industrialisation particularly in the short run – we have to forgo their deeper investigation.

However, from the point of view of another complex problem – also not treated in detail – it seems justified to raise at least the fundamental issues.

Foreign enterprises play an important role in the industry (industrialisation) of the developing countries. As is known, their profits – or part of them – are transferred abroad, and this reduces domestic savings. In addition, the foreign enterprises always represent economic power, and this economic power may easily support political and economic tendencies contrary to the interests of the country. This is particularly dangerous because the foreign capital is backed by its own state which can put political and economic pressure (through foreign trade, aid, etc.) on the government of the developing country. In addition, in order to attract foreign capital, the conditions suitable for this type of investment must be created. These conditions, however, are not necessarily favourable for the economic growth of the developing countries; for example, it is well known that foreign capital dislikes stronger and more determinate government control and the measures accompanying it. From all this follows a tendency restricting the role of foreign capital.

But the problem has another aspect. For the time being, and for a considerable time to come, the developing countries need foreign capital. The volume of savings (investment) in the developing countries is insufficient by comparison to their development requirements and needs. As has been mentioned above, in 1962–4 total investment in the developing countries amounted to 11 per cent of national income, and 3 per cent of it originated from abroad. The developing countries can hardly renounce more than a quarter of their investment. Foreign capital is needed not only for expanding investment possibilities, but also for expanding imports: it makes possible the importation of products, machinery and equipment which could not otherwise be purchased by the developing countries at all, or only by renouncing other important import items. The developing countries also need foreign enterprises (capital) because it helps to procure the know-how necessary for technical progress.

Finally, foreign enterprises are needed in many cases also because they have the marketing organisation necessary for developing exports, and the necessary experience. This is why there is a definite tendency in most developing countries to stimulate foreign investment.

How to solve the contradiction outlined above is a basic problem of industrialisation policy in the developing countries. Even without detailed investigation and without wishing to give advice to the developing countries, there is a possibility to make a step forwards in the solution of the problem. It is not immaterial for the developing country what type of foreign enterprise it has to deal with. To simplify the complicated reality, there are the big international companies exploiting some valuable natural resource of the country; these are active mainly in the extraction of raw materials (oil, non-ferrous metals, etc.). They produce mainly for export, and are more part of the world market than of the economy of the country where they are located. Such enterprises represent tremendous power, particularly in small and underdeveloped countries, if only because a considerable part of tax revenue, and even more of foreign exchange receipts, derives from these companies. But their interests are frequently opposed to those of the country, e.g. development of production or even full utilisation of capacity is not in their interests if the international monopoly wishes to keep prices high, or wants to develop its plants—or utilise its plants already established—in some other country.

Since these enterprises do not become integrated into the economies of the developing countries, the government can hardly influence them with purely economic measures, while the business policies of the company in question, for example the reduction of production, may seriously affect the foreign exchange position or tax revenues of the country.

As a rule, the governments of the developing countries make efforts to bring such companies under their influence. The most direct method for that is, of course, nationalisation. With this, however, the developing country may lose part of the advantages mentioned above. They often therefore prefer partial nationalisation (acquiring a part or the majority of shares). It also frequently occurs that independent national enterprises are founded in the industry in question. This makes possible the training of specialists and, in case of necessity, the operation of the foreign enterprise if it is later nationalised or if the foreign personnel are recalled.

The situation is different with industrial enterprises, mainly manufacturing ones, which are integrated into the economies of the developing countries and produce mainly for the domestic market. Here a single enterprise represents much less power than in the preceding case; and because it is an integrated part of the economy, the government may control its activities also with indirect measures such as import licences, customs duties, etc. The strategy of the developing country in safeguarding its interest may in such cases be directed to diversification, partly in the sense that a single enterprise should not monopolise the domestic market, and partly that there should not be present capital from only a single foreign country. In addition, 'joint ventures' come more and more to the fore, where foreign capital co-operates with private or public domestic capital.

There is another field where the basic problems are worthwhile mentioning, namely the role of the state in developing the economy and industry. Development of *infrastructure* has been traditionally, and is becoming increasingly a government task, even in the now developed countries. It needs no separate explanation that the development of infrastructure is indispensable for the development of the whole economy, and thus for industry.

Let us briefly review the special problem of the developing countries in this field. In these countries, infrastructural investment is almost exclusively financed from public funds, while in the advanced countries, or at least in some of them, private capital played a great role in it at the start of industrialisation (e.g. in railway and canal construction in England and the U.S.A., and partly also in Germany). At that time, however, the role of the state in the now developed countries was unimportant in productive investment, while – as has been pointed out several times – in the developing countries public funds have a major share in productive investment either directly or through official credits. The fundamental problem is thus how, in what proportion and by what criteria, resources should be allocated between directly productive and infrastructural investment.

Solution of the problem is made difficult by several circumstances. Calculation of investment efficiency is not easy even for productive investment. With infrastructural investment, however, efficiency cannot be directly measured or compared with the efficiency of productive projects. The 'efficiency' or result of the infrastructural investment shows in its indirect effect on the growth of national income, welfare, etc. With productive investment, at least in principle, it can be shown if they are inefficient, because they are not paid off, or not paid off rapidly enough, their discounted (present) value is not positive, etc.—according to the formula used for project evaluation. But there is always certain usefulness in infrastructural investment, since education, road building, etc., are always useful, though the best use is not necessarily made of the given funds. In addition, the developed capitalist countries, at least when granting official credits, and the international organisations which are strongly under their influence, like the World Bank, have shown a marked preference for infrastructural investment, at the expense of productive industrial projects. In this also the circumstance that such investment does not create competition for the exports of the developed countries, but even promotes them, may have played a role. A special problem is the *indivisibility* of a great part of infrastructural investment. Initially, the capacity of a road, a bridge or a railway line cannot be fully exploited, this only happens in the course of economic development, with the growth of this type of demand. Because of all these difficulties, in the developing countries we can often meet with an overemphasis on infrastructural investment – of course, in relative not absolute terms, but we can also meet with its neglect.

No general recipe can be given for the solution of this problem. The essence of the matter is naturally that infrastructural investment really serves economic growth, that it should be properly used, and that it should come about in the order and to the extent that it is actually needed. This requirement takes us back to the necessity of detailed economic planning, since infrastructural investment can be properly evaluated only in the framework of such a plan.

REFERENCES

1. It must be noted that this approach, though undoubtedly correct as regards the recognition of the importance and possibilities of planning, not infrequently also brought about a dangerous illusion, namely that it is sufficient to draw up some economic plan for accelerating development and liquidating backwardness. Frequently the sacrifices the socialist countries had to make in the interest of economic growth, and the social circumstances of building socialism, are forgotten.
2. In India and Burma, for example, the policies of governing parties have developed in the fight for national independence. This was fought against British imperialism and, identifying British imperialism with capitalism, it has become anti-capitalistic in many respects. Already in 1947, the constitution of Burma established that a certain part of the means of production should be in social ownership, allowing the functioning of private ownership only to the extent it does not work against public interest. From the social ownership of the means of production economic planning followed quite naturally, as a method of implementing the objectives accompanying national independence, i.e. increasing welfare, and a greater equality in the distribution of goods.
3. *World Economic Survey 1965*, Part I, U.N., New York, 1966.
4. It must be noted that the thirteen countries listed present a somewhat better picture than would be characteristic for the totality of developing countries. The circumstance itself that data on the plan and even more that statistics on plan implementation were available, indicated more advanced methods of planning.
5. 'Development Plans: Appraisal of Targets and Progress in Developing Countries', *World Economic Survey 1964*, Part I, U.N., New York, 1965.
6. See, for example, E. Hagen Everett, *Planning Economic Development*, Irwin, Homewood, Ill.
7. N. V. Sovani, 'Planning and Planners in India', *Indian Economic Journal*, 1966, No. 4.
8. See, for example, B. C. Tandon, *Economic Planning, Principles and Problems*, Chaitanya Publishing House, Allahabad, 1963, p. 223.
9. In Jamaica 5 per cent increase of G.N.P. was planned against 8·4 per cent in the preceding period; in Trinidad and Tobago 5 against 10·4 per cent.

10. In the national income statistics published in 1965 by the U.N., there were no data for 1963 for such relatively important and developed countries as Indonesia, Iraq, Uruguay, Algeria and Congo. In respect of the smaller and less developed countries the situation was even worse.
11. This is true even for the two-level programming of Kornai, tried in Hungary; though as far as we know, no attempt has been made in developing countries at such detailed programming.
12. Gunnar Myrdal, *Asian Drama*, Pantheon, New York, 1968, p. 716.
13. Certain aspects of the problem were mentioned in Chapter III, in connection with the application of capital-intensive and labour-intensive technologies.
14. Part of the studies submitted were published by United Nations Industrial Development Organisation under the title *Evaluation of Industrial Projects*, U.N., New York, 1968.
15. Such data are contained, for example, in the volume *Profiles of Manufacturing Establishments*, U.N., New York, 1967. Sales No. E. 67.II.B. 17.
16. Thus, for example, in 1958 this rate was 48 per cent in Afghanistan, 53 in Ceylon, 43 in Indonesia, 76 in Iran, 69 in Ghana, 59 in Nigeria. (Hinrichs, 'Determinants of Government Revenue Shares in Less-Developed Countries', *The Economic Journal*, Sept. 1965.)
17. According to the information given by the competent offices, e.g. the number of sectors separately considered in planning production, is five in Hungary, twenty-eight in France, forty in the Netherlands and 129 in Norway. (Jan Tinbergen, *Central Planning*, New Haven and London, Yale University Press, 1964, p. 122.) In Hungary the five sectors given were industry and mining, agriculture, construction, transport and trade. It is quite obvious that the plan is worked out in greater detail. It is also well known that in France the plans are drawn up in greater detail than in Holland or Norway. Thus, by 'sector' quite different things were meant in the countries concerned.
18. According to Myrdal, in comparison to developed capitalist countries, 'Planning in South Asia is . . . not the result of development, but is employed to foster development. It is envisaged as a *pre-condition* – indeed, is motivated by the assumption that spontaneous development cannot be expected.' (G. Myrdal, op. cit. p. 739.) Myrdal's contrast is perhaps not quite exact since by economic planning it was intended to serve development even in the advanced capitalist countries.
19. A. Maddison, *Economic Growth in the West*, The Twentieth Century Fund, New York, 1964.
20. H. H. Hinrichs, 'Determinants of Government Revenue Shares Among Less-Developed Countries', *The Economic Journal*, Sept. 1965, No. 299, Vol. LXXV, p. 552.
21. See Chapter III/1.
22. *U.N. World Economic Survey*, 1965.
23. Centre for Industrial Development: *Preliminary Study on the Patterns of Industrial Development in Developing Countries*, New York, 1964 (mimeographed).
24. Under colonial rule in Brazil, in the nineteenth century, industrial activity was expressly forbidden and behaviour in respect of industry did not change much even in independent Brazil, since it was not in the interest of the ruling stratum of landlords and merchants. Economic policy in Argentina was indifferent or even hostile to industrialisation up to the beginning of the twentieth century, and the Argentinian system of customs tariffs worked more against industrialisation than in its favour.

V

PAST AND FUTURE INDUSTRIAL GROWTH IN THE DEVELOPING COUNTRIES*

For a discussion of the past and future industrial growth of the developing countries it seems necessary to review the phenomena in question, the internal structure of industry in the developing countries, and other interrelations, in somewhat greater detail.

For the sake of brevity, the review of past development will be kept short and restricted mainly to a survey of the main statistical data in the Annex, treating separately the periods up to the middle of the twentieth century and the years since 1950. Beyond that, only some basic problems will be dealt with in connection with industrial development, and an attempt will be made to forecast the development of industry and its major branches up to 1985.

1. *Industry at the Time of Colonial Rule*

Only for the recent past can the industry of the developing countries be examined with the help of reliable statistics. For the whole of the developing countries and for the major regions, data are available only beginning with 1938 (collected by the U.N.); and as regards Africa, even data from 1950 on are restricted to certain industries. Some information, however, is also necessary regarding earlier periods, since industrialisation started in some form or other already in the nineteenth century or at the beginning of the twentieth, particularly in Latin America and Asia.

We have at our disposal little reliable information about the period before the twentieth century and, particularly, about the pre-colonial period. Obviously, there existed even in those times some industrial activity (small-scale cottage industries) in the countries in question. Indeed, especially in Central and South America as well as in Asia, there existed advanced civilisations, with towns –

---

* As in the preceding chapters, by developing countries those of Africa, Asia and Latin America are meant, excluding the Republic of South Africa, Japan and the Asian socialist countries.

large states that were centrally governed, and together with these there was division of labour, and industrial articles were consumed by the population and in other fields, including warfare. It is more difficult to tell what was the *relative development* level as compared to Europe.

The colonisation of Latin America falls into the period prior to the industrial revolution. But the general level of productive forces and, within that, the level of industry was obviously lower than in the colonising countries (in this case, Spain and Portugal), since otherwise the conquerors would have met greater difficulties and they could hardly have perpetuated their power so easily. In the next phase, the colonising countries themselves (namely, Spain and Portugal) lagged behind the industrial and general economic development of Western Europe; in their colonies, naturally, industry could develop even less.

Colonisation of large areas of Asia was already taking place in the period of the industrial revolution or after it. Information regarding the development level of the Indian economy prior to colonisation is rather contradictory. According to some sources the development level of India was similar to that of Europe before the industrial revolution; commerce and credit were well advanced, and the quality of industrial products attained or even surpassed that of their European equivalents, even in such complex industries as shipbuilding. According to other data, however, the standard of living was essentially higher in Western Europe than in India already at the time of the industrial revolution (even if the difference was not so great as later in the nineteenth and twentieth centuries). This contradicts somewhat the image of an advanced economy and developed industry in India.

Africa, particularly Black Africa, was more backward at the time of colonisation than either South America or Asia; therefore, industry was hardly separated there from agriculture, and its technologies also remained primitive.

Whatever may have been the state of industry in the African, Asian and Latin American regions at the time of colonisation, the difference separating the colonial and semi-colonial areas from the developed countries *increased* from the beginning of colonisation and as a consequence of it. In this respect, economic backwardness is precisely the consequence of colonisation and of the imperialist system.

The earlier colonising countries do not like to acknowledge this responsibility. They refer to the fact – perhaps not without some justification – that the colonisers penetrated into countries stagnating both economically and socially, pushed them out of the trough, linked them to the world economy, built railways and roads, and even achieved something in the field of health and education – though not too much, particularly in education. It is correctly pointed out by T. Szentes that 'in the given historical period, at the beginning of imperialist development, in the case of countries still underdeveloped today, the question was not whether they would find themselves as dependencies at all, but rather which of the great imperialist powers would conquer them.'[1] Here Szentes is right to extend Marx's statement on India, according to which: 'The point is obviously not whether the British had the right to conquer India, but whether it would be preferable if India were conquered by the Turks, Persians or Russians rather than by the British.'[2] But the powers which took over the government of the developing countries cannot be relieved in any case of their responsibility for the further development of the countries conquered.

Instead of the former colonisers acknowledging their responsibility for the stagnation of the economy, the peoples of the countries in question are frequently still blamed. Speaking about economic stagnation in India, Allen wrote: '. . . finally, and probably this is the most important reason: the social tradition and the establishments in India were not favourable for the home-enterprises in the modern industry.'[3] But this can hardly be considered the *main* cause of backwardness, though it would obviously be incorrect to neglect entirely the retarding effect of tradition and institutions. In reality, domestic entrepreneurs soon set themselves in India too to develop industry; in the second part of the nineteenth century they had already built a considerable cotton industry, and at the beginning of the twentieth an important amount of steel was produced, a development due to Indians – not to mention other industries where, although factories were built by foreign capitalists, Indian personnel were working. But development was slow and, particularly at the beginning, it took place rather against the will of colonial government than with its support.

The governments of the colonial countries, and their representatives in the colonies, represented the interests of their own capitalists in the colonies governed by them, and thus even the development carried out often did at least as much harm as good. In India, for example, for military and economic reasons, the British built between 1853 and 1900 25,000 miles of railway, the length of which had increased by 1914 to 35,000, and by 1939 to 43,000 miles. In other countries, as in Germany and the U.S.A., railway construction generated a strong development of the domestic economy, and the growth of metallurgy and engineering may be largely attributed to it. In India, however, railway building did not start the development of local heavy industry; only some coal mining has come about, and the absolutely necessary repair shops were built, otherwise everything was imported from England. As against that the railways opened up the Indian market for British manufactured goods, mainly textiles, and helped to ruin the domestic cottage industry (which was, of course, technically inferior) and helped the export of agricultural products and also their transport within the country.

Thus, the colonial countries, having taken over the government of the colonies, exercised their power not in the interest of the country's population, but in the interest of domestic capitalists. It is customary to explain the neglect of industrialisation with the fact that '. . . the ruling economic philosophy of the West was opposing the idea that the Government should take part in the manufacturing industry directly'.[4] In reality, this was *British* 'philosophy' in the period when it corresponded to British interests, because when Germany, and much more Japan,[5] started their industrialisation, the governments of those countries actively participated, not only with protective customs duties, but with direct support given to industry, not infrequently by founding industrial enterprises. The real explanation of backwardness may be found much more in what is also mentioned by Allen, namely that 'the British government treated hostilely every procedure which might threaten the ever increasing sale of British finished products since India . . . should be considered as a supplier of raw material and market for the British industrial products'. It was essentially because of identical or similar reasons that the worldwide division of labour between advanced capitalist and colonial or semi-colonial countries developed, so characteristic for the second half of the nineteenth and the first half of the twentieth century, conserving backwardness and even increasing its relative extent. As is well known, this division of labour made of the colonial country a raw-material-producing and industrial-article-purchasing appendage of the capitalist mother country. Industrialisation was not incompatible with this type of development, but rather the emphasis was on comparative advantages in the static sense – as has been explained at length in Chapters I and II. In this context there was not much difference between the colonial and the semi-colonial (politically independent) countries. Colonial government did not help but, if by no more than limiting imports, it hindered industrialisation. In this policy, however, it also had to rely in the colonial countries on groups whose interests were related to an unchanging political situation and economic structure. In the politically independent countries (e.g. in Latin America) the maintenance of the existing division of labour was similarly in the interest of the ruling landowner groups.

But colonisation, while hindering industrialisation, also brought about its preconditions in many respects. Though, by force and in the interest of exploitation, it liquidated social systems that had become rigid and incapable of economic development, it unified major areas both politically and economically; it introduced and spread the imported products of modern engineering, and certain elements of modern technology (e.g. in the export industries, in transport, in maintenance and repair works), and in some places even created certain industrial activities. As a result, industrialisation could start when, for one reason or another, it became necessary to supplement some industrial goods which were lacking, and which had been imported earlier.

The imperialistic type of division of labour between the advanced and the backward countries first changed as a consequence of the First World War. Up to the First World War there was no industrial import substitution. In India, where the consumption of industrial goods was very low, the share of imports in consumption even increased: from 1899 to 1913 industrial imports increased by 70 per cent, while domestic industrial production only did so by 50 per cent.[6] However, in Argentina – which was not a poor country – industrial production rose quickly, doubling between 1904 and 1914; this growth was not of an import substitution character. There was some industrial growth also in Brazil, but not such as to affect the domination of industrial imports.

At the time of the First World War, as a result of the diminished export capacity of the advanced countries (mainly Britain), import substituting industrialisation started in India. From 1913 to 1929 industrial production increased by 80 per cent, while the use of industrial articles did so by only 16 per cent. Similarly, industrialisation of an import substituting character was triggered off by the First World War in Brazil, where industrial output doubled between 1914 and 1919. The war had an opposite effect on Argentina, where industrial production declined in this period. This was related to the more developed character of the Argentine economy and to the fact that the war reduced capital imports and imports of important industrial raw materials, as well as the output of certain branches connected with exports.

The economic crisis between the two world wars again released import substituting tendencies. In India industrial production increased from 1929 to 1937 by 54 per cent (the use of industrial products by 34 per cent); in Argentina it grew from 1927/9 to 1937/9 by 46 per cent, characteristically in the direction of import substitution. The situation was similar in Brazil, which had been heavily afflicted by the depression. After some relapse, industrial output

F

in 1934 already exceeded the 1928/9 level and in certain branches (since consumption rather decreased) it partly replaced imports.

The earliest *comprehensive* figures covering the whole industrial production in the developing countries are those compiled by the Statistical Office of the United Nations Organisation for the year immediately preceding the Second World War, i.e. 1938.[7]

In this period, the African, Latin American and Asian countries contributed only 7 per cent to the total industrial output of the world (exclusive of the socialist countries). The share of Africa was negligible, of Latin America 3·7 per cent and of Asia – excluding Japan – 2·9 per cent.[8]

The data relating to Africa are rather uncertain. Industry of any importance was to be found only in the North African countries (Egypt, Morocco, Algeria), where general economic development was at a higher level, even at this time, than in Black Africa; or in the Belgian Congo and Rhodesia – in the latter mainly due to the exploitation of mineral wealth. In Latin America, 60–70 per cent of the total industrial output of the region was contributed by three countries: Argentina, Brazil and Mexico; and in Asia the share of India in the whole region was about 55 per cent. The industry of the developing countries employed about 18–19,000,000 people, against about 60,000,000 industrial workers in the developed countries. This also indicates – as would be expected, under given conditions – the low productivity level in the developing countries. The general economic (and within that the industrial) development level of the developing countries is characterised in Table V/1, with the aid of some comprehensive indicators, in 1938, 1948, 1961 and 1970 – comparing these indicators with the similar indicators in developed (capitalist) countries.

As can be seen from the table, *per capita* national income in the developing countries was about 11 per cent of that in the developed countries in 1968 ($85 and $769), while net industrial output *per capita* was only 5 per cent ($16 and $304). Similarly, the share of manufacturing in total industry was lower in the developing countries (79·6 and 84·9 per cent) as well as the share of heavy industry in manufacturing (31·3 and 49·2 per cent, respectively).

Some idea can be obtained of the relative development level of the industries of developing countries, if the shares of the individual industrial sectors in total world output of the sector are compared with the share of industry as a whole in total world industrial output – which was about 7 per cent, as mentioned. In comparison to this average, the share of mining was high (14·8 per cent) mainly due to the 24·8 per cent share of ore mining and to the 19·9 per cent

Table V/1

SOME INDICATORS OF NATIONAL INCOME AND INDUSTRIAL PRODUCTION
IN DEVELOPED CAPITALIST AND DEVELOPING COUNTRIES

(values in 1958 U.S. dollars)

	1938		1948		1961		1970	
	Developed	Developing	Developed	Developing	Developed	Developing	Developed	Developing
Per capita national income (G.N.P.)	769·0	85·0	958·0	94·0	1337·0	121·0	1874·0	151·0
Industrial employment per 1,000 inhabitants	99·7	21·0*	112·6	27·3	120·6	28·8	—	—
Per capita industrial output (value added)	304·0	16·0	404·0	19·0	666·0	36·0	1024·0	54·0
Share of manufacturing in industrial output, per cent	84·9	79·6	86·6	78·1	87·6	70·7	87·9	69·6
Share of heavy industry in manufacturing output, per cent	49·2	31·1	57·8	32·9	64·1	44·3	68·8	45·4

* Estimate.

Source: The Growth of World Industry, U.N., 1965, 1970.

share of oil and gas extraction. The share of coal mining was only
2·5 per cent, i.e. lower than the combined industrial average. Owing
to the greater share of mining, the weight of manufacturing was relatively smaller (6·6 per cent) while that of the food industry was
somewhat higher (9·7 per cent); the shares of paper industry and
engineering were particularly low (1·5 and 2·6 per cent).

From 1938 to 1948 and 1950 the total industrial production of
the developing countries increased at a somewhat slower rate than
that of the advanced capitalist countries:

INDEX NUMBERS OF INDUSTRIAL PRODUCTION
1938 = 100

	Developed capitalist countries	Developing countries
1948	144	138
1950	167	154

(Date taken from Annex V/1).

From 1938 to 1948 the industrial production of developed capitalist countries increased by 44 per cent, while that of developing countries only by 38. As can be seen from Table V/1, though *per capita*
national income increased in the developing countries in comparison
to the preceding period, its rate was slower than in the developed
countries. While in 1938 *per capita* national income in the developing
countries amounted to 11 per cent of that in the advanced countries,
by 1948 this fell to about 10 per cent. The situation is similar in respect of *per capita* industrial output, which fell from 5·3 per cent
in comparison to the developed countries in 1938 to 4·3 per cent by
1948.

2. *Growth of Industry since 1950*

In the second half of the twentieth century the total economic (and,
within that, the industrial) development of the Afro-Asian and Latin
American countries entered a new phase. The colonial system – at
least politically, and apart from a few exceptions – gradually came
to an end. Vast forces are at work in the backward countries aimed
at independent economic development and at the liquidation of one-
sided economic structures. This circumstance is reflected also in the
development of their industrial production. While in the eighteenth
and nineteenth centuries and even in the first half of the twentieth
century, industry increased faster in the now developed countries
than in Africa, Asia and Latin America, the situation changed around

the turn of the century and *the industrial growth rate of the developing countries has exceeded the growth rate of industry in developed countries (more exactly advanced capitalist countries)*. This can be seen in Table V/2.

Table V/2
GROWTH OF TOTAL INDUSTRY AND MAJOR INDUSTRIAL BRANCHES, 1950–66
(Index numbers of Industrial Production in 1966; 1950 = 100)

I.S.I.C.	Group or branch of industry	World total (excluding socialist countries)	Developed capitalist countries	Developing countries
1–3, 511–512	Total industry	242·8	233·2	338·5
1	All mining	198·6	151·8	405·4
11	Coal mining	99·0	92·1	213·4
12	Metal mining	195·7	195·8	195·6
13	Crude petroleum and natural gas	276·5	178·0	541·6
2–3	All manufacturing	242·2	237·3	310·0
20–26, 28–30, 39	Light manufacturing	192·3	185·0	243·9
27, 31–38	Heavy manufacturing	281·8	274·5	417·5
20–22	Food	177·5	172·6	222·3
23	Textiles	170·8	160·3	224·2
24	Textile and leather garment industry	180·4	174·6	
25–26	Wood products and furniture	187·1	176·4	
27	Paper	237·0	229·5	470·7
31–32	Chemicals	371·3	371·3	363·2
33	Non-metallic mineral products	230·9	217·5	360·8
34	Basic metals	197·5	188·6	378·6
35–38	Metal products	293·6	286·1	513·3
511–512	Electricity and gas	355·7	343·3	506·8

In the following pages, a short review will be given of industrial growth in the developing countries between 1950 and 1966, and of the particular features of their industries, comparing the latter mainly to those of the developed capitalist countries. From the statistical point of view, the analysis is based on U.N. sources, mainly on the publications *The Growth of World Industry 1938–1961*[9] and on later data by using the *Monthly Bulletin of Statistics of* the U.N.

The combined industrial output of the advanced capitalist and developing countries amounted in the period under review to about 70–80 per cent of the world total, while the production of the socialist countries (more exactly, of the Soviet Union and the European socialist countries) was 17·4 per cent of the world industrial total in 1950, 27·2 per cent in 1958, and 29·3 per cent in 1961.[10] It seemed more advisable to compare the results achieved and the expected development of industry in developing countries with that of the advanced capitalist countries and not with the world as a whole (inclusive of the socialist countries), because – at least as regards the past and the near future – the major results can be assessed and the fundamental tendencies disclosed better in this way owing to the closer relations between the two major regions in question. As has been mentioned in Chapter III, in the years 1960–4 two-thirds of the industrial exports of developing countries went to developed capitalist countries, and more than 80 per cent of their industrial imports came from the same countries; only about 7 per cent came from the socialist countries.[11]

Table V/2 presents the growth of total industry and of major industrial branches between 1950 and 1966.[12] By 1966 industrial production in the developing countries increased to almost 340 per cent of the 1950 level. In the advanced capitalist countries the index number was only 233 per cent. In terms of average annual growth rates, this is 7·9 per cent for the industry of the developing countries and 5·5 per cent for that in advanced capitalist countries, i.e. industrial growth was fast – seen in historical perspective – also in the advanced capitalist countries. In some shorter periods since 1938, the growth rates developed as follows:

Table V/3

AVERAGE ANNUAL GROWTH RATES OF
INDUSTRIAL PRODUCTION, 1938–1966*

(*percentages*)

Years	Total	Capitalist countries	Developing countries
1938–50	4·3	4·4	3·7
1950–5	6·3	5·9	7·3
1955–60	4·5	4·0	8·0
1960–6	6·3	6·2	8·4
1950–66	5·7	5·5	7·9

* Based on Annex V/2.

Thus, up to 1950 the industry of developing countries increased slower, but since then faster than in the developed capitalist countries.

In somewhat greater detail, still relying on Table V/2, mining increased faster in the developing countries than total industry (more than fourfold); in the developed capitalist countries mining increased much slower. This can be traced back to two circumstances: partly to the very fast development of crude oil and natural gas extraction in the developing countries (production grew more than fivefold), and partly to declining coal production in the developed countries.

As regards the growth of manufacturing, the difference between the two main regions is not so great as with mining, though it cannot be neglected. (The relevant index numbers are: 310 per cent for manufacturing in developing countries, and 237 per cent in developed capitalist countries.) The rate of growth in developing countries exceeded that of the developed countries in every sub-period, though between 1950 and 1955 the difference was small.[13]

Within manufacturing, industry increased faster in the developing countries in all three main industrial groups: light industry, heavy industry and the food industry. In the case of light industry and the food industry the growth rate exceeded the corresponding figure of the developed capitalist countries by about 30 per cent, and in heavy industry by about 50 per cent. Otherwise, the growth of heavy industry exceeded that of the light and food industries in both the developed capitalist and the developing countries.

As regards individual industries, growth was faster in the developed than in the developing countries only in the chemical industry. The textile, paper, non-ferrous mineral and metallurgical industries, engineering production, as well as electric energy and gas, grew faster in the developing than in the developed capitalist countries. The fastest-growing industry in the developing countries was engineering (the metal-working industries), while in the developed capitalist countries this place was occupied by the chemical industry. The growth rate of engineering exceeded the industrial average and also that of manufacturing to a greater extent in the developing than in the developed capitalist countries.

Of course, growth of production was different in the three regions of the developing countries.[14] There are no data available on the whole of *African* industry, but only for its two mining industries, for metallurgy and for the production of electricity and gas. In Asia, total industrial production increased somewhat quicker than in Latin America, mining grew somewhat slower, while manufacturing, particularly light and heavy industries, grew considerably quicker. From among the manufacturing branches, only the chemical industry increased more quickly in Latin America than in Asia. Data by countries – far from complete – could be gathered only for the period 1953–63.[15] It appears from these figures that anything may be found from very slow growth (e.g. 0·3 per cent annually in Uruguay) to very fast (18·2 per cent in the U.A.R.), but, at least in the twenty-five developing countries for which data could be collected, growth rates under 5–6 per cent annual average were exceptional.

The developing countries as a whole were characterised by a stability, an enduring dynamism in the growth of industrial production. From 1948–50 onwards, industrial production increased throughout the whole region, in contrast with the developed capitalist countries where it stagnated in 1954, and declined in 1958. A growth rate smaller than 4 per cent occurred only in 1953 in the region as a whole, and only in four years can we find growth rates below 7 per cent.

The internal structure of industry has the characteristics of underdevelopment in these countries.[16] Within the total industry of the developing countries, the share of mining was about 25 per cent in 1961; in the advanced ones, this ratio was only about 7 per cent. Within manufacturing, the share of light industry is about 55 per cent in developing countries and only 35 per cent in developed capitalist ones. Accordingly, the shares of the food and textile industries are higher within manufacturing, and that of engineering is lower; the latter ratio is 30–35 per cent in the advanced countries and only 14–16 per cent in the developing ones.

As regards the *tendencies of structural changes* in industry, the most essential difference is that the share of mining considerably diminished in the advanced capitalist countries while it significantly increased in the developing ones, primarily owing to growing crude oil and natural gas extraction. In *manufacturing, the main tendencies were the same in the two regions*, i.e. the ratio of heavy industry increased in both regions, that of light industry diminished, and within these the shares of the food and textile industries declined and that of engineering increased. Another considerable difference is that the share of the chemical industry increased fast in the developed capitalist countries, while this growth was considerably slower in the developing world.

The average data relating to the developing countries as a whole cover very diverse phenomena considered by individual countries. This relates both to the industrial structure by branches and to the tendencies and rates of structural changes.[17]

Let us give a few examples for illustration. In the developing countries as a whole, the share of the textile industry was around 12 per cent within manufacturing in the 1960s. But this average is composed of very different values: 1·7 per cent in Ghana, 4·8 per cent in Ceylon, 7·3 per cent in Nigeria, but 66 per cent in Pakistan, 32 per cent in the U.A.R., 22 per cent in Turkey, almost 40 per cent in Ethiopia, and almost 32 per cent in India. These wide differences appear also in the tendencies of structural changes. In general, the share of the textile industry decreased, i.e. the growth of this industry was slower than that of total manufacturing. However, between 1953 and 1963 textile industry increased faster than total manufacturing in Ceylon, Colombia, the Philippines and Venezuela – to mention only the major countries. There is a – not very strong – tendency discernable that the pattern by branches does not get differentiated, but becomes rather similar in the individual countries.

Finally, a few words about the relative importance of industry, or rather about the tendency of changes in its importance in the developing and the developed capitalist countries. As a first approximation, this can be characterised by the contribution to G.D.P. In the developed capitalist countries, manufacturing and mining combined contribute about 46 per cent to G.D.P., while within that figure the share of manufacturing is slowly increasing and that of mining is slowly decreasing. In the developing countries the share of manufacturing has grown, though its ratio is still much lower. It was about 10 per cent at the end of the 1950s in Africa, 20 per cent in Asia and 23 in Latin America. As should be obvious from what has been said above, the share contributed by mining has been increasing in the developing countries.

Of course, these average data again hide very different ratios in the individual developing countries. For example, in Argentina the contribution of industry was more than 36 per cent in 1964, while in Ceylon it was only 6·5 per cent; it was almost 50 per cent in Iraq in 1963 – owing to the large share of mining; in Ethiopia it was barely above 7 per cent. The differences are related not only – or in this case we may venture to say 'not so much' – to the special endowments of the countries but rather to the relative development level of the countries, reflected in the contribution of industry to gross domestic product. Otherwise the main tendency, the growing share of industry appears quite unequivocally and generally.

To sum up, it can be said that at the time of colonial rule the economies of the developing countries were suppliers of raw materials to the developed capitalist countries and markets for the industrial products of the latter. As a consequence, their domestic industries did not develop to any significant extent. The backward economy was not at all or by no means sufficiently modernised by the colonial governments. Even the governments of the countries which have retained or acquired political independence (e.g. in Latin America) carried on similar economic policies, either because they were forced

F*

to do so by the imperialist countries or in the interest of the ruling (generally landowner) classes. (In this respect the only exception is Japan.) Thus, the differences in respect of industrial development levels continued to grow, though some industrial development started to satisfy certain domestic needs and to complement non-industrial activities. This industrial development obtained a new impetus in the first half of the twentieth century, when the 'traditional' division of labour between the developed and the colonial and semi-colonial countries suffered a setback owing to war and depressions.

Since the Second World War the situation has changed; on the basis of political independence, the developing countries definitely strive to accelerate their economic growth and, within it, to industrialise. The whole region is characterised by a sustained dynamism of industrial development and by a faster industrial growth than in the developed capitalist countries, though, owing to extremely rapid population growth, relative backwardness in terms of *per capita* industrial production has not diminished. While the developing countries in general are quickly industrialising, there are great differences among individual regions and, particularly, among individual countries. From among the regions, the level of industrial development is highest in Latin America, followed by Asia, and is lowest in Africa. The growth rates are higher in Asia than in Latin America and – as far as one can conclude by the growth rate of energy production, since there are no comprehensive data on total industry – the African growth rate approaches that of Asia. The structure of industry is characterised, in comparison with the developed countries, partly by a relatively greater weight of mining and, within manufacturing, by the greater importance of light industry in comparison with heavy industry. The tendency of changes in industrial structure points towards growing similarity in the sense that the industrial structure in developing countries (i.e. their macro-structure) approaches that in developed countries. However, the product-pattern (the micro-structure) continues to reflect backwardness. The chemical industry is an exception, growing faster in the developed capitalist countries than in the developing ones. It seems that faster growth of the chemical industry takes place only at higher stages of development; this is indicated by the circumstance that in Latin America it increased faster than in the developing countries in general. Otherwise, as will be explained later, growing similarity in the macro-structure does not at all mean a similar approximation as regards the standard of living or the general level of economic development.

3. *The Size of the Market and the Development of Individual Industries*

Problems of growth are mostly specific to the individual industries, but there are, of course, also more general problems. From among them, only a single one will be dealt with here in detail, namely the connection between the size of the market and the development of industry and individual branches of industry. It is through this relation that the relative development of individual industries, their past development tendencies, and – at least partly – their expected future trends can best be explained.

For individual national economies, particularly at a lower stage of development, the sales of industrial articles are determined mainly by the domestic market. The process of developing manufacturing industry (i.e. industrialisation) is, at the same time, also a process of substitution, partly substituting products of the small-scale (handicraft, cottage-industry) and partly substituting imported products by the products of domestic large-scale industry. Every late-industrialising country strives at the start of industrialisation to secure expanding markets for its own manufacturing industry, and small-scale industry is partly or entirely displaced.

Initially, owing to low national income and the concomitant low consumption of industrial articles, the domestic market is narrow. This is why the size of the domestic market is a prime condition of industrialisation. This market, of course, expands with industrialisation, similarly to the fact that economic growth is also more or less a function of industrialisation. The starting of large-scale, mechanised manufacturing production is made possible by the size of the domestic market at different stages in each industry, at different levels of economic development. It is mainly this circumstance which determines – in a longer historical perspective – the course of industrialisation, from the viewpoint of the industries emerging and the changes in industrial structure.

It is a general rule that the market for consumer goods can attain the size suited for large-scale manufacturing production sooner than the means of production. Within consumer articles, the 'traditional' products – i.e. the textile, clothing and food products – attain this critical size earlier than durable consumer goods created by technical progress (radio, television, refrigerators, washing machines, cars, etc.) or the chemical goods (plastics and synthetic fibres). Accordingly, large-scale light industry can be created earlier than heavy industry. This is what happened also in the first industrialising countries, and this is repeated in the now developing countries. The process, of course, is influenced by natural and historical circumstances; it may be affected by political decisions, but only in the framework of objectively given conditions and general rules.

As is known, the costs of production, and particularly of investment, decrease with the size of plants, Therefore, to increase the size of the plant is advantageous until higher transport costs or the management problems accompanying growing size (diminishing flexibility, and smaller possibility for adaptation) do not counterbalance the advantages. There are therefore rational plant sizes below which plants are not viable under the given economic and technical conditions. The lowering of costs is particularly steep where production is carried on with a few big units, since the costs of these quickly diminish with growing sizes, i.e. mainly in chemical and metallurgical processes. The lowering is not so steep, and the advantage of larger scale of production ceases sooner in production carried out with several machines, i.e. where the increase in the scale of production consist mainly in increasing the number of machines. Production technology is generally of this latter type in the traditional industries, that is, in those which produce directly for consumption, as for example the textile or the clothing industries. This is also one of the reasons why the domestic market reaches sooner the size necessary for large-scale production.

A further, not negligible, viewpoint is to what extent small-scale industry remains competitive and retains the market. This depends partly on the character of technology and partly on that of demand. As regards the textile industry, in Western Europe also mechanical production supplanted hand operations sooner in spinning than in weaving. The same is now repeated in the Asian countries (e.g. India and Pakistan), in which small-scale industry has a stronger tradition. In the clothing industry, however, the small-scale industry retained for a relatively long time part of its market, beyond technological causes, also because it could adapt itself better to the special requirements of the buyers.

These circumstances account for the outstanding importance of the *textile industry* in the developing countries, where this industry generally emerged and assumed factory-scale character sooner than other industries. Today it can already satisfy domestic needs and, in certain countries, it can export. Relying greatly on domestic raw material, the textile industry is the only branch in the developing countries which has a considerable share in world production. As regards the whole textile industry, the developing countries employ in it more people than the developed capitalist countries. Of course, owing to low productivity, their share in production is much lower; in 1964 it was somewhat above 20 per cent by value added and somewhat below 40 per cent by the weight produced. The two shares differ so much because the developing countries produce less labour-intensive products than the developed ones. Of the output of jute products, three-fourths are turned out by the developing countries. Also among textiles for clothing they produce mainly the cheaper cotton fabrics; the share of wool and of synthetic fibres is lower. Within the cotton industry, coarser, cheaper cloth is made than in the developed countries.

The growth of market size – and, consequently, the growth – of the textile industry is already slower in the developing countries in comparison to the whole of industry, though it is still faster than in the developed countries. Between 1950 and 1966 the textile industry of the developing countries increased at the average annual rate of 5·2 per cent (against 3·4 per cent in the developed capitalist countries) while industry as a whole increased at 7–9 per cent p.a. Of course, the situation is different in the different regions. In Latin America, particularly in the bigger countries, the process of import substitution had mostly come to an end by the middle of the twentieth century; cotton spinning capacity increased after 1950 only by about 35 per cent. In Africa, however, the textile industry is relatively young and import substitution has not yet ended. As a result, from 1950 the spinning capacity has grown about threefold. Growth has been similar since the turn of the century in the countries of the Near East. In Asia, where the textile industry has the greatest traditions, spinning capacity has grown about twofold since 1950.

The size of the market can be expanded with the aid of exports, which is necessary not only to increase production but also to procure the equivalent necessary for imports. The textile exports of the developing countries are considerable in comparison to both their total exports and to world trade in textiles. In the exports of some countries, textiles are of outstanding importance (mainly the export of cotton fabrics); thus 33 per cent of the exports of India, 21 per cent in Pakistan and 13 per cent in the U.A.R. are textile products.

The growth of the textile industries of developing countries was facilitated by the circumstance that the raw material, at least part of it (mainly cotton) is available within the country; so in this respect the natural conditions are favourable.

Thus, in the textile industry the domestic market is big enough to allow production to develop, and with domestic production as a basis, exports have also developed. But the domestic needs increased relatively slowly and, owing to the world-wide slow increase in consumption, as well as the protectionist policies of the developed countries (to be reverted to later), exports also increased at a relatively slow rate.

For the products of the iron and steel industry, the domestic markets of the developing countries are small, but consumption increases fast. As is known, this sector is of strategic importance in industrialisation, since it induces growth in the supplying sectors as well as in the sectors where its products are used. The main consumers of steel are the machine building industry, mining and construction, which all increase fast in the developing countries. The growth of steel production was therefore dynamic.

But, to start production, to 'enter' the market, critical plant sizes are rather big in ferrous metallurgy. Therefore the share of the developing countries is still low in world production (though it is growing quickly, since in 1953 it was about 1·6 per cent and in 1966 about 3·7 per cent). Iron and steel production started late in the developing countries and mainly in the bigger ones; before the First World War it existed only in India, it became established before the Second World War in Mexico and came about after the Second World War first in Brazil and then in Argentina. It is in these countries that we can find annual steel production above 1,000,000 tons. In seven or eight more countries there is still considerable production (above 100,000 tons per annum). The steel exports of the developing countries are at present not significant; on the other hand, about half of the total domestic consumption is imported.

In this case, the domestic market is relatively narrow, but it is dynamic, and grows at a fast rate. The natural conditions – more exactly, the raw materials – present a special problem. In the past, ferrous metallurgy developed mainly where the two most important raw materials, iron ore and cokeable coal, could be found near or could easily be procured. This limitation gradually diminished, partly with the growth of consumption and thus with the growing advantages of a site near to consumer centres, partly with the relative reduction of transport costs, and finally with the exhaustion of the traditional iron ore deposits and the discovery and exploitation of new ones mainly in the developing countries. At present an ever-growing share of iron ore originates in the developing countries and the richness in iron ore promotes the development of ferrous metallurgy – although it is mainly delivered for the time being to the developed countries.

Export-oriented industries. The main basis of industrialisation is generally the domestic market, and production can be shifted towards exports only gradually, after it has been developed for the domestic market. There are also, however, special export-oriented industries in the developing countries. For the development of such industries special conditions were necessary – as will be proved by closer investigation – such as advantageous natural conditions, a dynamic growth of demand, monopolised markets on a world scale and the activity of big international firms in exploiting the natural resources.

The extraction of crude oil, as the most characteristic of this kind of export industry, developed through the exploitation of natural resources in developing countries by international firms. A few great oil firms have for a long time ruled the markets (and exerted a degree of political sway over the countries where the oil deposits are to be found). Recently, the monopolistic position of the big firms has been diminishing, and the developing countries have increasingly the possibility to dispose of their oil resources. The exploitation of existing deposits and, particularly, the opening up of new ones, as well as the selling of oil, continues, however, to take place mostly with the participation of the big international firms, because neither the necessary capital nor the knowledge and, particularly, the commercial organisation for exports, can be found in the developing countries.

Another such characteristically export-oriented industry is non-ferrous metallurgy, where big international firms also play an outstanding role. In 1964, for example, the share of the developing countries was 7 per cent of world copper consumption, but 40 per cent of metal production and about 44 per cent of ore production. As regards tin, the corresponding ratios were 2, 68 and 95 per cent. The situation is similar with lead and zinc, though with these the share of the developing countries is higher in utilisation and lower in metal production and ore mining. It should, however, be obvious from these ratios that we have here mostly export industries. They are of strategic importance in economic development, particularly because the countries producing for export are mostly small and the metals and ores amount to a large proportion of their total exports. The freedom of movement of the developing countries, their ability to dispose of their own resources, has grown also in respect of non-ferrous metals, but they have not eliminated the international firms from production and sales altogether.

In aluminium production the situation is somewhat different: the developing countries as a region are net importers of the metal, though the greater and growing part of bauxite production is coming even now from the developing countries. It may, however, be expected that in the next one or two decades a situation similar to that regarding the other non-ferrous metals will develop, and the share of the developing countries in world aluminium output will rise from its present level of about 3 per cent to about 18 per cent. The big producers will not be the countries which are at the same time also big consumers, but small countries such as Ghana, Cameroon, Congo and Guinea, where favourable natural conditions (mainly hydro-energy and cheap bauxite) make production profitable. For these countries aluminium exports will have the same strategic importance for their whole economic development as oil and copper have in the case of other small countries. But the starting of aluminium production took place or will take place in these small developing countries with the participation of the few international firms ruling the capitalist world market, since it is these that have the necessary capital, knowledge and market organisation.

There is another industry also where the possibilities of an export-oriented development emerge, namely in the petrochemical industry, mainly in the field of producing fertilisers based on natural gas. New fertiliser plants are being built using the raw material resources of the developing countries, e.g. in Kuwait, Iran, Saudi Arabia, Lybia and several Latin American countries. In these, at least in some of them, the scale of production exceeds domestic needs and will continue to do so in the foreseeable future, hence development takes place from the begining with the aim of exporting – also with the participation of international firms.

The developing countries are, of course, interested both in exploiting their natural resources and in export earnings. It is also obvious that export industries may contribute to raising the technical level of the whole country, though experience up to now has shown that these industries function within the backward economy as separate modern islands, their relations being more intensive with the world market and the colonising country. With proper economic policy this phenomenon can be reduced, as can be the danger menacing the actual independence of a small country from the big foreign firms active in their territory. But the danger persists, and in industrialising the developing countries this must be considered.

The production of export industries is independent of the domestic market, the scale of production not being determined by the domestic demand. But there are only a few such industries, and the influence of the domestic market is mostly decisive even if it is not exclusive. This is particularly so when some new industry is established in the developing countries.

The starting of production is made possible by the domestic market in individual industries with different development levels and population sizes. We illustrate this with the examples of steel-making and the cotton-textile industries.

Let us start from the assumption that steel production becomes economically rational with a capacity of about 200,000 tons p.a. It can be assumed that annual consumption of about 400,000 tons of steel is necessary to build a furnace producing 200,000 tons for domestic use, since it is obvious, particularly with such a small volume of production, that full self-sufficiency is inconceivable.

For the cotton industry we assume that the rational plant size is determined by the spinnery, and the size is 20,000 spindles or 3,600 tons of thread p.a. Here we assume also that about half of the domestic consumption is met by domestic production.

Both in steel and textiles, *per capita* consumption grows with increasing *per capita* national income. Income elasticity is high with steel and relatively low with textiles.

On the basis of international data, the following interrelation may be assumed between *per capita* national income and the use of steel and textiles.

Per capita national income, $	100	200	400	800
Per capita steel consumption, kg.	9	33	100	250
Per capita textile fibre consumption, kg.	3	4·8	7	9·4

From these assumptions the size of the population can be worked out that allows for the starting of textile and steel production at various levels of *per capita* national income:

National income per head, $	100	200	400
Population (in millions) at which the production of			
of steel	45	11	4
of textiles	2·4	1·5	1
can be started			

As can be seen, textile production can be started with a much smaller market, particularly on lower levels of economic development; later, however, the difference quickly diminishes.

The *engineering* industries show perceptibly the decisive importance of the domestic market's size. Since this industry is made up of different sectors, the structural changes among its sectors can easily be studied as a function of the size of the market. As is known, the engineering industries are closely related to every branch of the economy, supplying them with the machinery and equipment necessary to increase production and productivity. Here is the starting point also for many new kinds of production processes, and this industry also contributes to the training of the specialists necessary for modern production in other branches.

The backward economic structure of developing countries is also reflected in the fact that their share in world production is smallest in this branch, only about 4 per cent. As has been mentioned, the share of engineering is also low in the total industrial output of the developing countries (14–16 per cent on average, while in developed

Table V/4

ENGINEERING INDUSTRIES IN INDUSTRIALISED AND LESS INDUSTRIALISED COUNTRIES: SELECTED INDICATORS OF DEVELOPMENT

	Engineering industries		Total yearly steel consumption (thousand metric tons)	Engineering goods		Value added in engineering production (million U.S. dollars)	Value added in total manufacturing (million U.S. dollars)
	Number engaged, in thousands	Percentage in total manufacturing (value added)		Percentage imports in domestic consumption	Percentage exports in domestic production		
Less industrialised countries	Over 200	25–30 or more	1,000 or more	10–50	20–50	—	—
I. Developed and diversified engineering production	Over 200	15–20	1,000 or more	50–75	Insignificant	400–800	2,000–5,000
II. Engineering production at initial stage	20–50	8–12	400–800	80–90	Insignificant	50–100	400–1,000
III. No engineering production or engineering restricted to repairs and simple metal manufacture	20 or less	8 or less	400 or less	85–100	Insignificant	up to 50	up to 400

countries this ratio is above 30 per cent). The rate of growth, however, is fast: between 1950 and 1966 it was almost 11 per cent annually. The basis of growth was the increase of the domestic market (and partly, of course, also import substitution), since the engineering exports of the developing countries are at present negligible.

From the point of view of the level of their engineering industries, the developing countries can be classified into three groups, which can be distinguished clearly from one another and from the industrially developed countries by characteristic criteria (see Table V/4).

Demand for the products of the engineering industries can be roughly characterised by the size of the 'modern' sector of the economy, and the latter by the size of manufacturing (by the G.N.P. created by manufacturing), and by domestic steel consumption. Regarding these criteria, Group I of the developing countries had a rather sizeable domestic market for engineering products, the G.N.P. created by manufacturing was in 1961 between 2,500 and 3,000 million dollars, and steel consumption was above 1,000,000 tons p.a. (this group comprises India, Brazil, Mexico and Argentina, see details in Table V/5).

Table V/5

DEVELOPING COUNTRIES: SELECTED STATISTICAL INDICATORS OF INDUSTRIAL DEVELOPMENT

| Country | Value added (million dollars) | | Share of metal products in total manufacturing (per cent) | | Steel | | Number of persons engaged in total manufacturing (thousands) (d) |
	All manu-facturing I.S.I.C. 2–3 (a)	Metal products I.S.I.C. 35–38 (a)	Value added (b)	Number engaged (b)	Produc-tion Thousand metric tons (c)	Con-sump-tion (c)	
Group I:							
India	4701·8	753·3	14·5	12·9	4,071	5,154	1870·5
Brazil	3643·3	645·2	14·3	11·5	1,843	2,701	1547·0
Mexico	2999·4	557·0	14·3	13·8	1,728	1,840	1978·0
Argentina	2412·7	480·0	20·7	25·3	441	2,379	1411·0
Group II:							
Turkey	1012·6	100·1	7·4	10·9	282	549	295·3
Venezuela	886·6	85·9	6·1	6·0	—	448	137·8
Pakistan	803·1	101·6	8·6	11·6	9	192	397·8
Colombia	658·2	70·8	8·0	12·6	176	405	236·8
Chile	643·4	71·1	9·7	13·3	363	506	206·6

Table V/5—continued

Country	Value added (million dollars) All manufacturing I.S.I.C. 2–3 (a)	Value added (million dollars) Metal products I.S.I.C. 35–38 (a)	Share of metal products in total manufacturing (per cent) Value added (b)	Share of metal products in total manufacturing (per cent) Number engaged (b)	Steel Production Thousand metric tons (c)	Steel Consumption (c)	Number of persons engaged in total manufacturing (thousands) (d)
Korea (Rep. of)	571·6	58·5	9·9	10·3	61	—	260·6
U.A.R.	497·6	44·6	6·0	7·0	—	373	260·8
Philippines	447·6	53·3	10·7	11·2	—	504	228·4
Indonesia	—	—	10·9	11·6	—	439	334·5
Iran	—	—	—	—	—	351	—
Group III:							
Peru	367·6	28·4	6·1	7·8	—	246	116·3
Federation of Rhodesia and Nyasaland	356·4	57·4	24·6	22·4	60	244	109·6
Cuba	351·8	—	—	—	277	—	—
Algeria	341·4	66·1	22·0	20·2	—	402	146·7
Uruguay	313·7	57·6	—	18·9	—	86	191·4
Morocco	303·1	50·8	19·0	—	—	152	—
Thailand	253·5	—	—	10·3	—	257	189·8
China (Taiwan)	253·1	39·7	6·1	8·2	198	287	173·0
Burma	181·8	—	2·8	3·6	—	—	120·9
Ceylon	180·6	32·2	23·6	36·0	—	89	49·9
Ecuador	121·2	—	1·5	1·7	—	—	30·4
Syria	92·6	—	—	—	—	—	—
Guatemala	71·7	—	3·9	6·9	—	—	27·6
El Salvador	48·3	—	4·1	3·8	—	—	60·3
Honduras	41·1	—	2·8	3·0	—	—	20·1
Nicaragua	31·1	—	1·3	2·1	—	—	18·9
Paraguay	24·2	0·3	3·7	5·3	—	—	34·3
Ethiopia	23·2	—	—	—	—	—	20·0
Nigeria	—	—	5·4	—	—	182	—
Tunisia	—	—	—	—	—	79	12·9
Ghana	—	—	9·3	13·8	—	67	21·7

Sources: (a) Unpublished estimates of the statistical Office of the U.N.
       (b) *The Growth of World Industry 1938–1961*, U.N., 1964.
       (c) *Statistical Yearbook 1962.*
       (d) Same as in (b).

These countries imported 50–60 per cent of their engineering product requirements; the share of engineering in manufacturing was 15–20 per cent, domestic engineering was adequately developed and diversified, i.e. it produced many kinds of engineering products. It is precisely this circumstance that allows a considerable part of domestic demand to be met with domestic production.

Group II sharply deviates from Group I. Here the value added by manufacturing was 400–1,000 million dollars, and steel consumption was 400–800 tons p.a. The characteristic share of engineering within manufacturing was 8–12 per cent, engineering was in the initial stages of development, with a rather narrow product pattern. Imports amounted to 80–90 per cent of domestic use. (Here belong, for example, Turkey, Venezuela, Pakistan and several other countries.)

Group III cannot be unequivocally distinguished from Group II. Some countries which are smaller as regards the size of manufacturing seem to be more developed as regards the share of engineering. It is characteristic of this group of countries that both its manufacturing and its steel consumption were lower than in the preceding group, the share of engineering within manufacturing was 8 per cent or less, and the engineering industries were underdeveloped, restricted mainly to repair work and the production of simple mass products.

The development level of engineering seems to be related not so much to the general development of the country (in terms of *per capita* national income), but much more to the size of the domestic market, influenced not only by *per capita* income but also by the size of population. This is why in India, a poor country in terms of *per capita* income, and in Brazil, equally relatively poor, we find a more developed, diversified engineering industry, with a higher share in manufacturing than in many richer countries.

The developing and the industrially developed countries can be unequivocally distinguished in our classification. The share of engineering within manufacturing is higher in the developed countries; in addition, and perhaps even more important, the industrially developed countries have considerable exports in engineering products, while exports are insignificant even in Group I of the developing countries.

The three groups mentioned can also be understood as characteristic stages in the growth of engineering in the developing countries. Development is principally determined by the size of domestic demand. First, the production of simple mass products becomes technically possible and profitable (iron-constructions, pots and pans, containers, locks, etc.). In this field, domestic manufacturing can quickly attain a level of quality and costs that is more favourable than that of small-scale industry; it also quickly becomes competitive with imports. Quality requirements are not too high, and with part of the mass products mainly those made from sheet metal and rather bulky, domestic production is relatively favourable because of the higher transport costs of the manufactured goods compared to the raw material.

Beyond the production of simple mass articles, the third group (the lowest stage of development) is characterised by repair-maintenance works, a kind of activity that may be considered as the basis for developing engineering production, contributing to indigenous workers becoming acquainted with engineering technologies and skills.

At a higher stage of development, demand is growing for engineering products that are more complicated both in the means of production and as consumer goods. The growing demand makes it possible to start the production of more complicated engineering equipment. With further growth in demand for increases in the means of production in the countries belonging to Group I industrial equipment, energy-producing and -transforming machinery, machine tools, etc. start being produced, and engineering production becomes more diversified. Thus, in the engineering industries *there is a possibility to shift gradually*, on the basis of experience gained in mass goods production and in repair and maintenance work, to the production of more complicated products. The scale of production can be gradually expanded. It is also possible to introduce new products (particularly those to be produced in series) beginning with the importation of part of the components and then gradually substituting imports by domestic production.

Experience has shown that the engineering industries of the developing countries grow gradually and on the basis of increasing domestic demand. This gradualness also shows in respect of the characteristic internal structure of engineering production. In industrially developed countries about 6 per cent of engineering production consists of simple metal products, 33 per cent consists of machinery (excluding electrical machinery), 24 per cent of electrical machinery and equipment, 33 per cent of transport equipment, and 4 per cent of instruments and precision engineering products. In Group I of the developing countries, the share of simple metal products is essentially higher: about 20–30 per cent may be considered as characteristic. The share of electrical machinery is usually greater than that of machine building. In Groups II and III the share of simple metal products is even higher, 35–40 and 50 per cent respectively.

It can be generally observed that the internal structure of engineering industries in countries at lower levels of development is approaching that of the countries at higher development levels. A similar phenomenon can be observed also in respect of engineering exports. The machine exports of countries in the first group, i.e. Argentina, Brazil, India and Mexico, have increased recently at a rate far exceeding that of world exports or that of the developed countries, though as regards the exports volume or their proportion relative to domestic production they are as yet rather modest.

It is much debated whether the engineering industries should be, or can be, developed in the developing countries. According to the arguments against such policies, they should not. The reasoning runs as follows:

(a) The domestic market is small; if the scale of production is not large enough, costs will be high.

(b) In addition it is not worth while, since 'developing the engineering industries in a backward country usually does not yield any absolute cost-advantage, as the working out and control of new production technologies enabling the realisation of a higher surplus value is taking place in the industrial centres'.[18]

(c) Finally, there is also reasoning such as that it is not worth while to develop the engineering industries to any significant extent, since they have no natural markets in the developing countries, as agriculture is not a consumer; owing to overpopulation, mechanisation is not necessary; therefore, attempts are made to create a market by establishing other engineering branches. This sector, established on the basis of the conception of 'engineering for engineering', has no proper links either with the domestic market or with the world market, and its efficiency is therefore unsatisfactory.[19]

To what extent are these objections justified? The internal markets of the backward countries are narrow indeed, and these countries are compelled to adapt their scale of production to that fact; hence productivity is lower than in the developed countries. But it is particularly in the engineering industry that there is some possibility for growth in every country and at every level of development, just because of the flexibility of this branch. It is thus not the development of engineering that is lacking in economic rationality, but such development that does not rely on the level once achieved and on the actual possibilities, but breaks away from them. It is true that the technological knowledge, the 'know-how', must in most cases be procured from abroad, but this was done by every 'late industrialising' country. It is not necessary that the advantages accompanying the application of up-to-date methods should get lost in this way. Otherwise, either development is put off, and in this case know-how must be imported later, or domestic technological development is attempted which may either be impossible or much more expensive.

Reference to the concept 'engineering for engineering's sake' does not seem to be justified. There is not, and never can be, any such concept. At a lower level of development, the engineering industries are buyers of their own products mainly in respect of machine tools (machine tools are, of course, also used in other branches for repair and maintenance), inter-industry shipments within the country are growing precisely at the higher stages of development. Machine tool production is not very great in engineering as a whole, and particularly not in the developing countries. As against that, in the engineering production of developing countries, simple metal products, which are mostly consumer goods, are of great importance together with electrical machinery and equipment. The share of non-electrical machines grows only in later phases of development – and of that only a part consists of machine tools.

Nor can such 'engineering for engineering's sake' be discovered in more detailed reviews of development. For example, in Cambodia, a small country at a low level of development, factories have been built in recent years for the production of the following products:[20] (a) agricultural implement workshop; (b) mechanical engineering shops (with foundries, mainly for construction and mining machinery); (c) wire products, nails, nuts and bolts, and metal furniture; (d) aluminium ware; (e) metal containers; (f) sheet metal and sections, mainly into larger containers; (g) weighing machines; (h) sewing machines and bicycles.

Pakistan, a much bigger country than Cambodia, already has a sizeable engineering industry and wishes to develop it further. It also produces simple machine tools, which are easily absorbed by the home market, hence the overwhelming part of machine tools will still have to be imported in the future. The production of non-electrical machinery (the smaller part of which is machine-tool production) amounts in this country to 18–19 per cent of total engineering output.[21] It says much for developing engineering that in the developing countries there is use for less sophisticated products that are no longer used, and have therefore gradually been dropped from production, in the developed countries.

It is still worth noting that – although agriculture is not a major customer of the engineering industries even in the developed countries, and although big-scale mechanisation – i.e. capital-intensive, labour-saving mechanisation – is not yet of any great relevance in the developing countries, it would not be correct entirely to neglect the agriculture of developing countries as a market for engineering products. Some machines have the direct effect of increasing production; and there is an absolute economic justification for supplying agriculture with the necessary tools and implements, irrigation equipment, etc. (as has been referred to in Chapter III), since these are necessary for increasing agricultural yields.

In the foregoing, exports have frequently been mentioned as a tool for expanding the market; it was mainly exports to the developed countries that we had in view, since that is where the greatest market for industrial products is to be found. In principle, however, there also exists another possibility for expanding the market, namely with the aid of regional or sub-regional co-operation among developing countries. Such co-operation is obviously desirable, as it would facilitate expansion of the market, help to avoid the creation of too small or not fully used production capacities, and in general help faster industrialisation.

In principle the possibility for such co-operation does exist, but in the field of practical experience it has not yet been much exploited. This circumstance has both techno-economic and socio-political causes. In export-oriented industries (e.g. non-ferrous metallurgy), particularly in smaller countries, because of the narrow domestic market, only those new plants can be efficient which are directed towards exporting to markets in developed areas – in comparison to which the markets of the developing countries are unimportant. In engineering, the international division of labour would have great significance; however, it seems that vested interests are too strong in the countries which already have some engineering industry and we do not know of any outstanding results in this sector, though some initial results are known. In Latin America, for example, intraregional trade in machinery increased between 1961 and 1965 from $11,000,000 to $50,000,000. In 1965, however, the total exports of machinery of the region amounted to $11,100,000 while imports were $3,410,000,000.

In the textile industry, international co-operation has not such great importance from the viewpoint of rational plant size as, for example, it has in engineering: it would have greater importance for the smallest or the least developed countries. Greater specialisation in the textile industry would have advantages also for larger countries, but co-operation is hindered by the fact that a similar pattern for the industry has developed in individual countries: namely, complementarity is small, with the result that part of the products would have to be imported from outside the region or sub-region even in the case of integration or customs union. In addition, an already well-established textile industry can exert greater pressure against infringement of its real or assumed interests (i.e. the monopolisation of the domestic market).

It seems that neither the political will to establish effective international co-operation, nor the organisation of international planning, particularly organisation for plan-implementation, is sufficiently strong at present to bring about actual co-operation. In the case of steel production being started in the smaller African countries, development could surely be faster and sounder economically if the countries united and pooled their resources and their domestic markets.

There is no lack of initiative in this direction, yet I doubt whether much of it will be implemented in the near future. In individual developing countries the decision to start steel production is taken rather quickly, even if the restricted scale of production makes the efficiency of the venture doubtful. But proposals on co-operation usually result in new discussions rather than in actual steel production. For example, West Africa (where the greatest user is Nigeria, which has some steel production and where the creation of new production capacity has been planned) was the subject of a study made under the auspices of the African Economic Commission of the U.N. with the aim of selecting the best site for the whole region. Comparing the feasible sites in Liberia, Gabon, Ghana and Nigeria, the specialists proposed Liberia. This was discused in October 1964 by the 'Industrial Co-ordination Conference for West Africa', following which the Liberian government appointed a committee in August 1965 to discuss the problem, where a new specialist committee was formed which convened in October 1965 and decided to convene for new discussion again in March 1966.[22]

4. Some Characteristic Features of Industrialisation in Developing, Advanced Capitalist and Socialist Countries

Industrialisation is an economic process which, by and large, has been completed in the advanced capitalist countries and in the European socialist countries. The question may be raised whether the developing countries indeed undergo industrialisation, transforming and modernising their economies, and if so, what are the similarities and the differences between industrialisation processes taking place in various periods, various regions and under different economic and social conditions; furthermore, what conclusions do the analysis and comparison of these processes permit us to draw concerning the expected industrial expansion in developing countries?

According to a frequently quoted statement by Marx: 'The country that is more developed industrially only shows to the less developed the image of its future.'[23] Of course, Marx did not mean this statement to refer to the long-term and world-wide tendencies of industrial growth, but spoke about the general validity of the 'natural laws of capitalist production', saying that the German readers of his work should not be complacent, thinking that the situation in Germany was much better than that prevailing among the British industrial and agricultural working class. However, it is not unjustified to interpret the validity of Marx's statement somewhat more widely. It can be proved that the process of industrialisation shows many similarities, even if it has taken place in various countries in different periods and under different conditions. The similarity is, of course, the greater the more general our approach to the process. For example, the definition adopted by the Committee for Industrial Development of the U.N., referring to technological up-to-dateness, a diversified economic structure and a dynamic manufacturing industry, is of general validity.[24] On the other hand, the deeper we go into details and the more concretely we analyse industrialisation in the individual countries, the greater do we find the differences, even between countries undergoing industrialisation almost simultaneously, at the same cultural level and under the same social system.

In the present comparison, the main characteristics of industrialisation will be examined from three aspects, namely the relation of industrialisation (*a*) to the growth of total and *per capita* national income, (*b*) to the changes in economic structure (of the whole economy and within industry), and (*c*) to the widespread application of scientific and technological results in practice.

(*a*) The most important criterion of industrialisation and, at the same time, of economic growth is *a lasting and rapid growth of total and* per capita *national income*. National income, of course, does not only grow in a modern industrial economy. According to some authors, production prior to the industrial revolution remained unchanged and productivity was determined by the number of population: 'When population increased, the *per capita* product diminished, and when population decreased, the *per capita* product increased.'[25] This statement, even if true for some shorter period, certainly cannot be accepted for a longer period. The world's population also increased before the industrial revolution. (According to Kuznets, from 275,000,000 in the year 1000 to about 730–750,000,000 by 1750.[26] Even if the data are not accurate, the fact of growth cannot be denied.) However, population growth is hardly conceivable without the growth of production and of national income. It is probable that productivity also increased for a long time – although slowly. Again, according to Kuznets, *per capita* national income increased in England[27] between 1700 and 1780, i.e. before the industrial revolution, by 2 per cent every ten years.

However, it is an important fact that *since the industrial revolution*,

*and owing to industrialisation, the rate of economic growth has greatly
accelerated – in terms of both total and* per capita *national income.*
In England the growth of *per capita* national income grew from 2
per cent every ten years before the industrial revolution to a ten-year
growth rate of 13·4 per cent in 1780–1881; it was 17·9 per cent in
France (1841/50–1960/62), 9·2 per cent in Germany in a first (1851/5–
1871/5) and 17·9 per cent in a later period (1871/5–1960/2). In the
other advanced countries the growth rates were similar and in some
cases even higher.[28]

These ten-year growth rates correspond to annual compound
rates of 0·9–2·0 per cent. For somewhat later periods, more detailed
data covering more capitalist countries are available. According
to Maddison, the annual growth of *per capita* income in twelve
developed countries[29] was 1·6 per cent on an average from 1870 to
1913, 1·1 per cent from 1913 to 1950, and 3·1 per cent from 1950
to 1960.[30] The rate of economic growth (of *per capita* national income) did not attain 2 per cent annually in any of the developed
capitalist countries between 1913 and 1950. Even between 1870 and
1913 it was surpassed only in Denmark (2·1 per cent), Sweden (2·3),
Canada (2·0) and the U.S.A. (2·2).

Against this picture the economies of the developing countries
did not grow, or grew extremely slowly up to the middle of the twentieth century. Of course, there are no reliable data available for this
period; only the very approximate estimates of some authors
can be relied upon. According to Kuznets, the *per capita* income in
underdeveloped countries has increased by 50 per cent in the past
century, i.e. by about 0·4 per cent annually. According to Patel,
growth was even slower,[31] only 20 per cent between 1850 and 1960,
that is, 0·1 per cent on an annual average.

Compared to this situation, the 2 per cent annual growth rate of
per capita national income in the developing countries after the
Second World War (in fact, 2·2 per cent between 1955 and 1960
and 2 per cent between 1960 and 1966) is a decisive turn, even if this
rate is lower than that of the advanced capitalist countries (3–4 per
cent) or of the socialist countries (5·5–6·5 per cent).[32] *Thus, the process
of industrialisation in the developing countries started in the middle
of the twentieth century and the growth of* per capita *national income
was no slower than it had been in the initial stage of industrialisation
of the now developed capitalist countries,* though it was slower than
the rate of industrialisation of the socialist countries and slower
than the present growth of the advanced capitalist countries.

At the beginning of industrialisation, however, the developing
countries started in many respects from a more difficult situation,
from a lower level than that experienced in the countries which first

industrialised. A comparison of *per capita* income levels between countries situated very far from one another or between remote periods is well known to be extremely uncertain, and we can only rely on the bold estimates of a few authors. The *per capita* national income in developing countries may have been around 75–100 dollars in the middle of the nineteenth century. At the same time the figure for the avanced capitalist countries, according to Kuznets, was about 340 dollars, while according to Patel it was 150 dollars in 1850 in the countries which are now industrialised. (The gap between the two estimates is not so great as it would seem from the two figures, since what Kuznets has in mind are the early industrialising and most advanced capitalist countries, while Patel includes all countries now industrialised, not only Western Europe and the U.S.A., but also the Scandinavian and European socialist countries.)

In spite of the ambiguity of the estimates, it seems unequivocal that *the advanced capitalist countries were richer at the beginning of industrialisation than the developing countries are now.* The situation is less unequivocal in respect of the European socialist countries, since they had attained highly different economic levels when they started to industralise. It seems, however, that their economic level was rather higher than that of the developing countries at the start of the process.

Let us now look at the growth rate of industry. There are no reliable data available on the 'early industrialising' countries, but the tendency is sufficiently clear. The growth rate of industrial production in England was 2–3 per cent between 1793 and 1817, 3–4 per cent between 1818 and 1855 and again 2–3 per cent between 1856 and 1875.[33] In France, the figures are the following: 2·1 per cent for 1815/24–1845/54, 2 per cent for 1845/54–1865/74 and 1·5 per cent for 1865/74–1885/94.[34]

Such relatively moderate industrial growth rates were quite usual in the early industrialising countries. *Late industrialisation is characterised by quicker growth rates.* For socialist industrialisation, particularly in its initial stages, we find annual growth rates at least 9–10 per cent; in the developing countries it was almost 8 per cent annually between 1950 and 1966.[35]

(b) It is a characteristic tendency of *changes in economic structure* that, together with industrialisation, economic growth and the growth of population, the ratio of those employed in the primary sectors (agriculture, fishery, etc.) gradually diminishes, and so does the share of their contribution to national income, while the importance of the secondary sector (manufacturing) and later of the tertiary one (services) increases. This structural change is one of the possible criteria for a numerical characterisation of the industrialisation process.

At the start of the transformation process of economic structure, about 80 per cent of those economically active were still engaged in the primary sector. Such is the situation even today in quite a few developing countries. According to economic historians, this was also the situation in the now developed countries. However, this had changed by the time of the first population censuses. In England, for example, agriculture engaged only about 35 per cent of the population and contributed to national income 32 per cent of the total in 1801, but even in the seventeenth century, i.e. before the industrial revolution, agriculture yielded only 40–45 per cent of national income. With the progress of economic growth and industrialisation, the share of those engaged in the primary sector has gradually diminished to around 10 per cent in the most advanced countries, while the share of industry has gradually increased and stablised at around 30–40 per cent.

Comprehensive data on changes in the structure of employment are available for 1860 and 1880 for the major regions of the advanced capitalist countries, and for 1900 and 1920 for the developing countries.

Around 1880, only 50 per cent of those employed in the developed capitalist countries worked in agriculture and about 25 per cent in manufacturing. From that date, the share of agriculture has been decreasing while that of industry has been growing. However, the absolute numbers of the agricultural labour force continued to grow up to 1920, both in Europe and in the E.E.C. – which comprises the more developed countries – as well as in North America.

For the socialist countries no similar comprehensive data are available for long periods, but the main tendencies can be established from the data relating to individual countries.[36] In the Soviet Union, the structure of employment did not change between 1913 and 1928; rather, the share of industrial employment declined somewhat, from 9 to 8 per cent, while that of agriculture slightly increased, from 74·9 per cent to 79·8 per cent. From 1928 on, the share of industry increased quickly and that of agriculture diminished. In the smaller European socialist countries, industry increased rather slowly up to the years following the Second World War, and the share of agriculture also decreased slowly. For example, the share of industrial employment in the total increased from 8·1 per cent in 1934 to 10·3 per cent in 1946 in Bulgaria, from 17 per cent in 1910 to 20·1 per cent in 1941 in Hungary, and from 16·9 per cent in 1931 to 18·8 per cent in 1950 in Poland. The rapid change in structure started after the Second World War.

The absolute numbers in agricultural employment increased in the Soviet Union up to 1928, and in Bulgaria, Yugoslavia and Hungary till the years after the war (the data for Poland are not comparable). *In the European socialist countries the rapid change in economic structure and the decline in the absolute numbers in agricultural employment are the consequences of industrialisation.*

As can be seen from Table V/6, it is characteristic of the developing countries that the ratio of agricultural employment is high and that of manufacturing is low. The share of the latter very slowly increased up to about 1950; in South and East Asia it even declined, from 9·9 per cent in 1900 to 7·3 per cent in 1950. The same tendencies can be found when individual countries are examined. In India, industrial employment fell from 12·4 per cent in 1911 to 10·5 per cent in 1931 and 9·5 per cent in 1951, and only started to grow later.

Table V/6

LONG-TERM CHANGES IN THE STRUCTURE OF EMPLOYMENT

(*Ratio of those engaged in agriculture and industry to total employment*)

(*percentages*)

Area	1860	1880	1900	1920	1930	1950	1960
Europe:							
agriculture	—	55·7	50·6	47·2	43·6	39·2	31·8
manufacturing	—	20·0	22·3	22·8	23·7	24·4	27·5
European Economic Community:							
agriculture	—	50·8	44·4	40·0	35·1	30·5	20·5
manufacturing	—	27·2*	25·6	26·9	27·7	27·6	32·1
North America:							
agriculture	60·5	50·8	38·3	28·2	23·3	12·9	7·3
manufacturing	18·3	18·6	22·5	26·8	23·7	27·4	28·7
Latin America:							
agriculture	—	—	—	65·9	63·4	54·1	50·1
manufacturing	—	—	—	13·0	13·4	13·8	14·5
South and South-East Asia:							
agriculture	—	—	76·4	77·5	76·8	75·3	73·1
manufacturing	—	—	9·9	9·4	9·2	7·3	8·8
North Africa:							
agriculture	—	—	—	76·8	76·0	72·9	69·6
manufacturing	—	—	—	6·3	6·3	7·4	7·6

* Including construction.

Source: P. Bairoch and I. M. Limbor, 'Changes in the Industrial Distribution of the World Labour Force, by Region, 1880–1960', *International Labour Review*, October 1968.

In Mexico, the ratio was 10·9 per cent in both 1921 and 1940, 12·
per cent in 1950 and 15 per cent in 1960. In Turkey, there has been
hardly any change since 1935. *Thus, industrialisation affecting the
economic structure in the developing countries only started to any
serious extent in the mid-1950s.*

Of course, the population of the developing countries has grown,
particularly in recent times, much more quickly than it did in the
advanced capitalist countries at the start of their industrialisation.
The annual average of population increase in these countries was
0·4–0·8 per cent at the end of the nineteenth and the beginning of
the twentieth centuries, while in the developing countries it now
exceeds 2 per cent annually. This undoubtedly affects the changes in
economic structure and prolongs the extensive growth of agriculture, i.e. the period when agricultural employment is growing in
absolute terms.

The main tendencies of changes in the internal structure of industry are generally known, and will not be dealt with here in detail.
They can be outlined as follows: heavy industry usually grows
quicker than light and food industries. In the course of growth,
first metallurgy and engineering were the dynamic branches –
metallurgy later increasing, though slowly – and the chemical industry has finally become the most dynamic branch of industry.

Of course, there are many deviations from this general scheme.
At the start of industrialisation the 'leading sector' may differ from
country to country. In England, for example the textile industry was
initially the leading sector, giving impulses to machine building and
indirectly to transport, and it was the most important branch in
exports. In Germany, however, no such part was played by the textile industry, even at the start of industrialisation in the last century,
since it had to cope with British competition; engineering showed a
quite rapid development, partly owing to state subsidies, railway
construction, etc., and became an important export branch.

Before the First World War, the textile industry in Hungary was
underdeveloped owing to the competition put up by the Austrian
industry, but relatively modern machine building and metallurgy
shaped up, partly to supply domestic railway construction and mining; in compliance with the agricultural character of the country,
the share of the food industry was considerable. After the First
World War – owing to protective customs duties – the share of the
textile industry jumped from 4·8 per cent in 1913 to 12·6 per cent by
1925 (calculated on the 1920 area of the country).[37]

In highly industrialised countries the share of heavy industry is
usually greater than in others, though this ratio is not an unequivocal indicator of the industrial development level. To quote a few

examples: the share of the heavy industry (including mining) in 1964 was 38·2 per cent in Ireland, 48·8 per cent in Austria, 72·4 per cent in the U.K. and 70·7 per cent in West Germany.[38]

Industrialisation in the socialist countries first led to the rapid development of heavy industry, mainly metallurgy and engineering. A U.N. study examining the 'typical' pattern by branches of industry in several countries, as a function of economic development level (in terms of *per capita* national income) and the number of population, established that, on an average, the shares of metallurgy and engineering are high in the industry of the socialist countries while those of the textile and the food industries are relatively low.[39] In Hungary, for example, the share of heavy industry was 70·5 per cent in 1964, i.e. about the same as in the industrially more advanced countries. The share of engineering is also characteristic of the development level: it was 15·5 per cent in Ireland, 14·3 in Greece, 21·0 in Finland, 23·6 in Austria, 34·5 in West Germany, 36·9 in the U.K. and 32·1 in Hungary in 1964.

The industrial structure of developing countries may also be seen to follow that of the developed ones. The structural change is quicker than economic development, particularly in large countries. In other words, the internal structure of industry approaches that of the developed industrial countries quicker than the general growth of the economy. In India, for example, the share of engineering within industry amounted to about 20 per cent as early as in 1962, and in Brazil also to 20 per cent in 1963, which is undoubtedly higher than it was in the now developed countries when at a similar level of economic development; it attains or approaches the proportions of much more advanced capitalist countries (e.g. of Finland or Austria). The situation is, on the whole, similar with respect to heavy industry: in India its share is almost 50 per cent, and in Brazil more than 50 per cent.

(*c*) *The large-scale application of scientific and technological achievements* coincided with the initial stage of industrialisation, the industrial revolution, in the now developed capitalist countries. Here we should distinguish two stages. In the *preliminary stage* of industrialisation, the material and socio-political conditions suitable for applying modern technology came into existence. Material conditions should be understood as scientific and technological discoveries, or rather their wide diffusion; socio-political conditions as a system, or changes in the system, enabling modern technology to be more generally applied. In the course of history, however, this later date did not necessarily coincide with *the massive spread of modern technology, with the predominance of large-scale production methods* continuously developing within industry and relying on the

G

application of modern scientific results. A characteristic feature of the first industrialising, pioneering countries is that this preliminary stage is short, and the first appearance and the spread of modern technology can hardly be told apart. It was precisely the possibility of the spreading of new inventions, the social demand that brought them about and made it possible that new ideas should find application, should be experimented with and thereby mature and spread (without these, an invention would be, at best, a technical curiosity soon to be forgotten).

If we can speak at all about a preliminary stage in England, it may have lasted ten to twenty years, not more. It was longer in all the other late-industrialising countries of Western Europe. In Germany, the industrial revolution began in the thirties of the nineteenth century.[40] Thus, the preliminary stage lasted thirty to forty years, since the material conditions for the application of the new technology were present as early as the end of the eighteenth century, mainly under the impact of the industrial revolution going on in England. The general economic and cultural development level in Germany was favourable for the application of new technological methods, and the use of machines began, mainly cotton-weaving machines and steam engines. But a greater spread of manufacturing industry was hindered by the Napoleonic wars and by the tiny states that constituted feudal Germany and split up its economy. Industrialisation, therefore, could not be started without surmounting postwar difficulties, liquidating the feudal framework and, especially, creating an economic unity of Germany through the Zollverein in 1834.

In the United States of America, the political and social conditions for industrialisation were created by the War of Independence and the separation from England. Production based on the use of machinery made its appearance in the late eighteenth and early nineteenth centuries, but the quick spread of factory methods started only about 1820, thanks to the protective customs duties introduced in 1816. As in England, industrialisation evolved mainly in the textile industry, which had a central importance for stimulating other branches, mainly machine building.

France, where in the wake of the British industrial revolution the conditions of industrialisation had been created already in the late eighteenth and the early nineteenth centuries, lagged behind England and even behind Germany, in spite of the bourgeois revolution. It is difficult to establish the exact date when industrialisation started, or to link it to any political or economic event. We will not go too far wrong, however, if we put the real start of industrialisation round the mid-nineteenth century, when industrial output almost doubled in thirty years, industrial employment increasing at the same time by only 40 per cent. In Belgium industrialisation evolved earlier than in France and Germany, in the Scandinavian countries later. At any rate, we may establish that *the preliminary stage of industrialisation was concluded before the end of the nineteenth century in both Western Europe and the U.S.A. – the leading countries even in the first half of the nineteenth century – and before the mass production and application of machines and of mechanical large-scale factory production was begun.*

A general, somewhat neglected characteristic of industrialisation is that, with the exception of England, every country was a 'late industrialising' country for a longer or shorter period. The late industrialising countries took over the technological methods, and partly also the economic ones, from the pioneer country or countries. Compared to England, the other Western European countries and even the United States were late in industrialising, but compared to the European socialist countries, and particularly the developing ones, the late-comers are 'early industrialising' countries.

In the other countries of the world, both the preliminary stage of industrialisation and industrialisation proper (that is, the mass use of machinery techniques) started later. In Eastern Europe the preliminary stage started, in general, with the liquidation of feudalism. In Hungary, for example, it began after the abolition of serfdom, or rather after the compromise of 1867 with the Habsburgs. In these countries, however, the system of latifundia and the reactionary policies related to them (and possibly other circumstances, such as Hungary's political dependence on Austria) hindered industrial development. Real and fast development started only with socialist industrialisation.

In the developing countries, the preliminary stage started with colonisation, since it was then that the old social framework, which hindered the application of modern technology, was broken down, opening the way for the use of modern technology, though in a narrow scope and serving mainly the interests of the capitalists of the colonising country. Colonisation at the same time hindered the emergence of a modern economy, as has been mentioned. This applies particularly to Africa and Asia, where industrialisation proper started only after the end of colonisation.

The late industrialising countries apply the technology established in industrialised countries. *This task is more difficult; the later industrialisation starts, the longer the preparatory stage lasts and the greater the difference in development levels.* Fast development cannot be achieved by applying the technology initially used by the pioneer country; it requires modern technology existing in the given period, which results in certain contradictions that are difficult to solve. Modern technology is more capital-intensive (per worker) than the old, and its application requires greater skill, and special qualifications and training. The later industrialising countries, however, are short of capital and of skilled and qualified labour.

This problem of late industrialisation had to be faced also by the socialist countries. Speaking in general terms, their industrialisation strategies – relying on the social ownership of the means of production and on economic planning – were aimed partly at a maximum utilisation of existing resources (mainly manpower) and at putting them to productive use. This involved raising the quality of labour, particularly industrial labour, by training skilled workers and engineers. In the early stage of industrialisation, this was carried out mainly by the non-conventional means of *adult education*, i.e. by re-training during work, on evening courses, etc. Another aspect of development strategy was to secure a high rate of accumulation and to channel a considerable part of accumulation into industry. Finally, efforts were made to utilise intensively the capacities created by introducing several shifts, and to eliminate seasonal fluctuations and other uncertainties with the aid of planning. Obviously, a development of this type, which has essentially solved the basic task, namely rapid industrialisation, could not be carried on without losses. With quick mobilisation of labour resources, there was no time for proper training, and since the efficiency of the various courses was not high, a great part of those re-trained left their new trades. Also the intensive utilisation of capacities involved indirect and less measurable losses, inasmuch as the flexibility of the economy – the adaptive capacity of the productive apparatus to changing requirements – was reduced.

As is known, the growth of the scale of production, i.e. concentration, was one of the general forms of technological development. It may be observed that the late industrialising countries frequently build up a productive apparatus which is highly concentrated compared to their general development level. This has occurred already in capitalist Hungary. Before the First World War Hungarian industry, which lagged behind in productive capacity and the volume of industrial production, and had not yet really entered the stage of rapid industrialisation, attained and even surpassed more developed capitalist countries with respect to the concentration of her industry. For instance, in Germany thirty-six out of a hundred industrial workers were engaged in enterprises employing more than fifty workers, in Austria this figure was twenty-five, and in Hungary forty-four. In Germany 6·6 per cent of industrial workers were employed in plants with more than 100 workers, while in Hungary this was

10 per cent. The situation was similar in respect of mechanical energy, if calculated by horse-power per worker: the Hungarian figures are almost level with the British, and are higher than the French and the German ones.[41]

Socialist industrialisation was accompanied by even greater concentration. A statistical measurement, and especially an international comparison of concentration, is of course rather difficult, because the various data (e.g. average number of workers in a plant, or the distribution of plants by size) are not necessarily changing in the same way and do not give the same results. But the general tendency is unequivocal. The development of the average number of workers between 1942 and 1965 in Hungarian manufacturing plants is, for example, a characteristic indicator:

AVERAGE NUMBER OF
WORKERS PER PLANT[42]

1942	1955	1960	1965
97	169	177	195

At any rate, it may be established that in the period of socialist industrialisation, concentration quickly increased in Hungary – similarly to the other socialist countries. The extent of concentration in Hungary is high by international standards. The share in employment in plants with more than 1,000 workers was 51 per cent in Hungary (1965), contrasted with 39·8 per cent in West Germany (1964), 30·3 per cent in Italy (1961), 23·3 per cent in Belgium (1963) and 16·9 per cent in Finland (1963). Beside its unquestionable advantages, concentration also involved certain disadvantages (at least in Hungary) because a large-scale plant cannot adapt itself to changing demand as quickly and flexibly as a small-scale one. Of course, the relative importance of advantages and disadvantages varies by branches.

As far as the situation can be surveyed on the basis of statistical data, concentration, as a result and as a means of applying modern technology, increases also in the developing countries, though its extent is very much smaller than in the developed capitalist countries, and particularly in the socialist ones. The ratio of the small-scale handicrafts is particularly great. It can be stated unequivocally that with economic and industrial development, the share of small-scale industries and handicrafts decreases while the extent of concentration increases. According to available data, the share of employment in factories with more than 100 employees is 60 per cent in the more developed Latin American countries; 51 per cent in the moderately developed ones and 35 per cent in those on the lowest level of development. The Hungarian data, which on the whole are comparable with these, show 80 per cent for 1942 and 85 per cent for 1960.[43]

In general, countries embarking late on the road of industrialisation (in which respect the European socialist countries and the developing countries are alike) have adopted and continue to adopt a higher technical level than that which the now developed countries evolved at the start of their own industrialisation. As a consequence, both the national economic and the industrial structure (macroscructure) quickly approached that of the advanced countries. In the socialist countries this was a consequence of deliberate preferences, but in the developing countries it was due precisely to the adoption of more advanced technology. This tendency is likely to assert itself also in the future.

Owing to technological progress, it is potentially possible for late industrialising countries to skip over certain stages and use more up-to-date technology right at the start, not only with respect to a larger-scale production, or higher technological equipment of labour, but also as regards the character of the technology employed. It seems, for instance, that in the developing countries – at least, in some of them – more up-to-date transport and communication techniques are being introduced, insofar as trucks, cars and airborne transport play a greater role than the capital-intensive railway investment with long pay-back returns. In the developing countries also, energy supply is built to a greater extent on hydrocarbons, and coal mining has less significance than in the developed capitalist or the socialist countries. (This may, of course, have geological reasons.) It seems, however, that later the structures will come closer to one another. A certain degree of railway development will obviously become necessary in the developing countries, and coal mining will also evolve. This is indicated at least by the fact that in the developed capitalist countries coal mining has stagnated or been reduced in recent years, while it has grown in the developing countries at annual rates of 5 per cent. Apart from the effect of natural, geological conditions, the main tendency of the branch (macro-) structures is that the patterns of industry in individual countries approximate to one another. This is of considerable importance, because the specialisation deriving from micro-structures (product structure) is playing an ever greater role in the international division of labour.

Both socialist and developing countries are characterised by a quick growth of industrial production which, in the later industrialising countries, is due not, or not only, to spontaneous economic development but also to political decisions: it is a tool in the service of economic growth, national independence and social progress. Thus, structural change and the rate of industrial development display similar tendencies in both the socialist and the developing countries. But this is not necessarily the case regarding the concentration of plants.

As has been explained in Chapter IV, the social conditions and the role of the state in the capitalist countries are different from what they are in the developing countries. According to the ideology originally prevailing in the capitalist countries, progress is best served if the state interferes as little as possible in the economy; the interference of the state, its economic role, and its planning activity developed only later. In the developing countries, no such ideas hinder the economic role of the state from asserting itself, but on the contrary, while in the developed capitalist countries planning is a consequence of development, in the developing countries it is an indispensable tool of economic growth.

In the socialist countries, planning is closely related to the social ownership of the means of production. Among the developing countries, however, the scope of social ownership, as well as the efforts to increase the role of social ownership, differ widely. Fast concentration in the socialist countries was also a consequence of the social ownership of the means of production. In the developing countries the extent of concentration depends partly on the future development of social ownership in industry, partly on planning and on economic policies. It is quite conceivable that in this connection tendencies differing from country to country and from industry to industry will develop. In India, for example, the state-owned enterprises in heavy industry have acquired an important role and there are considerable efforts at concentration. In light industry, however, particularly cotton weaving, Indian planning and economic policy aim precisely at maintaining and even expanding small-scale and cottage industry, which is obviously a tendency opposed to concentration.

5. Tentative Forecast of Future Industrial Growth in the Developing Countries

Relying on the data presented in the preceding chapters and on other information, an attempt will now be made to forecast the expected development of industry in the developing countries in the next fifteen to twenty years. The main aim of the exercise is to present the *major tendencies* which, owing to industrialisation, will influence the internal economic structure of the developing countries and the relations between the developing and the industrially developed countries.

METHODS OF THE PROGNOSIS

Various methods may be applied to forecast the expected development of a branch or branches of the economy. Here we have used trend-extrapolation, and to justify this procedure, we survey some methods and the possibility of their application for the prognosis of the expected development of the industry.

For an international prognosis *the national plans and prognoses* may be used, e.g. to prognosticate the expected production of electrical energy, since such plans or prognoses have been drawn up in many countries (at least in the developed regions). But as regards the whole industry or the main branches, the situation is different; development plans or prognoses, particularly such as would cover longer periods, are not known to exist.

In principle, production can also be estimated *on the basis of existing and known future production capacities, together with prognoses relating to capacity utilisation.* This method can be applied in practice only where production is homogeneous and the whole production or the bulk of it is turned out by a few major plants, i.e. in the case of heavy chemicals, in metallurgy, paper mills, cement, etc. A study prepared for the African Regional Industrialisation Symposium, for example, contained a detailed list by countries of the aluminium producing capacity existing in 1964 and of that in the process of building, or planned.[44] Such compilations can be made, if proper information is available, for other industries, like ferrous metallurgy, fertiliser production, etc. In the present case, however, no such surveys were possible. But for the whole of industry or for each of its branches, no such assessment can be made, since in many industries, as for instance in engineering, the number of plants (capacities) is too great, and neither the range of products to be turned out in given plants, nor the productivity of the plants with respect to the different products, is known in advance with sufficient accuracy.

The expected production (or consumption) can be estimated for some branches with the aid of projecting a major economic indicator and using *elasticities of demand.* It is usual, for example, to forecast in this way the development of energy demand (or demand for electrical energy) on the basis of the growth in national income or in industrial production.[45] In using this method, one starts from the assumption that the major economic indicator, for example the development of national income or of industrial production, can be more safely planned than the production of energy, and that the coefficient of elasticity, i.e. the percentage growth in demand for energy generated by 1 per cent growth in national income, can also be exactly projected – either on the basis of past data (i.e. the coefficient is stable), or with the aid of international comparisons. If no prognosis but a plan is drawn up, only the existence of the second condition – the possibility of being able to plan the coefficient – is necessary, since in this case the problem is the growth in demand for energy accompanying a planned growth in national income. In essence such a method was applied in a study in preparation for the second development decade of the U.N.,[46] where the elasticities of the main economic sectors, within the sector of manufacturing (and, separately, within light and heavy industry) were established from international data, as a function of *per capita* national income and population increase. With the aid of these elasticity coefficients, growth was estimated with different assumptions regarding population growth and *per capita* national income.

This method is acceptable as long as the branches figuring in the prognosis are sufficiently aggregated, i.e. as long as the prognosis relates to agriculture on the one hand, and to industry on the other. But even in this case, the expected growth rates vary considerably, even with assumptions between rather narrow limits, and even if the elasticity coefficient is considered to be constant – a rather doubtful assumption over a longer period. But the growth of individual industries cannot be unequivocally linked to the growth of national income, or *per capita* national income or the growth of population. With industrial products, needs vary not only as a function of national income, but also as a function of technical progress, i.e. the same national income may involve at various dates bigger production and consumption in one branch and smaller in another. In the case of the developing countries, a substitution process also takes place, which is at least partly independent of the growth in national income, and which cannot be properly reflected by elasticity coefficients relating simply to the past or relying on international comparison.

Finally, expected growth can be estimated on the basis of *trend-extrapolation*, i.e. on the basis of past growth. While in the application of elasticities the basic assumption is that the relation between certain economic phenomena (e.g. between the growth of national income and the demand for energy) will not change, the fundamental assumption of trend extrapolation is that development over a period will take place in the future in the same manner as in the past. It is no doubt a weakness of such prognoses that the expected development of industry is not linked to the development of other branches of the economy, to foreign trade, labour supply, import and export possibilities, etc. But all that would be a major deficiency only if the aim were not a forecast (in order to scrutinise the change of internal economic structures and of international economic

G*

interrelations), but planning and the most rational allocation of resources.

In the present prognosis, the latter method was used and trends were extrapolated on the basis of data available for the entire industrial production of the developing countries and for individual industries, up to 1985. For checking and correcting the results obtained, prognoses based on capacity data were used in certain cases, and those made by international organisations in other cases.

The prognosis was worked out for industry as a whole, for mining and manufacturing, for light and heavy industry and the food industry within the manufacturing sector, and in greater detail for three mining branches and nine other industries, relying on the industrial index numbers of growth given in Annex V/1. Among the manufacturing branches, the basic data on developing countries were missing for the textile and leather garment industries and the wood and furniture industries, but were available only for the developed capitalist countries and the two areas combined. Thus, a more detailed prognosis was made only for three mining and seven manufacturing branches (including also the production of electrical energy and gas).

Past data were available for 1938 and from 1948 for each year up to 1966. Linear and exponential equations were calculated for 1938–66 and for 1948–66. The correlation of the exponential equations with the actual data are better than that of the linear equations. As is known, the linear trend expresses a growth of the same *volume* each year, while the exponential one expresses a growth of the same *rate* (percentage). Checking the results of trend equations also showed that a closer correlation can be obtained for 1948–66 than for the years 1938–66; growth seems to have been 'more regular' in the later periods.

For each data series, four kinds of prognoses were made. Owing to what has been said above, in the following only the prognosis of the exponential trend for 1948–66 will be used. It must be noted that this yields the highest values, i.e. the quickest rate of growth. The prognoses were made for the years 1970, 1975, 1980 and 1985.

Table V/7 contains the forecast of industrial production in developing and developed capitalist countries. The first column of the table shows the growth rate in developed capitalist countries for certain industries and groups of industries. The second shows the same for the developing countries, while the third contains certain data corrected on the basis of some considerations to be reviewed below.

In the first column there is no figure for coal mining. In the developed capitalist countries, the volume of coal production has diminished, as is shown in Annex V/1, by an annual 6–7 per cent since 1956–7. It cannot be justified to project this decrease forward to the future, since we can assume that for a not inconsiderable period coal mining will remain important. Thus, the tendency of the past ten to twenty years provides no satisfactory orientation in this field. In the second column, comprising the trend prognoses of the developing countries, there are no data for the textile and leather garment or the wood and furniture industries, since international statistics on past growth rates have not been published.

In the third column the trend prognoses for the developing countries have been corrected in several cases – mostly upwards. We shall discuss the reasons for this below.

Table V/7

EXPECTED AVERAGE ANNUAL GROWTH RATES OF
INDUSTRIAL PRODUCTION IN DEVELOPED CAPITALIST AND
DEVELOPING COUNTRIES

(*percentages*)

	Trend prognosis		
	Developed capitalist countries	Developing countries	Corrected prognosis
Total industry	5·3	7·9	8·0
All mining	2·5	9·3	9·0
Coal mining	—	5·0	—
Metal mining	4·4	4·3	—
Crude petroleum and natural gas	3·3	11·7	10·0
Manufacturing	5·4	7·3	7·5
Light manufacturing	4·0	5·7	6·0
Heavy manufacturing	6·2	9·5	10·0
Food	3·5	5·1	—
Textiles	3·2	5·0	6·0
Textile and leather garment industry	3·7	—	—
Wood products and furniture	3·8	—	—
Paper	5·7	10·7	—
Chemicals	8·5	8·6	—
Non-ferrous mineral products	5·1	8·4	—
Basic metals	3·8	9·0	10·0
Metal products	6·3	11·0	12·0
Electricity and gas	8·1	10·6	—

Metallurgy. For Asia international organisations (E.C.A.F.E.) expected a 13 per cent future growth in *ferrous* metallurgy. In Latin America production was 7,000,000 tons in 1963, but capacities existing or shortly operating were estimated at about 16,000,000 tons. *Aluminium* producing capacities in developing countries will rise from about 200,000 tons in 1963 to more than 2,000,000 tons, taking into account new investments, extensions and planned projects.[47] If it is assumed that this growth will take place up to 1985, that is, in twenty-two years, we arrive at a growth rate of 11 per cent. If the capacities were completed by 1980, the growth rate would be 14·5 per cent p.a.

Considering these more detailed estimates it seems justified to correct the prognosis upwards to about 10 instead of 9 per cent, i.e. expecting a faster growth than in the past.

Engineering. The trend-prognosis is an 11 per cent growth rate. The estimate of international organisations for 1965–75 is 15 per cent for Asia, 10 per cent for Africa and 14 per cent for Latin America. These estimates are rather optimistic, yet again it seems justified to raise the prognosis of 11 per cent to at least 12 per cent. Relying on similar considerations, the prognosis for the *textile industry* has been raised from 5 to 6 per cent. (International organisations estimated that production in the developing countries as a whole will double between 1964 and 1975, i.e. it will grow at a rate of about 6·5 per cent p.a.)

Considering the preceding reflections and our general knowledge on technical progress which indicates an accelerated growth in the *chemical industry* in the future, the prognoses for total manufacturing, as well as those for light and heavy industry, have been rounded upwards. As opposed to that, the expected growth rate of mining has been reduced, in view of the expectation that the rapid growth of oil extraction will slow down somewhat, though it will certainly remain fast enough.

Some data of our prognosis have been checked against those of the study already mentioned related to the preparation of the second U.N. development decade. This study drew up prognoses for the years 1965–80, – relying on the growth of total and *per capita* G.D.P. – for agriculture, all non-agricultural sectors, manufacturing, and within the latter for light and heavy industry as well as services. The growth of the individual sectors was estimated with the aid of elasticity coefficients from the assumed population growth and the growth in *per capita* national income. For 1970–80 the lowest variant of the prognosis (about 6 per cent annual growth of G.D.P.) the growth in manufacturing was 7·75 per cent, in light industry 6·9 per cent and in the heavy industry 9·3 per cent p.a.[48]

AVERAGE ANNUAL GROWTH RATES
(*per cent*)

	U.N. prognosis 1970–80	Corrected trend prognosis
Manufacturing	7·75	7·5
Light industry	6·9	6·0
Heavy industry	9·3	10·0

The forecast in Table V/7 and the U.N. prognosis – particularly that relating to the whole of manufacturing – are quite close to each other. But the growth rates of light and heavy industry deviate noticeably when compared to each other. In the first case the ratio is 9·3 : 6·9 = 1·35, in the second case 10 : 6 = 1·66.

It is, of course, not surprising that prognoses prepared by different methods should yield different results, even if on the whole identical data are taken for basis – namely past development. During several periods since 1938, however, heavy industry always increased in the developing countries at least 50–70 per cent faster than light industry. For the future, it is perhaps even more justifiable to estimate an acceleration in the relative growth rate of heavy industry, rather than a deceleration, and we therefore considered it unnecessary to correct our prognosis in this respect.

Prognoses obviously do not serve the purpose of establishing the production level for some given year in advance, but – as has been mentioned above – to analyse the expected development of industry and the whole economy.

Let us first examine the expected changes in the economic *structure* of the developing countries by main sectors. We can start from the assumption that industry at present contributes about 20 per cent to national income and agriculture about 50 per cent. (In reality, the share of industry is higher in Latin America: in 1960, for example, it was 25·8 per cent in Brazil, 28 per cent in Argentina and 25 per cent in Colombia, while it was lower in Asia and Africa: 9 per cent in Nigeria (1954), 18·5 per cent in India, 12·8 per cent in Pakistan.) Let us further assume that the average annual rate of growth will be, according to our prognosis, 8 per cent in industry and 3 per cent in agriculture, and that the share of the other sectors in the economy will not change. *In this case, after twenty years the internal structure of the economy will radically change*, insofar as the share of industry will rise to 35 per cent, that of agriculture will fall to 35 per cent, and the share of the other sectors will remain, according to our assumptions at 30 per cent. From these assumptions a 5 per cent

growth rate derives for the national income as a whole, corresponding on the whole to what the developing countries experienced from
1950 on.

Table V/8

DISTRIBUTION OF NATIONAL INCOME BY
MAIN BRANCHES OF ORIGIN

| | Percentage distribution of national income of year 0 | Increase | | Percentage distribution of national income in 20th year |
		Average rate of growth, per cent	Total in 20 years, 0 year = 100	
Industry	20	8	466	35
Agriculture	50	3	180	35
Other	30	5	265	30
National income, total	100	5	265	100

This structure of the economy corresponds on the whole to that in
countries which have arrived at the threshold of a modern economy.
Let us compare this with the share of agriculture and industry in
the national income of certain countries.[49]

	Agriculture (per cent)	Industry (per cent)
Romania (1938)	38·5	30·8
Finland (1948)	31·6	39·1
Portugal (1950)	33·4	35·2

*Development of the economic structure, in comparison to the econo-
mic development level in terms of* per capita *national income, will be
faster.* Average *per capita* national income in the developing countries was – according to U.N. data – about $150 (at 1960 U.S. dol-
lars). In the case of a 2·0–2·2 per cent annual growth rate, this would
increase to $220–230, which is less (perhaps not much less than in
Portugal and Romania) than it was in the now more developed
countries when they had a similar economic structure.

It is worth while to point out that *the economic growth potential of the
country increases as the share of industry grows.* This can be illustrated
in purely qualitative terms. Relying on the figures of our preceding

example, the growth rate of agriculture is 3 per cent and that of industry 8 per cent, and the relative share of the other sectors is invariable; at the beginning of the twenty-year period, i.e. when the share of agriculture is 50 per cent and that of industry is 20 per cent, and national income increases at the annual rate of 4·6 per cent. In the twentieth year, however, when the shares of agriculture and industry are both 35 per cent, the growth rate is 5·35 per cent, i.e. it is 16 per cent higher than the initial one, though the growth of the individual sectors did not change at all. In reality, the impact of industrial growth is considerably greater since it affects the potential growth of other sectors. It is also obvious that we can have here only a numerical illustration of economic interrelations, the figures used being more or less arbitrary. It is sure, at any rate, that industry will grow faster than agriculture, and its increasing share involves the effects mentioned. It is by no means sure, on the other hand, that the share of the 'other' sectors will remain unchanged. Since these too grow faster than agriculture, their growing share would also strengthen the tendency mentioned.

Let us now examine the *changes of the internal structure of the industry*. If we start from the fact that within manufacturing the share of light industry (including food industries) is about 55 per cent in the initial period and that of heavy industry is 45 per cent, while light industry increases on average at an annual rate of 6 per cent and heavy industry at 10 per cent, the share of heavy industry will grow in twenty years to 63 per cent. This ratio already approximates the 1964 data of developed capitalist countries (U.S.A. 74 per cent, U.K. 75 per cent, West Germany 76 per cent, Italy 67 per cent), that is, of countries where the economic development level in terms of *per capita* income is much higher than can be expected in the developing countries in the next two or three decades.

As is known, the share of engineering within industry tends to be characteristic in some countries of the industrial development level. Let us examine how, from this point of view, the economic structure of the developing countries will change in the case of our forecast. Let us assume that the share of engineering within the industry of the developing countries is about 15 per cent. (In reality it was 20·4 per cent in India in 1963, 15–16 per cent in Iran in 1963–4, 12·5 per cent in Mexico in 1960, 10·5 per cent in Colombia in 1963.) According to our prognoses, engineering will grow at the annual rate of 12 per cent while industry as a whole grows at 8 per cent. In this case the share of engineering after twenty years will be about 30 per cent, which again approaches the 1954 level of developed countries (Italy 28·5 per cent, U.S.A. 33·3 per cent, West Germany 34·5 per cent, U.K. 36·9 per cent).[50]

Thus, in a historically brief period, the macro-structure of the developing countries will become 'modern'. However, their real backwardness will not cease, and – according to the hypotheses on the growth rates – it will be reflected not only by a relatively low national income, but also in their continued low share in the total world industrial production. If, therefore, we start from the data in Table V/7 regarding the industrial growth in developing and developed capitalist countries, the following results will be arrived at for the changes in the share of industrial output in the next twenty years:

Table V/9

SHARE OF DEVELOPING AND DEVELOPED CAPITALIST COUNTRIES IN INDUSTRIAL WORLD PRODUCTION

(excluding socialist countries)

		Share in percentages		Increase	
		0 year	*in 20 years*	*Average growth rate per cent*	*in 20 years, 0 year = 100*
Manufacturing	*Developed capitalist*	90	85	5·4	286
	Developing	10	15	7·5	425
Metallurgy	*Developed capitalist*	95	86	3·8	210
	Developing	5	14	10·0	673
Engineering	*Developed capitalist*	96	89	6·3	339
	Developing	4	11	12·0	965
Textile industry	*Developed capitalist*	80	70	3·2	190
	Developing	20	30	6·0	321

Accordingly, the share of the developing countries in manufacturing will rise from 10 to 15 per cent, in metallurgy from 5 to 14 per cent, in the engineering industries from 4 to 11 per cent, and in the textile industry from 20 to 30 per cent. *This is a serious change, but it does not yet decisively alter the role of the developing countries in industrial production and thus in the international division of labour.*

The prognoses relating to the industrial growth of the developing countries were based on data of 1939–66 and 1949–66, respectively, since at the time of writing the study which served as a basis for the Hungarian edition only these data were available. In the meantime, however, data on industrial growth were published up to 1969 and partly even including 1970 – even if not for the whole year.

It would be possible to complement our data series up to 1969, and to carry out the trend calculations anew. It is however, possible to confront the original prognoses with the actual growth in the years 1967–9 and examine whether the development of these three years shows considerable deviation from the prognoses. It seems that the latter method is more sensitive, giving a better control of the prognoses, since a completion of the sixteen-year data series with another three years only slightly modifies the value of the prognoses. Obviously, no final conclusions can be drawn from the data of three years either as regards changes in the process reflected by the prognoses, or on their stability, but it can be stated whether some break has appeared in the long-term development tendencies.

In Table V/10 we find the trend prognoses and the corrected trend prognoses of average growth rates based on Table V/6, as well as the average growth rates for 1966–9 and the growth from 1968 to 1969; the latter are based on the *Monthly Bulletin of Statistics* of May 1971. Relying on these data an attempt will be made to answer the question whether there is an essential change in tendency in relation to the prognoses, and whether it is necessary to change these prognoses – considering, however, to what extent a three-year period can indicate changes in tendency at all.

As can be seen from the Table, the growth of the whole industry has slowed down somewhat in the period 1966–9 to 7·25 per cent p.a., but it seems that this slow-down was transitory. In the whole region of developing countries, industrial output increased from 1966 to 1967 by 5·5 per cent, but in the next year growth was 8 per cent and, as can be seen from the Table, 8 per cent again from 1968 to 1970. (The data for 1970, incomplete as they are, again indicate some deceleration.)

In view of the data for the three years 1967–9 and those relating to 1969, a significant deviation from the prognosis on industrial growth can be seen only in the case of a single industry, paper, where the prognosis was a growth of 10·7 per cent p.a. and actual growth was only 6·2 per cent in 1967–8 and 7·5 per cent from 1968 to 1969. The information available is insufficient to judge whether the change is lasting and what are its causes.

However, it can be seen from the data that the qualitative statements drawn from the prognoses continue to hold. Similarly, according to the *Monthly Bulletin of Statistics*, average industrial growth in the developed capitalist countries was 4·6 per cent on average in the period 1967–9, i.e. industry continued to grow much faster in the developing countries. In the developing countries mining still

Table V/10

INDUSTRIAL GROWTH IN THE DEVELOPING COUNTRIES

(*percentages*)

	Trend	Corrected trend	Actual growth rates	
			Average of 1962–9	1966–9
	Prognosis			
Total industry	7·9	8·0	7·25	8·0
All mining	9·3	9·0	8·6	8·5
Coal mining	5·0		3·1	4·5
Metal mining	4·3		4·2	8·0
Crude petroleum and natural gas	11·7	10·0	10·0	10·0
Manufacturing	7·3	7·5	6·3	9·0
Light manufacturing	5·7	6·0	5·1	6·5
Heavy manufacturing	9·5	10·0	8·0	13·0
Food	5·1		4·8	8·0
Textiles	5·0	6·0	5·7	8·0
Textile and leather garment industry			4·2	4·0
Wood products and furniture			6·3	3·0
Paper	10·7		6·2	7·5
Chemicals	8·6		8·7	8·5
Non-ferrous mineral products	8·4		8·6	10·0
Basic metals	9·0	10·0	8·6	14·0
Metal products	11·0	12·0	8·4	12·5
Electricity and gas	10·6		11·3	10·0

grows quicker than manufacturing, mainly due to the lasting high growth rate in crude oil and natural gas extraction. Otherwise, the growth rate has diminished against the 11·7 per cent of the prognosis, which supports the justification for the corrections made. (Of course, it is mere coincidence that growth was 10 per cent both for 1967–9 and from 1968 to 1969, i.e. exactly the value of the corrected trend prognosis.) Heavy industry also continues to increase quicker than light industry in the developing countries. The ratios for the three-year period are 8 : 5·1 = 1·57. It seems that this also justifies keeping the ratios in the trend prognosis as against the U.N. estimates. Otherwise, these ratios seem also to depend on the rate of growth: both the dynamic development and the slow-down can be felt more in heavy industry than in light industry. This is indicated by the circumstance that in the three-year period 1967–9 a considerable deceleration appeared in comparison to the data of the trend prognosis and the corrected trend prognosis, while the acceleration in 1969 was particularly noteworthy in these sectors.

REFERENCES

1. T. Szentes, *A gazdasági elmaradottság* (Economic Underdevelopment), Közgazdasági és Jogi Könyvkiado, Budapest, 1965, p. 28.
2. K. Marx and F. Engels, 'Az indiai brit uralom eljövendő eredményei' (Future results of British rule in India). In Collected Works, Vol. I., Szikra, Budapest, 1949. p. 329.
3. G. C. Allen, *The Industrialisation of the Far East*, The Cambridge Economic History of Europe, Vol. VI, Part II, Cambridge University Press, 1965, p. 909.
4. Op. cit., p. 909.
5. See, for example, Henry Rosovsky, 'Japan's transition to modern economic growth, 1868–1885' (Rosovsky, ed., *Industrialisation in two systems*, John Wiley, New York, 1967).
6. A. Maizels, *Industrial Growth and World Trade*, Cambridge University Press, 1963.
7. *The Growth of World Industry 1938–1961*, U.N., 1965.
8. Op. cit., p. 234.
9. *The Growth of World Industry 1938–1961*, National Tables, U.N., New York, 1963, and *The Growth of World Industry 1938–1961*, International Analyses and Tables, U.N., New York, 1965.
10. *The Growth of World Industry*, International Analyses and Tables, p. 230.
11. *Industrial Development Survey*, U.N.I.D.O., I.D./Conf. 1/46, Sept. 1967, p. 129.
12. Detailed series on the whole period can be found in Annex V/1.
13. See Annex V/2.
14. See Annex V/3.
15. See Annex V/4.
16. See Annex V/5.
17. See Annex V/6.
18. Béla Kádár, *Gazdaságfejlesztés és nemzetközi munkamegosztás a fejlődő országokban* (Economic development and international division of labour in the developing countries), Közgazdasági és Jogi Könyvkiadó, 1967, p. 92.
19. Op. cit., p. 95.
20. *Industrial Development in Asia and the Far East*, Vol. IV, U.N., New York, 1966, p. 104.
21. Op. cit., p. 131.
22. *Industrial Development in Africa*, U.N., 1967.
23. K. Marx, *Capital*, Preface to the first German edition, Vol. I, Foreign Languages Publishing House, Moscow, 1961, pp. 8–9.
24. 'Industrialisation is a process of economic development, where a growing part of national resources is mobilised for shaping a technologically up-to-date and diversified economic structure. This economy is characterised by a dynamic manufacturing industry, producing means of production and consumer goods, capable of securing the rapid growth of the whole economy, and economic and social progress.'

200 STRATEGIES FOR INDUSTRIALISATION IN DEVELOPING COUNTRIES

25. W. A. Cole and Ph. Deane, 'The Growth in National Income', *Cambridge Economic History*, Vol. VI, p. 2.
26. S. Kuznets, *Modern Economic Growth: Rate, Structure and Spread*, Yale University Press, New Haven and London, 1966, p. 35.
27. The data refer to national product.
28. G. Cukor, *A fejlődő orságok iparositásának néhány kérdése*. (Some questions of industrialisation in developing countries), Akadémiai Kiadó, Budapest, 1970, pp. 64–5.
29. Belgium, Denmark, France, Germany, Italy, the Netherlands, Norway, Sweden, Switzerland, the U.K., Canada, the U.S.A.
30. A. Maddison, *Economic Growth in the West*, The Twentieth Century Fund, Now York, 1964.
31. S. J. Patel, 'Economic Transition in Africa', *The Journal of Modern African Studies*, 1964, No. 3.
32. Review of International Trade and Development, 1967, U.N., New York, 1968, T.D./5/Rev. 1.
33. W. G. Hoffmann, *British Industry 1700–1950*, Basil Blackwell, Oxford, 1955.
34. J. Kuczynski, 'Lange Reihen aus Frankreich', *Jahrbuch for Wirtschaftsgeschichte*, 1968, Teil III, Akademie-Verlag, Berlin, 1968.
35. See Annex V/2.
36. E. Ehrlich, *Nemzetközi elemzések a magyar távlati tervezéshez* (International analyses to be used in Hungarian long-term planning), Publications of the Institute of Economic Planning, National Planning Office, Part C, 1968, No. 2.
37. T. I. Berend, and Gy. Ránki, *Magyarország gazdasága az első világháboru után, 1919–1920* (Hungary's economy after World War I, 1919–1920), Akadémiai Kiadó, Budapest, 1966.
38. *Az ipar ágazati szerkezete* (The pattern of industry by branches), Budapest, 1966, C.S.O.
39. *A Study of Industrial Growth*, U.N., New York, 1963.
40. According to Mottek, in 1834. H. Mottek, H. Blumberg, H. Wutzmer, and W. Becker, *Studien zur Geschichte der industriellen Revolution in Deutschland*, Akademie-Verlag, Berlin, 1960.
41. Zs. P. Pach, (ed.), *Magyar gazdaságtörténet* (Hungarian Economic History), Part II: 1848–1944, Tankönyvkiadó, Budapest, 1963, p. 173.
42. *Az ipar koncentrációja* (Concentration of Industry), Periodical Publications of the C.S.O., 1967, No. 3.
43. In Hungarian statistical practice, plants with more than nineteen employees are considered as factories, while Latin American statistics set the limit at five employees. By making the necessary corrections, the difference between the two sets of data would be even greater.
44. *Industrial Development in Africa*, United Nations, 1967.
45. See Cukor and Sági, *Az energiaszükséglet és távlati tervezése* (Demand for energy and its long-term planning). Közgazdasági és Jogi Könyvkiadó, Budapest, 1964.
46. *Developing Countries in the Nineteen-Seventies: Preliminary Estimates for some Key Elements of a Framework for International Development Strategy*, E./A.C.54 (L.29), Rev. 1, 14 June 1968.
47. *Industrial Development in Africa*, U.N., 1967, pp. 191–2.
48. *Developing Countries in the Nineteen-Seventies* . . . op. cit.
49. Source: *The Growth of World Industry 1938–1960*, National Tables, U.N., New York, 1963.
50. Source: *Az ipar ágazati szerkezete* (The pattern of industry by branches), K.S.H., 1966.

VI

INDUSTRIALISATION IN THE EUROPEAN SOCIALIST COUNTRIES

The two decades or so following the Second World War were a period of fast industrial growth and of structural transformation of the economy in the Central European socialist countries (East Germany, Czechoslovakia, Poland, Hungary, Romania, Bulgaria, Yugoslavia). In the economy – particularly in industry – processes took place which are similar in many respects to those taking place at present (and probably those which will take place in the next decades) in the developing countries. It will therefore be worth while to attempt a survey of the main characteristics of this industrialisation, to see whether some useful conclusions can be drawn regarding the industrialisation of the developing countries. The industrialisation of the Soviet Union will not be dealt with in our analysis since the transformation had mostly taken place there prior to the Second World War. Because of its size and huge industrial potential, the Soviet Union can hardly be compared with the developing countries; not only with the majority of them but neither with the few countries that have a large population or a large area. Nor shall we discuss Albania, on account of its small size and for lack of detailed data.

The question naturally arises to what extent economic growth and industrialisation – taking place in different countries, at various dates, under different political and social circumstances and in different geographical and climatic environments – can be compared at all. Interpretation of the comparison is not a treatise in economic history but – in conformity with the main purpose of this book – to draw conclusions for the economic policy and industrial development strategy of the developing countries. *The question thus arises: what can a country learn, if it can learn anything at all, from the economic experience of another country?*

No attempt will be made here to give an exhaustive, well-founded or final answer to this question. From the viewpoint of the present exercise a few brief and general remarks will suffice. In another connection we have already mentioned that the more similarities that can be found in the economic development taking place in individual countries, the more general interrelations we have in view, and differences will grow the more closely we examine details. It has been similarly mentioned that economic growth and industrialisation yield several similar phenomena in every country and thus give rise to similar problems. Industrialisation is everywhere accompanied by a faster growth of national income than before and by changes in the economic structure. Problems emerge everywhere in connection with employment, savings, the foreign trade balance, and in particular the extent and character of import substitution and export promotion. It will also be clear, without any need for further proof, that problems will be the more similar the nearer to each other the individual countries are in their general conditions, mainly their economic and industrial development levels. It is similarly obvious that more meaningful generalisations can be made in respect *of the individual elements of development strategy*, since *the combination of elements* is unique for each country, and even unique for different periods in the same country.

Before reviewing the industrialisation experiences of the socialist countries, let us draw an approximative picture relating the economic and industrial development levels of the European socialist countries and the developing countries.

Industrial development levels and the process of development are complex, multi-dimensional phenomena which cannot be satisfactorily characterised by a single indicator. It is due to the complexity of the phenomena that the relative position of a country may be different if viewed from different aspects and measured by different scales.

The most general indicator of economic development level is per capita *national income*. This is closely related to industrial development levels since with economic growth – up to a certain, rather high level of development – a growing share of national income derives from industry. Owing to this interrelation, *a possible measure of development levels may be the share of industry in the creation of national income and in employment. The development level of the economy as a whole and that of industry may also be characterised by the character of the international division of labour.* With the exception of a few big countries which – precisely because of their size – are less dependent on foreign trade, with economic growth both the absolute and relative size of foreign trade (in comparison to national income) will increase too, *and also the share of manufactured products will grow within exports*.

International comparison of *per capita* national income is a rather uncertain and inaccurate operation. This is particularly so if countries at different development levels or having different social and economic systems are compared. The problems of comparison are well known and, therefore, will not be discussed here in detail. National income is expressed in terms of money, and the official rates of exchange mostly do not adequately reflect purchasing power. Though with the aid of more detailed analyses there is some possibility for corrections, exact comparisons cannot be obtained. The system of national income statistics are not uniform, and in particular there is a difference between the systems used in the West and in the socialist countries. In the majority of the developing countries the national income statistics are in themselves rather uncertain, just as in many countries even population statistics are unreliable. This latter circumstance may gravely distort the data on *per capita* national income. Finally, in the case of developing countries, the measurement of the national income produced and used in the subsistence sector is uncertain and relies only on approximative estimates.

The difficulties mentioned are partly eliminated by the method elaborated in Hungary by Ferenc Jánossy. This method approximates the level of national income in individual countries through the *consumption of major products expressed in physical units of measurement.*[1] The results of Jánossy are given in Table VI/1. For some of the countries in the table, the results of a more recent international comparison are also presented.[2] The data refer to 1955, in terms of U.S. dollars; Jánossy used 1954, Harbison 1964 dollar prices.

In the majority of cases, the data diverge greatly. The reason for the divergence is partly the difference in price levels and partly the difference in method. It may be stated, however, that – *with only a few exceptions – the ranking of the countries is identical in the two kinds of statistics.* (It should be noted that Jánossy considers his data to be reliable in the range of $200–1,000.)

According to Jánossy's data, the *per capita* national income of the developing countries in 1955 was between $50 and $400, according to Harbison between $50 and $650. (In 1965, according to Harbison, it was between $100 and $800.)

The difference in national income levels is not negligible even among the European socialist countries, though the differences are much smaller than among the developing countries. Within the group East Germany and Czechoslovakia are more developed. Hungary and Poland occupy medium positions, while Romania, Bulgaria and Yugoslavia are less developed. The figures published vary depending on the method of calculation. For information we present one of the calculations, referring to European socialist countries and – for comparision – to Portugal, Mexico and Turkey.

Table VI/1
PER CAPITA NATIONAL INCOME, 1955
(*U.S. dollars value at date shown*)

	Jánossy in 1955	Harbison in 1964
U.S.A.	1,700	2,655
Sweden	1,100	1,610
Australia	1,055	1,349
U.K.	860	1,218
Switzerland	800	—
Denmark	750	1,153
West Germany	720	1,048
France	690	1,101
Austria	530	—
Argentina	390	646
Italy	380	602
Japan	325	329
Hungary	320	362
Poland		353
Chile	315	383
Cuba	310	—
Spain	270	—
Portugal	245	228
Mexico	235	330
Brazil	220	184
Columbia	220	237
Jamaica	200	—
Philippines	174	125
Ecuador	165	—
Iraq	156	—
Turkey	155	192
Morocco	147	—
Honduras	144	—
Guatemala	140	240
Peru	124	—
Ceylon	123	—
Indonesia	100	—
Thailand	82	89
Pakistan	63	70
India	61	77
Burma	54	49

As mentioned above, one possible measure of development levels is the contribution of industry to national income or by the share of industrial total in employment. The contribution of industry to

Table VI/2

PER CAPITA NATIONAL INCOME

(in U.S. Dollars of 1960 international purchasing power)

	1937	1960	1965	1969
East Germany	500	700	840	1,032
Czechoslovakia	347	675	715	892
Hungary	244	400	500	660
Poland	204	370	466	574
Bulgaria	153	330	439	603
Romania	165	—	—	—
Yugoslavia	163	260	346	416
Portugal	190	284	366	431
Mexico	177	274	307	—
Turkey	122	142	158	—

Source: Sándor Ausch, C.M.E.A. Co-operation: Its Situation, Mechanism and Perspectives (in press), Publishing House of the Hungarian Academy of Sciences. The 1937 and 1960 data are the calculations of Eva Ehrlich with the improved dynamic variant of the Jánossy method, the 1965 and 1969 data are extrapolated from the 1960 figures with the aid of official index numbers.

See also: Eva Ehrlich: 'An examination of the interrelations between consumption indicators expressed in physical units of measurement and per capita national income'. Czechoslovak Economic Papers, No. 7, Prague 1966, pp. 109–137.

national income increased in Hungary between 1950 and 1970 from 26 per cent to 43 per cent, while the share of agriculture decreased from 48 to 17 per cent.[3]

In respect of employment the situation was the following in Hungary:

Table VI/3

DISTRIBUTION OF THE ECONOMICALLY ACTIVE POPULATION

(per cent)

	1950	1960	1965	1968	1970
Industry	19·4	27·4	32·2	33·0	36·5
Non-agricultural sectors, total	48·0	59·1	68·1	69·5	73·8
Agriculture	52·0	40·9	31·9	30·5	26·2
TOTAL	100·0	100·0	100·0	100·0	100·0

Source: Statistical Yearbook, 1967.

As regards the other socialist countries, the ratio of industrial employment increased in Czechoslovakia from 29·4 to 38·4 per cent (1948 and 1968), in Bulgaria from 7·9 to 26·8 per cent (1948 and 1965) in Yugoslavia from 12·6 to 18·2 per cent (1953 and 1961), and in Poland from 18·8 to 23·3 (1950 and 1960).

For the individual main regions of the developing countries Table V/4 contains data relating to employment and Annex V/7 shows the contribution ratios to national income in some countries.

Finally, *the share of manufacturing products in exports*, which also characterises development levels, increased in Hungary from about 30 per cent in 1948 to 70 per cent in 1965. In the developing world the differences among countries are great; the average may be around 18–20 per cent.

As a general conclusion we may say that the more advanced of the developing countries, the front group, have already surpassed the level attained by the socialist countries in the early 1950s, and the rest are gradually approaching this level. However, the countries of Black Africa and the densely populated Asian countries are still behind the starting level of the socialist countries. This level has been attained by the North African and Middle Eastern countries, by some Asian ones and by the majority of the Latin American countries, and has been considerably surpassed by a few countries in Latin America. In evaluting our comparison, these circumstances must be kept in view.

The experiences of socialist countries in industrialisation will be reviewed in the following from a few special points of view. (A *complete* survey would require a separate book, not a brief chapter.) These viewpoints are the following:

(*a*) In the analysis we shall mainly deal with the Hungarian experiences. These are best known to the author; the procedure is also justified by the circumstance that Hungary occupies a medium position, as it were, among the countries in question in respect of development level.

(*b*) Somewhat greater emphasis will be laid on the experiences of the initial period of socialist industrialisation, up to the 1950s, than on current problems. This is the period that is nearer to the developing countries, regarding economic development levels and other conditions. Hence the present problems are rather problems of an economy with a more complex structure, as well as problems related to the transition from the so-called extensive phase of development to the intensive one, when the labour reserves get exhausted and increase of production can be expected more and more from growing productivity and not from increasing employment, as was the case in the past. As is known, the latter situation is not a general characteristic of the developing countries.

(c) A few problems, essential for the industrialisation strategy of the developing countries, will be more closely examined. These are the following:

(i) the place and role of industrialisation in the development of the economy as a whole and, in this context, the allocation of resources, mainly of labour and investments among the main branches of the economy.

(ii) the size of plants and enterprises,

(iii) the choice of technology (labour- and capital-intensive technologies),

(iv) international division of labour (import substitution and export promotion).

Several problems, otherwise very important for the developing countries, as for example the forms of ownership of industrial enterprises (private or public ownership, domestic or foreign ownership), will not be dealt with in detail. These problems did not arise in socialist industrialisation; owing to the social and economic system, the role of non-state owned industry is negligible, nor does foreign property play any role.

THE ROLE OF INDUSTRIALISATION IN ECONOMIC DEVELOPMENT

Beginning in 1950 the economy and, particularly, industry increased at a fast rate in the European socialist countries (see Table VI/4). It was characteristic of development that the growth of industry exceeded that of the whole economy (see rows A and C in the Table).

The features of economic and industrial growth will be examined through the example of Hungary, with the aid of Tables VI/5–6. The major macro-economic interrelations are the following:

The period 1950–70 can be divided into two main sub-periods. The first sub-period, from 1950 to 1958, was characterised by a tumultuous development, which however was neither continuous nor sustained. A high rate of development in some years was interrupted by a slow-down or even a drop behind the level of the previous year. National income showed increases as high as 12–16 per cent a year but also decreases of 2 to 5 per cent compared to the previous year. Industrial development – rather high on the average – was also extremely uneven. However, this uneven growth of national income originated mainly in the contribution of agriculture to national income. The changing rate of development also, of course, affected the use of national income as shown by the fluctuating rate of growth in consumption and in the ups and downs of aggregate investment.

Table VI/4

GROWTH AND AVERAGE GROWTH RATES OF THE ECONOMY IN SOME SOCIALIST COUNTRIES

Country		1950 = 100				Average rate of growth per cent			
		1955	1960	1965	1970	1950/5	1955/60	1960/5	1970/
Hungary	A	138·7	190·3	237·1	330·2	6·7	6·5	4·5	7·0
	B	128·4	174·6	213·4	291·7	5·1	6·3	4·1	6·5
	C	193·3	277·8	397·8	307·9	14·1	7·5	7·4	7·6
Bulgaria	A	178·3	282·6	394·3	600·0	12·2	9·2	6·6	8·7
	B	171·4	259·2	350·0	513·0	11·4	8·6	6·9	8·0
	C	191·2	405·9	708·8	1275·0	13·9	16·2	11·8	12·5
Czechoslo-vakia	A	149·1	209·1	229·1	320·7	8·3	7·0	1·8	7·0
	B	140·0	188·3	200·0	277·4	7·0	6·1	1·2	6·8
	C	166·7	273·3	353·3	476·0ᵃ	10·7	10·4	5·3	7·6ᵇ
Poland	A	150·9	207·6	277·4	369·8	8·6	6·6	6·0	5·9
	B	137·7	173·8	219·7	281·6	6·6	4·8	4·8	5·1
	C	217·1	348·6	525·7	762·8	16·8	9·9	8·6	7·8
East Germany	A	172·3	240·4	285·1	367·2	11·5	6·9	3·5	5·2
	B	177·3	259·1	311·4	399·5	12·1	7·9	3·7	5·1
	C	208·1	327·0	435·1	573·0	15·8	9·5	5·9	5·7
Romania	A	195·7	269·6	415·2	597·4	14·4	6·6	7·5	7·6
	B	182·4	237·3	354·9	482·7	12·8	5·4	8·4	6·3
	C	214·3	368·6	711·4	1292·0	16·5	11·5	14·1	12·7
Yugoslavia	A	—	—	—	—	—	—	—	—
	B	—	—	—	—	—	—	—	—
	C	140·0	262·0	434·0	—	7·0	13·4	10·6	—

A = Value added (M.P.S.).
B = *Per capita* value added (M.P.S.).
C = value added by industry, according to official index numbers.

Source: A magyar ipar nemzetközi összehasonlitásban 10, (Hungarian industry: a international comparison), Central Statistical Office, Budapest, 196 pp. 102–3; for 1970: projections with the aid of official indices.

ᵃ· 1969.   ᵇ· 1969/75.

Table VI/5

MAIN INDICATORS OF ECONOMIC DEVELOPMENT IN HUNGARY, 1950–70

	National income		Industrial output		National income produced in industry		Agricultural output		National income produced in agriculture	
	1950 = 100	Previous year = 100	1950 = 100	Previous year = 100	1950 = 100	Previous year = 100	1950 = 100	Previous year = 100	1950 = 100	Previous year = 100
1950	100	—	100	—	100	—	100	—	100	—
1951	116	116	124	124	117	117	—	—	119	119
1952	114	98	150	121	137	117	—	76	74	62
1953	128	112	167	111	152	111	—	119	103	139
1954	122	95	170	102	146	96	—	102	98	95
1955	132	108	186	109	162	111	118	112	113	115
1956	117	89	170	91	137	85	102	102	94	83
1957	144	123	196	115	165	120	117	115	111	118
1958	152	106	217	111	184	111	123	105	114	103
1959	162	107	238	110	198	108	128	104	118	103
1960	177	109	267	112	228	115	120	94	106	90
1961	185	105	294	110	253	111	118	98	97	92
1962	196	106	317	108	273	108	122	103	105	108
1963	207	106	339	107	286	105	128	105	110	105
1964	215	104	369	109	307	107	134	105	113	103
1965	216	100	386	105	321	105	127	95	102	90
1966	233	108	412	107	351	109	139	109	112	110
1967	252	108	448	109	382	109	144	104	113	101
1968	265	105	472	105	404	106	145	101	112	99
1969	286	108	486	103	422	104	155	107	126	113
1970	300	105	521	107	458	109	146	94	110	87

Table VI/5—continued

	Consumption		Total savings		Fixed capital formation		Imports		Exports		Balance of foreign trade in percentage of exports*	Share of non-food products in exports
	1950 = 100	Previous year = 100	1950 = 100	Previous year = 100	1950 = 100	Previous year = 100	1950 = 100	Previous year = 100	1950 = 100	Previous year = 100		
1950	100	—	100	—	100	—	100	—	100	—	+3·9	60·8
1951	103	103	171	171	174	174	125	125	120	120	+0·4	—
1952	98	95	132	77	194	111	145	116	133	111	−4·9	—
1953	100	102	169	128	225	116	154	106	151	113	+2·2	—
1954	119	119	118	70	178	79	168	109	158	105	−2·4	71·9
1955	125	105	139	118	195	110	175	104	183	116	+7·8	71·6
1956	135	108	37	27	175	90	152	87	148	81	+1·2	74·8
1957	146	108	209	565	165	94	216	142	148	100	−39·8	78·2
1958	150	103	148	71	251	152	200	93	208	140	+7·7	77·6
1959	160	107	181	122	292	116	251	125	234	112	−3·0	79·9
1960	170	106	251	139	400	137	309	123	266	114	−11·6	81·2
1961	172	101	257	102	385	96	325	105	313	118	+0·3	81·5
1962	178	103	279	109	414	108	364	112	335	107	−4·5	77·9
1963	186	104	320	115	494	119	415	114	367	110	−8·3	79·2
1964	196	105	345	108	526	106	473	114	411	112	−10·6	79·3
1965	199	102	302	88	530	101	482	102	459	112	−0·7	78·6
1966	209	105	337	112	500	94	496	103	485	106	+1·7	78·3
1967	223	107	446	132	669	134	562	113	518	107	−4·4	78·8
1968	233	164	437	98	643	96	573	102	544	105	−0·8	77·1
1969	246	106	422	97	673	105	613	107	631	116	+7·5	77·2
1970	263	107	533	126	772	115	797	130	700	111	−8·1	

* import (−), export (+) surplus.

Source: *Statistical Yearbook, 1967, 1970.*

MAIN INDICATORS OF INDUSTRIAL DEVELOPMENT IN HUNGARY, 1950–1970

	Industrial output		Industrial employment		Labour productivity		Volume of industrial investment		Share of industrial in total investment	Share of main industrial branches in total industrial investment*				
	1950 = 100	Previous year = 100	1950 = 100	Previous year = 100	1950 = 100	Previous year = 100	1950 = 100	Previous year = 100		Basic material and energy	Engineering	Heavy industry	Light industry	Food processing
1950	100	—	100	—	100	—	100·0	—	37·6	61·4	29·2	90·6	3·9	5·5
1951	124	124	108	108	115	115	164·9	164·9	44·8	69·3	23·4	92·7	3·9	3·4
1952	150	121	119	110	126	109	206·0	124·9	47·3	77·1	17·0	94·1	3·8	2·1
1953	167	111	131	110	127	101	212·8	103·3	48·5	75·8	17·5	93·3	3·0	3·7
1954	170	102	140	107	122	96	137·6	64·7	44·4	75·9	12·4	88·3	5·3	6·4
1955	186	109	143	102	130	107	128·3	93·2	45·3	70·4	11·7	82·1	7·8	10·1
1956	170	91	145	101	117	90	143·8	112·1	49·6	71·0	15·0	86·0	5·8	8·2
1957	196	115	148	102	132	113	125·2	87·1	46·7	71·6	12·5	84·1	8·2	7·7
1958	217	111	154	104	142	107	149·2	119·2	44·6	69·2	15·2	84·4	8·6	7·0
1959	238	110	159	103	150	106	198·9	133·4	42·2	63·6	20·6	84·2	8·6	7·2
1960	267	112	167	105	160	107	220·9	111·1	40·0	64·2	19·5	83·7	9·6	6·7
1961	294	110	171	102	173	108	228·5	103·4	45·0	69·4	14·8	84·2	9·1	6·7
1962	317	108	175	103	181	105	254·2	111·2	43·3	69·2	14·5	83·7	8·4	7·9
1963	339	107	181	103	187	103	269·1	105·9	39·7	67·0	14·3	81·3	10·6	8·1
1964	369	109	187	103	198	105	284·6	105·8	40·1	65·1	13·3	78·4	12·1	9·5
1965	386	105	188	101	206	104	293·6	103·2	41·3	64·4	14·3	78·7	12·1	9·2
1966	412	107	190	101	217	105	332·9	113·4	38·6	62·6	17·5	80·1	11·2	8·7
1967	448	109	196	103	229	106	410·1	123·2	39·8	61·3	18·1	79·4	11·6	9·0
1968	472	105	190	104	231	101	383·0	93·4	36·6	66·1	17·8	83·9	8·1	8·0
1969	486	103	196	103	231	100	398·4	104·0	35·2	60·6	18·6	79·2	10·6	10·2
1970	521	107	204	100	247	107	439·3	110·3	33·2	59·0	18·8	77·8	11·6	10·6

* Investment Statistics, 1950–66.

Source: *Statistical Yearbook, 1967, 1970.*

From 1959 onwards, development became more even. National income increased by at least 5 per cent a year (except in 1964–5) and frequently by as much as 8 to 9 per cent. The rate of industrial development also became more even and, at the same time, somewhat slower. The tendency manifested by agriculture to maintain its output and its contribution to national income at a fairly high level and to withstand unfavourable climatic conditions should be considered as a particular achievement of the second sub-period. This was the result of the greater emphasis given to agriculture, the formation and stabilisation of large-scale collective farms, better organisational methods and, last but not least, increased industrial inputs in agriculture (for example, fertilisers). As a result of a more even growth rate for national income, there was a stable increase in consumption and also in savings (except for 1965 and 1968/9 as regards savings).

Industrialisation was in the centre of development policies, particularly in the first part of the period, in close connection with the possible maximum mobilisation and exploitation of resources. This development strategy was reflected mainly by the increase in employment and in structural changes. As can be seen from Tables VI/5–6, industrial employment increased in Hungary from 1950 to 1955 by almost 50 per cent; in the next period development was still relatively fast, particularly up to 1965 when it was on average 2–4 per cent p.a. Savings increased up to about a quarter of national income, amounting to 14 per cent in 1950, 20 per cent in 1960 and 25 per cent in 1970.[4] The share of industry in total investment was equally high in the other socialist countries. In 1961–5 it amounted to 48·7 per cent in Bulgaria, 44·4 per cent in Poland, 38·9 per cent in Yugoslavia, 52·0 per cent in East Germany and 53·2 per cent in Romania.[5]

Within the general industrial development policy, special priority was given in Hungary to heavy industry; this is reflected by the high share of investment in heavy industry. (Of course, this is mainly because heavy industry is very capital-intensive.) This tendency also underwent some change in the 1960s, when the investment shares of the light and food industries were increased.

The result of this development policy – regarding only the most important macro-economic interrelations – was a relatively fast increase of national income, at an annual rate of above 5 per cent. It should be noted that this growth rate – high as it is in itself – can only be considered as moderate in comparison to the other socialist countries. The difficulties and ups and downs of the first period were later successfully surmounted, with development becoming more even. The development policies, together with great efforts on the part of society, succeeded in fundamentally changing the economic structure. The share of agriculture has diminished and that of industry increased both in the creation of national income and in employment. To ensure further economic growth, savings and investment were stabilised at a relatively high level; but, except in the initial period, this high rate of saving did not take place at the expense of consumption which increased by 3–6 per cent annually. Structural change also showed in foreign trade, as we saw earlier. We will ¦deal with this aspect of economic development in somewhat more detail later.

Bulgaria is somewhat nearer to the developing countries, particularly as regards changes of the economic structure. In that country industrial employment – as has already been mentioned – increased from 7·9 per cent in 1948 to 26·8 per cent by 1965, while agricultural employment fell from 82·1 per cent to 44·3 per cent. Growth was faster than in Hungary, with similar fluctuations, with setbacks in some years, particularly in the first part of the period. The rate of savings was even higher than in Hungary; in 1960, for example, it was 27·5 per cent and in 1965 28·3 per cent. Incomes increased at about the same rate in the two countries.

Table VI/7

PER CAPITA REAL INCOME IN HUNGARY AND BULGARIA, 1952–65

(*1952 = 100*)

	Workers and employees		Peasantry	
	Hungary	Bulgaria	Hungary	Bulgaria
1956	148	151	172	107
1960	198	192	202	170
1965	233	215	248	242

Source: *A Bolgár Népköztársaság és a Magyar Népköztársaság népgazdaságának összehasonlitása az ágazati kapcsolatok mérlege alapján*, Statisztikai Időszaki Közlemények, 1962/2 (comparison of the economies of the Bulgarian and Hungarian People's Republics on the basis of input-output tables. Periodical Statistical Publications 1962/2).

This book does not aim at discussing general development strategies nor at raising such problems as can be met with, say, under the headings of balanced and unbalanced growth. A few short, general remarks still seem to be appropriate. The experience of the European socialist countries unequivocally proves that a relatively fast change

H

in economic structure is possible within a historically short period – one or two decades – and that industrial development has a central role in such changes in structure. For fast growth, and particularly for starting fast growth, great and concentrated efforts are needed. Such efforts put a great strain on the resources available to a country, which unavoidably causes tensions and invokes the danger of disequilibrium. An actual upsetting of equilibrium is by no means necessary, and even less is it desirable, but the danger is greater in periods of fast and concentrated development. The danger can be reduced by sound economic policy, but it cannot be completely eliminated. The lack of equilibrium may appear between the production and utilisation of national income, between exports and imports, in consumption, in investment, or in the field of an economic sector, product, or product group. Disequilibrium constitutes a serious danger if it results in declining living standards or in their lasting stagnation.

The main danger accompanying economic growth, which can slow down or hinder development, is perhaps not so much the lack of equilibrium, the emergence of tensions (apart from declining or stagnating living standards), but rather the lack of adaptation of economic policies to rapid changes in circumstances. Thus, a different policy is necessary for the introduction of new branches of production (i.e. a certain kind of protectionism) and a different one for stabilising their production and making them efficient (i.e. increasing participation in the international division of labour). Again, an economic policy is needed, when there is still abundant labour available to be drawn into production, that is different from the policy necessary when these resources are already exhausted. Precisely because the changes in structure are rapid, it is difficult to follow them flexibly with changes in economic policy and in economic institutions that are suited to them.

Choice of Technology. Capital and Labour-Intensive Technologies
As has been mentioned in Chapter III/2, in the socialist countries the problem of the choice between capital- and labour-intensive technologies emerged differently from the way it did in developing countries. At the beginning of the period under discussion, there were still mobile labour reserves in several socialist countries, partly in agriculture and partly among women in households, but unemployment in the more exact sense very soon ceased after the war and the ideas of applying so-called intermediate technologies, or technologies with zero or very low marginal productivity, were never raised. As in the developing countries, resources to be invested were scarce – at least, compared to needs – and thus the good utilisation

of resources (or, in other words, the efficiency of investment) became a focal point of attention.

In Hungary, in particular, labour was never as abundant as in the developing countries and the problems of unlimited supply of labour – a questionable concept even in the least developed countries – never arose. The situation in the whole period, but mainly in the beginning, was characterised by the relative scarcity of capital. Although unemployment was brought to an end very soon after the Second World War, mechanisation and large-scale units in agriculture freed important portions of the farm population. As already indicated, industry's share in total employment rose from less than 20 per cent to over 37 per cent in the period 1950–70. In addition, the proportion and number of economically active women rose considerably, mostly augmenting the labour force in industry, which was the most dynamic sector over the whole period. There was quite often a shortage of certain skills or in certain areas, but up to the second part of the 1960s, the overall labour shortage affecting industrial development as a whole – at least compared to the overall scarcity of capital – was less.

Unfortunately, it is difficult to answer the question how far the technologies actually used were capital- or labour-intensive, because relevant statistics or other information are not available. Output/capital ratios were decreasing for industry as a whole, but leaving out mining, there was some increase (see Table VI/8). We have to keep in mind also that these are a function not only of technology but also of capacity utilisation and changes in the pattern of production.

However, another indicator – namely the change in the value of productive equipment per employee – shows significant increases, pointing to the increase of capital compared to the labour force, i.e. to increasingly capital-intensive technologies. Detailed data are available for the sixteen-year period 1955–70.

As already mentioned, the really relevant alternative is very often not whether to select capital- or labour-intensive technologies but rather what plant size or what type of raw material (for example, fuel) to use, etc. Of course, in some cases just the former type of choice has to be made, and substitution of labour for capital is possible. It seems that in these cases the technology selected in Hungary was usually one or two steps behind the most 'advanced', i.e. the most capital-intensive and labour-saving technology; probably less as a result of some conscious policy or scientifically based project evaluation and more as a consequence of the necessity to economise on investment funds which were scarce in comparison to production targets.

Table VI/8

OUTPUT PER UNIT OF CAPITAL (*a*) AND VALUES OF
PRODUCTIVE EQUIPMENT PER EMPLOYEE (*b*) IN HUNGARY*

		1955	*1960*	*1965*	*1970*
Heavy industry	*a*	100	99·2	89·9	92·6
	b	100	122·5	174·9	206·4
Heavy industry, excluding mining	*a*	100	100·9	104·9	112·2
	a	100	122·1	163·1	—
Light industry	*a*	100	108·8	100·6	93·6
	b	100	101·5	125·5	145·3
Food industry	*a*	100	98·4	126·3	125·0
	a	100	129·1	139·4	141·9
Industry total	*a*	100	99·8	93·5	94·4
	b	100	123·7	161·6	185·5
Manufacturing industry	*a*	100	107·0	103·7	—
	b	100	118·8	152·5	—

* *Statistical Periodical Publications*, No. 15, Central Statistical Office, Budapest, 1966; *Source for 1970 figures:* Ipari Adattár Industrial data collection 1, Budapest, 1972.

In one respect, however, there seems to have been a general pattern, which was certainly not the result of conscious policies but of the above-mentioned contradiction between resources and targets. The pattern is the following: for basic production capacities – which, once installed, cannot be altered for the whole lifetime of the plant – up-to-date, efficient (i.e. if necessary capital-intensive) technologies are used. For auxiliary operations, like material handling – which can be added later – more primitive, capital-saving and labour-intensive methods are introduced. The evidence for such a pattern concerning capital- and labour-intensive technologies is more indirect than direct. International comparisons of productivity show that labour productivity in Hungarian industry is relatively higher in the basic operations, and relatively lower in the auxiliary operations – in particular in material handling. In consequence, a disproportionately large number of workers are engaged in material handling. On the other hand, the amount of equipment used in material handling is relatively small and an increasing lack of manpower for such operations – which require great physical strength – is being felt. There is, therefore, a pressing need to modernise such operations.

This pattern of using capital-intensive and labour-intensive technologies together is worth the consideration of the developing countries. If used as a conscious policy it allows capacities and production to be increased, without freezing capital in outdated technologies and in this way taxing the future, and it allows the more capital-intensive technologies to be introduced in the auxiliary operations at later stages, as capital becomes more abundant and labour more scarce.

Another reason why this kind of development strategy may be useful in the developing countries is because, owing to the growth of national income and thus of potential savings, the investment put off can be later implemented with relatively smaller efforts. With a 5 per cent annual rate of growth, for example, the volume of national income doubles in fifteen years and thus the same investment – relative to national income – can be implemented with half the effort fifteen years later.

SIZE OF PLANTS AND ENTERPRISES. SMALL-SCALE AND LARGE-SCALE PLANTS

In Hungary, particularly in the first period, socialist industrialisation was characterised by a definite advance in plant scales, based on a deliberate industrial development policy and priority given to large-scale plants. This can be illustrated mainly by the decreasing share of private small-scale industry and the growing share of state-owned manufacturing plants.

Table VI/9
EMPLOYMENT IN HUNGARIAN INDUSTRY*
(*thousands and per cent*)

Year	State industry		Industrial co-operatives		Artisans		Total	
	Number	Per cent	Number	Per cent	Number	Per cent	Number	Per cent
1950	666	80	14	2	151	18	831	100
1955	981	82	118	10	90	8	1,189	100
1960	1,142	83	161	11	81	6	1,384	100
1965	1,322	85	176	11	61	4	1,569	100
1970	1,517	84	238	13	61	3	1,816	100

* *Statistical Yearbook*, 1967, 1970, Budapest.

As can be seen from the Table, in 1950 small-scale industry still engaged 18 per cent of total industrial employment. This ratio fell to 3 per cent by 1970, and the decrease did not fully augment employment in state industry, since it went mostly to the industrial co-operatives, where employment increased from 2 to 13 per cent within industry. The co-operatives, however, although in general they operate smaller units than state industry, can not by any means be considered small-scale plants.

Not only did a shift towards large-scale forms of manufacturing occur in respect of industrial macro-structure, but the size of plants increased within the individual sectors, as is shown in the next Table:

Table VI/10

AVERAGE NUMBER OF WORKERS IN FACTORY-TYPE
INDUSTRIAL PLANTS IN HUNGARY

	1942	1955	1960	1965
Heavy industry	147	251	269	300
Light industry	81	122	115	137
Food industries	38	78	92	86
Total industry	97	169	177	195

Source: Statistical Periodical Publications, No. 3, 1967.

Otherwise, Hungarian industry is strongly concentrated even in comparison to the economically more advanced countries. Concentration can be measured with various indicators; for example with the average staff per plant (used above) or with the distribution of employment by plant-sizes, shown in Table III/3. A measure of concentration may be the share of workers employed in plants with 1,000 or more workers. According to this indicator, the following picture emerges if Hungary is compared to some developed countries:

Table VI/11

SHARE OF EMPLOYMENT IN PLANTS
WITH 1,000 OR MORE EMPLOYEES

(*industry total* = 100)

Country	Year	Per cent
Hungary	1965	51·0
West Germany	1964	31·8
U.K.	1958	35·4
U.S.A.	1958	31·6
Italy	1961	30·3
France	1962	20·6
Japan	1963	19·8
Canada	1961	19·3
Sweden	1963	18·5
Finland	1963	16·9

Source: Statistical Periodical Publications, No. 3, 1967.

The clear tendency towards an increase in the size of plants was the result of a belief in the general advantages of big plants in order to realise economies of scale, to use modern technologies, to reduce current costs and economise on capital requirements. These advantages undeniably exist and we can observe a world-wide increase in plant sizes in certain industries. This is the case, for example in heavy chemicals, electricity, steel plants, and generally in industries where the basic technologies are chemical or metallurgical, based on a small number of big producing units and where the increase in plant size results from the increase in the sizes (capacities) of these units. However, in other industries where the basic production unit is small and the increase of the plant size results rather from the increase of the number of units, the advantages of big sizes are much less apparent. Recently the attitude concerning the plant sizes underwent some changes, largely due to the evaluation of past experience. According to present thinking – directly relevant, of course, only to the present Hungarian situation – there are sectors where plant sizes are still considerably below the optimum, even if the article in question is produced by only one plant in the whole country (for example, some chemicals). In some other sectors, like textiles, food industries and perhaps the engineering industry, average plant sizes could be considered as too big or, more exactly, there is a certain lack of small and medium-size plants. The latter have – as already mentioned – a greater flexibility and adaptability, which the big plants lack.

A further problem related to the fast development of large-scale plants is a shortage of servicing, mainly maintenance activities, and this has taken acute forms in recent years. This shortage is due less to the development of large-scale plants and more to the labour shortage which is increasingly felt; recently this has led to special government measures aimed at promoting the small-scale (handicraft) activities of maintenance character. (Thus, for example, craftsmen may obtain preferential state credits, retired workers may perform maintenance work with licences issued for this purpose while keeping their pensions, etc.)

From all the foregoing certain general conclusions can be drawn, probably applicable also to the developing countries. There is, it seems, no principle that would be equally valid in respect of the most rational plant scale for every industry and for each individual case. Part of industrial production, mainly the production of energy, raw materials and certain mass products manufactured by engineering, is efficient only in the case of large-scale production, and in certain cases is only possible in a large-scale framework. In sections of manufacturing – in the textile industry, in the clothing and shoe industries, leather goods, and in certain branches of engineering where rapid adaptation is needed to meet the changing requirements of consumers – medium-sized and small-scale plants are also necessary. These medium-sized and small-scale plants are – owing to the character of technology – not at a disadvantage in respect of costs in relation to large-scale plants. In many fields, however, servicing and maintenance activity requires definitely small-scale units, although even here in many cases relatively bigger sizes and division of labour within the plant are more advantageous, as for example in the repair of radio and TV sets or private cars.

INTERNATIONAL DIVISION OF LABOUR

Some fundamental principles of the international division of labour, particularly import substitution in the closer sense (autarkic) and in the broader sense (relative), have been discussed in Chapter II. These will not be treated here again.

As we can see from Table VI/5, Hungarian imports doubled from 1950 to 1958 and increased again by almost four times from 1958 to 1970. There was thus thus no autarkic (or absolute) import substitution – i.e. no decrease of the total volume of imports – indeed, quite the contrary. As the great majority (around 80 per cent) of Hungarian imports consist of industrial goods, there was no autarkic import substitution for industrial imports either. If we compare the volume of imports to national income, which is a relevant aspect for such comparisons, we can ascertain that from this point of view there was also no import substitution; imports increased faster than national income. Now, if imports are compared to *industrial output*, and it is assumed as a first approximation that the share of industrial imports in total imports remain relatively constant, the interrelationships are somewhat different.

From 1950 to 1958 industrial output increased faster than imports (although the differences were not considerable – see Table VI/5) – indicating at least some tendencies to relative import substitution. The main trend changed later (from 1958 to 1970 industrial output increased by about 140 per cent, and imports by as much as 300 per cent) to a gradual and sustained increase in the share of imports in domestic consumption.

The volume of foreign trade has similarly grown in the other socialist countries. In comparison to 1951, for which the data available are comparable, imports have grown in Poland and in Czechoslovakia more than threefold, in Hungary more than fourfold, in Romania more than sixfold and in Bulgaria thirteen-fold. The growth of exports is on a similar scale.

But from the viewpoint of industrialisation, the changes in the pattern of foreign trade, particularly of exports, are more characteristic than the growth in volume, since these also reflect the changes in structure.

As can be seen from relevant statistics, the pattern of foreign trade has radically changed in the countries in question, and the *one-sided agrarian and raw-material exporting character of the economies has ceased*. The change is particularly great in the industrially less developed countries, Bulgaria and Romania, since against the very low level of the 1950s (2 per cent in Bulgaria and 5·5 per cent in Romania), in 1968 more than one-third of Romanian and almost half of Bulgarian exports consisted of manufactured goods.

As regards the individual major products and product groups, development tendencies are different in the various countries, largely according to their endowments. A somewhat more detailed analysis will be given for Hungary as regards some product groups. While it is impossible in this study to discuss the development of production and/or imports by products or product groups, it seems justified to give some further information on

       industrial raw materials,
       semi-fabricates (intermediate goods),
       investment goods (machinery and equipment),
       industrial consumer goods,

and to go into somewhat greater detail concerning the problems related to the extension of existing production and to the introduction of new products, which present somewhat different aspects from the point of view of economic efficiency.

Raw materials. Hungary is a country rather poor in natural (except agricultural) resources; industrial development could not, therefore, be based on the existing sources of industrial raw materials, and even less on some kind of import substitution in this field. As a consequence, imports of most industrial raw materials – fuel, ores, timber, copper, etc. – had to be increased not only in absolute but also in relative terms. For example, the share of imported fuel in domestic consumption was 9 per cent in 1949, 12 per cent in 1955, 22 per cent in 1958, 27 per cent in 1960, and 30 per cent in 1965. Industrialisation for Hungary meant an increasing dependence on imports (and, as a consequence, obviously on exports), in particular of raw materials and semi-fabricates which are current day-to-day requirements of industrial production and must not be missing under any circumstances.

Semi-fabricates. There are important differences between (mineral) raw materials and semi-fabricates, in particular that the production of the first is possible only if natural resources are available (although geological surveys and research may and usually do discover

H*

new resources) while the production of the second is mainly a question of productive capacity and can be done on the basis of imported raw materials. Development of the production of semi-fabricates and construction of new capacity (or the extension of existing capacity) received strong priorities in Hungary. As can be seen from Table VI/6, the share of 'basic materials' (also comprising mining and electricity) was close to or above 70 per cent of total industrial investment in most years in the period. Metallurgy, or more exactly iron and steel, was mostly emphasised in the first part of the period under investigation, the chemical industry in the second part. The absolute volume of imports of semi-fabricates also increased; but there are indications that some relative import substitution took place in certain fields.

The production of *investment goods* (machinery and equipment) was a rapidly increasing sector constantly from 1948–50. The output of the engineering industry increased at a yearly average rate of about 15 per cent in 1950–5 and by about 10 per cent in 1955–65. However, this did not result in any appreciable import substitution for investment goods taken together.

First, an increasing proportion of engineering production was exported. The engineering industries accounted for 23 per cent of exports in 1950 and for around 30 per cent or more in the 1960s, while the share of non-industrial exports in total exports declined sharply. Secondly, after the engineering industries of a country have attained a certain level of development – which can be characterised by a share of about 25 per cent in industrial production – and, as a consequence, can provide for a substantial part of domestic requirements, there is not much room left for further import-substitution in a global sense, except perhaps in the case of a very few big countries. (To indicate some orders of magnitude: the share of engineering production in total industry was about 32 per cent in the industrially developed countries and about 13 per cent in the developing countries around the mid-1960s; it was about 25 per cent in Hungary around 1948–50.) Because of the great diversity of investment goods it is usually rational to specialise in a relatively small number of goods which are produced for the domestic market, as well as for exports, and to import the rest.

Manufactured consumer goods represent the only field where definite import substitution policies prevailed for a certain time. Even here the definition given for import substitution – namely, domestic production substituting goods previously imported – is only partly applicable. We have to bear in mind that the greatest impulse for industrialisation in Hungary closely followed the Second World War and post-war reconstruction. Living standards were low in this period as a consequence of the war, and priority was given to the most essential goods, food and simple clothing, etc. International trade, which had been disrupted by the war, was only very partially re-established. At the beginning, therefore, there was not much import for what domestic production could be substituted. Now, as mentioned before, economic policies in the late 1940s and early 1950s put strong emphasis on economic development in general and on industrial development in particular, and as foreign currencies in such situations are usually scarce, priority was given to importing raw materials and investment goods, the consumer being provided basically with manufactured goods which the domestic industry was able to produce at the time. This resulted, on the one hand, in a somewhat narrow choice of the more conventional consumer goods (such as textiles, shoes, etc.) and, on the other hand, in the lack of such new consumer goods which either appeared only after the Second World War (products of the chemical industry like synthetic fibres and some plastics; TV-sets) or which became less expensive and thus more widely available to the consumer even in the richer and more developed countries only in the 1950s (refrigerators, washing machines, etc.). This situation changed gradually from the mid-1950s onwards, as a result of economic policies, putting greater emphasis on (private) consumption. Domestic production of some of the 'new' products started without the item in question previously being imported like TV-sets or detergents, thus substituting domestic production not for actual but for 'potential' imports. In the case of other products like washing machines or refrigerators, domestic production developed only after the product had been imported for some years. For example, the production of refrigerators was started only in 1957, with 12,000 units being produced in 1961, more than 113,000 in 1966 and 120,000 in 1967. The production of vacuum-cleaners started at the same time, and that of (household) washing machines somewhat earlier; TV receivers were first produced in 1956, with about 2,200 units, but the annual production had risen to almost 300,000 in 1966.

How can we evaluate this experience? The criticism of import substitution policies usually stresses the disadvantage that it goes with excessive protection of the domestic industry, which need not thus compete with imports at home, and partly on this account it does not compete for foreign markets (exports) abroad. This leads to stagnation of technological development, inferior quality of products, low productivity increase rates, etc. However, this diagnosis only partly applies to the Hungarian case. Domestic production of new products (i.e. import substitution) was usually closely followed by increasing exports and a substantial part of these products (TV-sets, refrigerators, etc) is actually exported. Sustained export performance is usually a proof of at least acceptable quality, and is thus also of benefit to the domestic consumer. Imported consumer goods – including English woollens, French silk and Italian shoes – were also increasingly available in the past years, although not at particularly low prices.

Now this of course does not mean that every new – or traditional – product found adequate export outlets or that the volume of imports can be considered as satisfactory. Foreign currencies are scarce, and there are central priorities in the plans for imports, and foreign trade controls to enforce them, implicitly protecting domestic industry in this way. The general tendency, however, is to ensure the equilibrium of the trade balance not so much by restricting imports as by increasing exports, and following the introduction of the economic reform of 1968 (which cannot be described here), to increase imports even of goods which are also domestically produced, in order to expand the range of choice on the domestic market.

The main tendency now, therefore, is export promotion and the increase of the international division of labour, to create industries whose size and technical level enable them to be efficient exporters; for a small country this circumstance, of course, means relying on imports for many products.

For an evaluation of the development described here, it is worth while to consider what problems have been solved, what are still waiting for solution, and what new ones have emerged. In the case of Hungary, we can consider as solved the change in the economic macro-structure and, in this connection, the full employment of the population of working age – and this not only for the present and the near future, but also for the more distant future. Similarly, the capacity of the economy for saving has reached a level which enables further, rather fast growth. A new problem which is emerging and which will persist for some time yet, maybe even increasing, is the shortage of labour. A further persistent problem is to increase the export potential of the country in a way which will enable increasingly efficient participation in the international division of labour. The developing countries too will meet this problem, at the stage in their economic growth when industrial growth does not have to be based on the internal market or on the inclusion of new labour into production as it does at present.

REFERENCES

1. F. Jánossy, *A gazdasági fejlettség mérhetősége és uj mérési módszere* (Measurability of economic development level and a new method of measurement), Közgazdasági és Jogi Könyvkiadó, Budapest, 1963.
2. Frederic H. Harbison, Joan Maranic and Jane R. Resnich, *Quantitative Analyse sof Modernisation and Development*, Industrial Relations Section, Princeton University, 1970.
3. Measured at 1968 prices (Árvai János, 'The New Indexes of National Income and Net National Production', *Statisztikai Szemle*, No. 6, 1970).
4. Árvay, op. cit.
5. *Nemzetközi Statisztikai Évkönyv*, Központi Statisztikai Hivatal, 1970 (International Statistical Yearbook. Central Statistical Office, 1970).

ANNEXES

Annex II/1
LENGTH OF THE PERIOD OF EXTENSIVE GROWTH IN AGRICULTURE

$\lambda = 0\cdot2$	$\beta - \alpha$	$\dfrac{\alpha}{\lambda\beta}$	$\ln\dfrac{\alpha}{\lambda\beta}$	T
$\alpha = 0\cdot02$				
$\overline{\beta = 0\cdot04}$	0·02	2·50	0·916	45·8
0·05	0·03	2·00	0·693	23·0
0·06	0·04	1·65	0·500	12·4
0·07	0·05	1·43	0·3576	7·2
0·08	0·06	1·25	0·2231	3·8
$\alpha = 0\cdot025$				
$\overline{\beta = 0\cdot04}$	0·015	3·12	1·138	92·0
0·05	0·025	2·50	0·916	36·6
0·06	0·035	2·08	0·7323	20·8
0·07	0·045	1·78	0·5866	13·0
0·08	0·055	1·57	0·4510	8·2
$\alpha = 0\cdot03$				
$\overline{\beta = 0\cdot04}$	0·01	3·76	1·3244	132·4
0·05	0·02	3·00	1·0986	55·0
0·06	0·03	2·50	0·916	30·3
0·07	0·04	2·16	0·7701	19·3
0·08	0·05	1·87	0·6259	12·5

Annex II/2

LENGTH OF THE PERIOD OF EXTENSIVE GROWTH IN AGRICULTURE

$\lambda = 0.3$	$\beta - \alpha$	$\dfrac{\alpha}{\lambda\beta}$	$\ln \dfrac{\alpha}{\lambda\beta}$	T
$\alpha = 0.02$				
$\beta = 0.04$	0·02	1·67	0·5128	25·64
0·05	0·03	1·33	0·2851	9·5
0·06	0·04	1·11	0·1043	2·6
0·07	0·05	0·95	−0·0513	−1·02
0·08	0·06	0·83	−0·1864	−3·1
$\alpha = 0.025$				
$\beta = 0.04$	0·015	2·08	0·7323	48·8
0·05	0·025	1·67	0·5128	20·5
0·06	0·035	1·39	0·3293	9·4
0·07	0·045	1·19	0·1739	3·9
0·08	0·055	1·04	0·0392	0·7
$\alpha = 0.03$				
$\beta = 0.04$	0·01	2·50	0·9163	91·6
0·05	0·02	2·00	0·6931	34·6
0·06	0·03	1·67	0·5128	17·1
0·07	0·04	1·43	0·3576	8·9
0·08	0·05	1·25	0·2231	4·5

Annex II/3
CHANGES IN THE NUMBER AND AVERAGE SIZE OF AGRICULTURAL ESTATES

		Percentage change in the	
	Period	*number*	*average size*
		of estates	
WESTERN EUROPE			
Belgium	1950–9	+2	−3
Denmark	1950–9	−6	+5
Finland	1950–9	+8	−5
West Germany	1949–60	−14	+12
Ireland	1949–60	−9	+8
Netherlands	1950–9	−5	+4
Norway	1949–59	−7	+15
NORTH AMERICA			
Canada	1951–61	−16	+20
U.S.A.	1950–9	−31	+40
OCEANIA			
Australia	1950–60	+3	+20
New Zealand	1950–60	−1	+3
LATIN AMERICA			
Argentina	1952–60	−14	+1
Barbados	1946–61	−15	+5
Brazil	1950–60	+62	−29
Colombia	1954–60	+32	−25
Costa Rica	1950–5	+10	−7
Dominica	1950–60	+64	−31
El Salvador	1950–61	+29	−20
Panama	1950–60	+6	+46
Puerto Rico	1950–9	−14	+7
Uruguay	1951–61	+2	−2
Venezuela	1950–61	+29	−10
ASIA			
India	1954–		
	1960–1	+10	−10
South Korea	1955–60	+6	—
NEAR EAST			
Iraq	1952–8	+102	−38
AFRICA			
Kenya	1954–60	+14	−3
South Africa	1950–60	−9	+16
Southern Rhodesia	1950–60	+42	−15
Zambia	1950–60	+16	−27

Source: F.A.O., *The State of Food and Agriculture 1965*, p. 64.

Annex II/4A

INDEX NUMBERS OF AGRICULTURAL PRODUCTION, WORLD TOTAL AND REGION

(*1952/3–1956/7 average = 100*)

	Pre-war average	Average 1948/9 1952/3	1953/4	1957/8	1960/1	1963/4	1964/5	1971/2
PRODUCTION *All Agricultural Products*								
Western Europe	82	86	101	107	118	126	126	155
European socialist countries	81	86	94	118	132	134	144	180
North America	68	93	99	98	109	118	116	136
Oceania	78	90	97	102	123	136	142	162
DEVELOPED COUNTRIES	76	89	98	106	119	126	128	156
Latin America	73	88	96	113	121	130	129	159
Asia	84	87	98	107	120	127	129	170
Near East	73	85	99	112	122	135	136	164
Africa	67	88	98	105	118	125	128	154
DEVELOPING COUNTRIES	77	87	97	109	120	128	130	162
TOTAL	76	88	98	107	119	127	129	158
Foodstuffs								
Western Europe	82	86	101	107	118	127	127	157
European socialist countries	82	87	95	119	134	135	146	182
North America	66	92	98	101	111	120	118	145
Oceania	81	92	99	99	122	137	146	168
DEVELOPED COUNTRIES	76	89	98	107	120	127	129	160
Latin America	69	88	96	112	118	128	130	165
Asia	82	87	98	107	122	128	129	165
Near East	73	85	101	113	120	133	131	165
Africa	69	89	98	103	116	121	124	147
DEVELOPING COUNTRIES	76	87	98	108	120	127	129	162
TOTAL	76	88	98	108	120	127	129	161

Annex II/4B

	Per-war average	Average 1948/9– 1952/3	1953/4	1957/8	1960/1	1963/4	1964/5	1971/2
PER CAPITA PRODUCTION								
All Agricultural Products								
Western Europe	93	89	102	104	112	117	116	135
European socialist countries	83	92	96	113	121	119	125	146
North America	88	100	101	93	98	102	98	106
Oceania	104	99	99	95	107	112	114	113
DEVELOPED COUNTRIES	85	94	100	102	110	112	113	128
Latin America	110	98	98	104	103	102	99	98
Far East	109	93	100	100	106	105	104	108
Near East	95	94	102	104	106	108	106	108
Africa	95	97	100	97	101	99	99	101
DEVELOPING COUNTRIES	104	95	100	102	105	104	103	105
TOTAL	96	95	100	101	106	106	106	113
Foodstuffs								
Western Europe	93	89	102	104	113	117	116	136
European socialist countries	84	92	96	114	123	119	127	148
North America	85	99	100	96	100	103	100	113
Oceania	108	102	102	92	106	112	117	117
DEVELOPED COUNTRIES	85	94	99	103	111	113	114	132
Latin America	104	97	98	103	101	101	101	102
Asia	106	93	101	100	107	105	104	105
Near East	96	93	103	105	104	107	102	109
Africa	98	99	101	96	99	96	96	97
DEVELOPING COUNTRIES	102	95	100	101	104	103	101	106
TOTAL	95	95	100	102	107	107	106	115

Source: F.A.O., *The State of Food and Agriculture 1965*, Rome, 1965, pp. 14–15 and *Monthly Bulletin of Agricultural Economics and Statistics*, January 1972.

Annex III/1

CALCULATION METHOD OF SOCIAL MARGINAL PRODUCTIVITY (SMP)*

SMP is the effect of the investment project on the growth of national income and on the balance of payments.

$$SMP = \frac{X+E-M_i}{K} - \frac{L+M_d+O}{K} + \frac{r}{K}(aB_1+B_2)$$

$$= \frac{V}{K} \qquad - \frac{C}{K} \qquad + \frac{Br}{K}$$

$$\quad (a) \qquad\qquad (b) \qquad\qquad (c)$$

The symbols are the following:

K = investment
X = increment of production
E = savings in other enterprises or sectors (e.g. in the case of transport investments the savings of suppliers above the transport charges paid, so-called 'external economies')
M_i = cost of imported materials
V = $X+E-M_i$ that is, the increment of domestic value
L = wage costs
O = other non-wage and non-material costs including amortisation
M_d = domestic material costs
B = $a.B_1+B_2$ the total effect on the balance of payments
B_1 = effect of investments on the balance of payments
a = interest and amortisation of principal
B_2 = effect of the functioning of the investment project on the balance of payments
r = marginal rate of substitution between national income
(Y) and the effect on the balance of payments (B), that is, the factor correcting the official rate of exchange.

The above formulae can also be written in the form:

$$SMP = \frac{V}{K}\frac{V-C}{V} + \frac{Br}{K}$$

$$\quad (a)\ (b) \qquad (c)$$

* Chenery, 'The Application of Investment Criteria', *Quarterly Journal of Economics*, February 1953.

Annex V/1A
INDEX NUMBERS OF WORLD INDUSTRIAL PRODUCTION, EXCLUDING THE SOCIALIST COUNTRIES
(*1950 = 100*)

	Total industry (I.S.I.C. 1–3, 511–12)		
	World total*	*Capitalist countries**	*Developing countries**
1938	60·0	59·7	64·9
1948	87·1	86·1	89·4
1949	88·5	87·4	93·0
1950	100·0	100·0	100·0
1951	109·9	108·3	108·7
1952	112·8	111·0	112·2
1953	121·4	120·7	117·5
1954	121·4	120·7	128·0
1955	135·7	133·2	142·1
1956	141·4	138·8	154·3
1957	145·7	143·0	164·9
1958	142·8	138·8	175·4
1959	157·1	152·7	187·7
1960	168·5	162·4	208·7
1961	174·2	167·9	228·0
1962	187·1	180·4	245·6
1963	197·0	188·9	264·8
1964	212·8	204·0	291·2
1965	227·0	217·9	314·0
1966	242·8	233·2	338·5
1967	250·0	240·0	347·0
1968	270·0	257·0	376·0
1969	292·0	278·0	413·0
1970	297·0	281·0	442·0

* Throughout Annex V/1, the three columns are to be taken as having these headings.

	Mining, total (I.S.I.C. 1)		
	World total	Capitalist countries	Developing countries
1938	72·9	76·5	57·4
1948	93·2	95·0	83·3
1949	91·9	91·3	88·8
1950	100·0	100·0	100·0
1951	109·4	108·6	111·1
1952	112·1	111·1	118·5
1953	116·2	113·5	127·7
1954	117·5	113·5	135·1
1955	128·3	122·2	151·8
1956	135·1	128·3	162·9
1957	139·1	130·8	174·0
1958	135·1	123·4	185·1
1959	140·5	127·1	199·9
1960	150·0	129·6	240·6
1961	156·7	132·0	268·4
1962	166·2	137·0	298·0
1963	172·9	139·4	320·2
1964	182·4	144·4	346·1
1965	189·1	148·1	368·3
1966	198·6	151·8	405·4
1967	202·0	152·0	419·0
1968	216·0	159·0	455·0
1969	228·0	163·0	500·0
1970	242·0	170·0	535·0
	Coal mining (I.S.I.C. 11)		
1938	95·9	97·0	70·1
1948	100·0	100·0	91·0
1949	94·9	94·1	98·5
1950	100·0	100·0	100·0
1951	105·0	104·9	102·9
1952	103·0	102·9	108·9
1953	102·0	101·0	111·9
1954	99·0	98·0	117·9
1955	103·0	101·9	123·8
1956	107·1	104·9	131·3
1957	107·1	103·9	143·2
1958	101·0	98·0	149·2
1959	98·0	94·1	155·2
1960	98·0	94·1	164·1
1961	97·0	92·1	171·6
1962	99·0	94·1	180·5
1963	101·0	95·1	195·4
1964	103·0	97·0	198·4
1965	102·0	95·1	207·5
1966	99·0	92·1	213·4
1967	95·0	88·0	219·0
1968	92·0	86·0	225·0
1969	92·0	84·0	233·0
1970	91·0	83·0	236·0

Annex V/1C

Ore mining (I.S.I.C. 12)			
1938	91·6	90·3	95·7
1948	91·6	93·1	88·5
1949	93·0	93·1	94·2
1950	100·0	100·0	100·0
1951	105·5	105·4	108·5
1952	109·6	106·8	117·1
1953	118·0	113·6	127·1
1954	113·8	108·1	128·5
1955	130·5	125·9	139·9
1956	138·8	135·5	147·1
1957	147·1	143·7	155·6
1958	138·8	136·9	142·8
1959	144·4	141·0	151·4
1960	161·0	157·4	171·4
1961	163·8	160·2	171·4
1962	170·7	168·4	171·2
1963	172·1	171·2	172·8
1964	181·8	180·7	182·8
1965	190·2	188·9	194·2
1966	195·7	195·8	195·6
1967	194·0	188·0	206·0
1968	206·0	204·0	212·0
1969	215·0	209·0	228·0
1970	227·0	224·0	232·0
Crude oil and natural gas (I.S.I.C. 13)			
1938	51·5	57·5	35·4
1948	90·6	95·8	75·0
1949	89·0	90·3	83·3
1950	100·0	100·0	100·0
1951	112·4	113·6	110·4
1952	118·7	119·1	118·7
1953	126·5	124·6	129·1
1954	131·2	125·9	141·6
1955	143·7	136·9	162·5
1956	153·1	145·1	177·0
1957	156·2	145·1	187·5
1958	156·2	136·9	208·3
1959	167·1	145·1	229·1
1960	184·3	146·5	287·4
1961	199·9	150·6	333·3
1962	217·1	156·1	379·1
1963	228·1	160·2	412·4
1964	243·7	165·6	452·0
1965	253·0	168·4	481·2
1966	276·5	178·0	541·6
1967	290·0	184·0	577·0
1968	317·0	194·0	652·0
1969	344·0	202·0	730·0
1970	374·0	211·0	808·0

Annex V/1D MANUFACTURING

	Manufacturing, total (I.S.I.C. 2·3)		
1938	59·1	58·3	67·8
1948	87·3	86·0	91·5
1949	87·3	87·4	93·2
1950	100·0	100·0	100·0
1951	109·8	109·6	106·7
1952	111·2	112·4	108·4
1953	121·1	120·7	113·5
1954	121·1	120·7	123·7
1955	133·8	134·6	137·2
1956	140·8	140·2	149·1
1957	145·0	144·3	159·2
1958	140·8	138·8	169·4
1959	156·3	154·1	181·2
1960	166·1	163·8	196·5
1961	171·8	169·3	211·7
1962	184·4	181·8	225·3
1963	194·3	191·5	243·9
1964	211·2	206·8	267·6
1965	225·3	220·7	291·4
1966	242·2	237·3	310·0
1967	249·0	245·0	315·0
1968	266·0	262·0	339·0
1969	288·0	283·0	368·0
1970	293·0	287·0	393·0
	Light industry (I.S.I.C. 20·26$\sqrt{+}$28·30$\sqrt{+}$39)		
1938	71·8	70·0	72·7
1948	88·5	87·5	93·9
1949	91·0	90·0	93·9
1950	100·0	100·0	100·0
1951	102·6	102·5	103·0
1952	103·8	102·5	107·6
1953	108·9	108·7	110·6
1954	111·5	111·2	119·7
1955	120·5	118·7	130·3
1956	124·3	122·5	137·9
1957	128·2	125·0	143·9
1958	128·2	125·0	151·5
1959	138·4	135·0	157·6
1960	144·9	141·2	169·7
1961	148·7	145·0	180·3
1962	156·4	152·5	187·8
1963	164·1	158·7	200·0
1964	174·4	168·7	215·1
1965	182·0	176·2	230·3
1966	192·3	185·0	243·9
1967	195·0	187·0	252·0
1968	207·0	198·0	266·0
1969	218·0	208·0	284·0
1970	223·0	211·0	300·0

Annex V/1E

Heavy industry (I.S.I.C. 27√∓31–38)

1938	50·0	49·2	56·8
1948	84·8	85·0	84·3
1949	84·8	85·0	92·1
1950	100·0	100·0	100·0
1951	115·1	114·9	109·8
1952	118·2	119·4	109·8
1953	130·3	131·3	115·6
1954	128·8	128·3	129·4
1955	146·9	146·2	149·0
1956	153·0	152·2	162·7
1957	159·1	158·1	178·4
1958	151·5	149·2	196·0
1959	171·2	168·6	217·6
1960	184·8	182·0	239·1
1961	190·9	188·0	258·7
1962	207·6	202·9	286·2
1963	219·7	214·8	311·6
1964	240·9	235·7	352·8
1965	260·1	253·6	386·1
1966	281·8	274·5	417·5
1967	292·0	286·0	418·0
1968	316·0	309·0	458·0
1969	345·0	337·0	511·0
1970	352·0	342·0	552·0

Food industry (I.S.I.C. 20–22)

1938	69·7	71·4	70·1
1948	89·4	89·6	91·0
1949	94·7	96·0	94·0
1950	100·0	100·0	100·0
1951	102·6	103·8	102·9
1952	106·5	106·4	110·4
1953	110·5	110·3	113·4
1954	113·1	114·2	114·9
1955	118·4	118·1	125·3
1956	123·6	123·3	134·3
1957	126·2	125·9	140·2
1958	131·5	129·8	149·2
1959	136·8	135·0	153·7
1960	142·0	140·2	164·1
1961	148·6	145·4	176·0
1962	153·8	150·6	177·5
1963	159·1	155·8	185·0
1964	165·7	162·3	196·9
1965	170·9	166·1	208·9
1966	177·5	172·6	222·3
1967	189·0	182·0	231·0
1968	196·0	190·0	240·0
1969	205·0	198·0	259·0
1970	216·0	206·0	277·0

Annex V/1F

Textile industry (I.S.I.C. 23)

1938	74·4	74·7	78·8
1948	87·1	84·5	101·5
1949	89·5	87·8	98·5
1950	100·0	100·0	100·0
1951	102·2	102·1	101·5
1952	98·8	96·6	106·1
1953	105·7	105·4	112·1
1954	108·1	105·4	124·2
1955	113·9	109·8	134·8
1956	117·4	114·2	140·9
1957	119·7	116·4	143·9
1958	116·2	109·8	151·5
1959	125·5	120·8	154·5
1960	131·3	124·1	166·6
1961	133·6	126·3	172·7
1962	141·8	135·1	178·8
1963	148·7	140·5	189·4
1964	155·7	147·1	204·5
1965	162·7	152·6	213·6
1966	170·8	160·3	224·2
1967	171·0	159·0	227·0
1968	183·0	171·0	244·0
1969	195·0	183·0	259·0
1970	196·0	181·0	276·0

Textile and leather garment industry (I.S.I.C. 24)

1938	82·9	80·7	
1948	91·4	89·1	
1949	93·9	92·7	
1950	100·0	100·0	
1951	100·0	98·7	
1952	102·4	102·3	
1953	107·3	105·9	
1954	107·3	105·9	
1955	114·6	114·4	
1956	120·7	119·2	
1957	124·3	122·8	
1958	121·9	120·4	
1959	132·9	132·4	
1960	139·0	137·2	
1961	142·6	139·7	
1962	148·7	145·7	
1963	157·2	157·9	
1964	165·8	161·3	
1965	175·5	169·8	
1966	180·4	174·6	
1967	174·0	169·0	
1968	181·0	175·0	
1969	185·0	180·0	
1970	182·0	177·0	

Annex V/1G

	Wood and furniture industry (I.S.I.C. 25–26)		
1938	65·6	64·7	
1948	89·9	88·2	
1949	86·3	85·8	
1950	100·0	100·0	
1951	104·5	102·3	
1952	102·1	101·1	
1953	105·7	105·8	
1954	110·6	109·4	
1955	120·3	118·8	
1956	122·7	120·0	
1957	121·5	117·6	
1958	121·5	117·6	
1959	134·9	130·5	
1960	139·7	134·1	
1961	142·1	136·4	
1962	150·7	144·6	
1963	157·9	150·5	
1964	170·1	161·1	
1965	181·0	170·5	
1966	187·1	176·4	
1967	189·0	179·0	
1968	202·0	188·0	
1969	212·0	197·0	
1970	210·0	197·0	
	Paper industry (I.S.I.C. 27)		
1938	57·1	57·7	47·9
1948	82·8	83·1	72·9
1949	84·2	84·5	83·3
1950	100·0	100·0	100·0
1951	107·1	107·0	106·2
1952	101·4	101·4	106·2
1953	111·4	111·2	114·6
1954	118·5	118·3	143·7
1955	131·4	130·9	154·1
1956	138·5	138·0	177·0
1957	141·4	139·4	188·5
1958	142·8	140·8	208·3
1959	157·1	154·9	225·0
1960	164·2	161·9	243·7
1961	172·8	170·4	274·9
1962	184·2	180·2	310·4
1963	195·6	190·1	345·8
1964	209·9	205·7	383·3
1965	222·8	216·8	433·3
1966	237·0	229·5	470·7
1967	245·0	238·0	418·0
1968	258·0	251·0	470·0
1969	276·0	266·0	515·0
1970	280·0	268·0	560·0

Annex V/1H

	Chemical industry (I.S.I.C. 31–32)		
1938	48·2	48·2	55·4
1948	82·1	82·1	83·9
1949	83·9	82·1	92·9
1950	100·0	100·0	100·0
1951	114·2	114·2	105·4
1952	114·2	116·0	100·0
1953	124·9	128·5	107·2
1954	133·9	135·7	116·1
1955	149·9	151·7	137·5
1956	162·4	164·2	150·0
1957	171·4	173·1	164·3
1958	178·5	178·5	178·9
1959	199·9	199·9	198·2
1960	217·8	219·5	216·1
1961	232·0	232·0	234·0
1962	257·0	258·8	246·9
1963	280·2	282·0	271·9
1964	308·8	310·6	298·8
1965	335·6	337·4	327·4
1966	371·3	371·3	363·2
1967	395·0	400·0	364·0
1968	440·0	446·0	400·0
1969	485·0	491·0	432·0
1970	507·0	510·0	473·0
	Non-metallic minerals (I.S.C.I. 33)		
1938	56·3	58·1	51·0
1948	84·5	85·1	78·4
1949	85·9	86·5	88·2
1950	100·0	100·0	100·0
1951	111·2	110·8	109·8
1952	109·8	108·1	115·7
1953	115·4	113·5	125·5
1954	119·7	116·2	141·2
1955	132·3	129·7	156·9
1956	139·4	136·4	170·6
1957	142·2	137·8	186·3
1958	140·8	135·1	196·1
1959	157·7	151·3	211·8
1960	166·1	159·4	223·5
1961	170·4	163·5	237·3
1962	181·6	174·3	249·0
1963	191·5	182·4	270·6
1964	211·2	201·3	307·9
1965	221·1	209·4	329·4
1966	230·9	217·5	360·8
1967	230·0	215·0	360·0
1968	245·0	230·0	387·0
1969	262·0	246·0	425·0
1970	268·0	248·0	463·0

Annex V/1 I

	Metallurgy (I.S.I.C. 34)		
1938	55·8	54·5	67·9
1948	88·3	89·7	83·9
1949	83·7	84·1	89·3
1950	100·0	100·0	100·0
1951	111·5	112·5	108·9
1952	106·9	107·9	110·7
1953	115·0	115·9	116·1
1954	106·9	106·8	130·4
1955	131·3	131·8	142·9
1956	133·6	134·0	153·6
1957	133·6	132·9	164·3
1958	116·2	113·6	178·6
1959	130·1	127·2	205·4
1960	141·8	138·6	225·0
1961	142·9	138·6	237·5
1962	148·7	143·1	275·0
1963	159·2	152·2	301·8
1964	180·1	173·8	330·4
1965	191·7	184·0	351·8
1966	197·5	188·6	378·6
1967	199·0	190·0	383·0
1968	213·0	204·0	416·0
1969	237·0	227·0	468·0
1970	237·0	227·0	474·0
	Metal-working industries (I.S.I.C. 35–38)		
1938	46·9	46·1	53·3
1948	85·9	86·1	84·4
1949	85·9	86·1	91·1
1950	100·0	100·0	100·0
1951	117·1	116·9	113·3
1952	126·5	126·1	115·5
1953	139·0	138·4	117·8
1954	134·3	133·8	137·8
1955	153·1	152·3	157·8
1956	159·3	158·4	173·3
1957	165·6	164·6	195·5
1958	156·2	153·8	222·2
1959	176·5	173·8	246·6
1960	192·1	189·2	277·7
1961	198·4	193·8	306·6
1962	215·5	210·7	348·8
1963	228·1	223·0	375·5
1964	245·2	239·9	437·7
1965	268·7	262·5	488·8
1966	293·6	286·1	513·3
1967	306·0	299·0	518·0
1968	328·0	321·0	574·0
1969	358·0	348·0	653·0
1970	360·0	350·0	698·0

Annex V/1J

	Electrical energy and gas (I.S.I.C. 511–512)		
1938	44·2	43·4	46·5
1948	84·6	83·0	83·7
1949	88·4	88·6	90·7
1950	100·0	100·0	100·0
1951	111·5	113·3	111·6
1952	121·1	120·7	120·9
1953	130·8	130·1	134·8
1954	140·4	139·6	151·1
1955	155·8	154·6	169·7
1956	171·1	169·7	190·6
1957	182·7	179·2	209·2
1958	192·3	188·6	232·5
1959	207·7	203·7	255·7
1960	228·8	224·4	279·0
1961	242·3	237·6	306·9
1962	263·4	256·5	334·8
1963	282·7	275·4	369·7
1964	307·7	298·0	413·9
1965	330·7	318·7	453·4
1966	355·7	343·3	506·8
1967	379·0	366·0	555·0
1968	416·0	399·0	640·0
1969	455·0	435·0	706·0
1970	492·0	468·0	784·0

Source: The Growth of World Industry 1938–1961, International Analyses and Tables 1938–62, U.N., New York, 1965 (p. 178) and 1970. Vol. I.: *General Industrial Statistics*.
1962–5: *Monthly Bulletin of Statistics*, U.N., New York, November 1967. (Special table: A.)

Annex V/2A

AVERAGE ANNUAL INCREASE IN INDUSTRIAL PRODUCTION

(1. = World total. 2.= Capitalist countries. 3. = Developing countries.)

Years	Industry, total			Mining, total			Coal mining		
	1	2	3	1	2	3	1	2	3
1938–50	4·4	4·4	3·7	2·7	2·2	4·75	0·4	0·3	3·0
1950–5	6·3	5·9	7·3	5·1	4·1	8·7	0·5	0·3	3·6
1955–60	4·5	4·0	8·0	3·2	1·5	9·6	−1·0	−1·6	5·8
1960–66	6·3	6·2	8·4	4·8	2·7	9·1	0·2	−0·4	4·5
1950–66	5·7	5·5	7·9	4·4	2·6	9·2	1·0	−0·5	4·9
1965–70	5·4	5·3	7·2	5·0	2·9	8·7	−2·1	−2·6	2·7
1955–70	5·4	5·2	7·6	4·3	2·2	9·0	−0·8	−1·2	5·0

Years	Ore mining			Crude oil and natural gas			Manufacturing total		
	1	2	3	1	2	3	1	2	3
1938–50	0·8	0·8	0·4	5·7	4·7	9·0	4·5	4·6	3·3
1950–5	5·5	4·7	7·0	7·5	6·5	10·2	6·0	6·2	6·5
1955–60	4·3	4·5	4·2	5·1	1·4	12·1	4·4	4·0	7·5
1960–6	3·3	3·7	2·2	7·0	3·3	11·1	6·5	6·4	7·9
1950–66	4·3	4·3	4·3	6·6	3·7	11·1	5·7	5·6	7·3
1965–70	3·3	3·4	3·1	8·1	4·7	10·7	5·4	5·3	6·4
1955–70	3·9	3·8	3·8	6·4	3·0	11·0	5·4	5·3	6·9

Years	Light industry			Heavy industry			Food industry		
	1	2	3	1	2	3	1	2	3
1938–50	2·8	3·0	2·7	5·9	6·1	4·8	3·1	2·9	3·0
1950–5	3·8	3·5	5·5	8·0	7·9	8·3	3·4	3·4	4·6
1955–60	3·75	3·6	5·4	4·7	4·5	9·9	3·7	3·5	5·6
1960–6	4·9	4·7	6·25	7·3	7·1	9·75	3·8	3·5	5·2
1950–66	4·1	3·9	5·7	6·7	6·5	9·4	3·6	3·5	5·1
1965–70	4·1	3·7	5·5	6·1	5·8	7·9	4·5	4·1	5·8
1955–70	4·3	4·0	5·3	6·0	5·8	9·1	4·2	4·0	5·3

Years	Textile industry			Textile and leather garment industry			Wood and furniture industry		
	1	2	3	1	2	3	1	2	3
1938–50	2·5	2·5	2·0	1·6	1·8		3·6	3·7	
1950–5	2·6	1·9	6·1	2·8	2·8		3·75	3·5	
1955–60	2·9	2·5	4·3	3·9	3·7		3·1	2·4	
1960–6	4·5	4·4	5·1	4·4	4·1		4·9	4·7	
1950–66	3·4	3·0	5·2	3·75	3·5		4·0	3·6	
1965–70	3·5	3·4	4·7	1·2	0·9	4·1	2·9	3·0	3·3
1955–70	3·8	3·5	4·5	3·1	2·9	6·1	3·9	3·7	6·3

I

Annex V/2B

Years	Paper industry			Chemical industry			Non-ferrous minerals		
	1	2	3	1	2	3	1	2	3
1938–50	4·8	4·7	6·3	6·25	6·25	5·0	4·9	4·6	5·8
1950–5	5·6	4·6	9·0	8·4	8·7	6·6	5·8	5·3	9·4
1955–60	4·6	4·3	9·6	7·75	7·7	9·4	4·7	4·2	7·3
1960–6	6·3	6·0	11·6	9·3	9·2	9·0	5·7	5·3	8·3
1950–66	5·5	5·4	10·2	8·5	8·5	8·4	5·4	5·0	8·3
1965–70	4·6	4·3	7·8	8·6	8·6	8·3	4·2	3·6	7·9
1955–70	4·9	4·9	7·6	8·4	8·4	8·0	4·9	4·6	7·4

Years	Metallurgy			Metal-working industries			Electrical energy and gas		
	1	2	3	1	2	3	1	2	3
1938–50	5·0	5·2	3·3	6·5	6·6	5·4	7·0	7·2	6·6
1950–5	5·6	5·7	7·4	8·9	8·8	9·5	9·3	9·1	11·1
1955–60	1·6	1·0	9·5	4·7	4·5	12·0	8·0	7·7	10·5
1960–6	5·7	5·3	9·1	7·3	7·2	10·75	7·6	7·4	10·4
1950–66	4·3	4·1	8·7	7·0	6·8	10·75	8·25	8·0	10·7
1965–70	4·1	4·1	6·1	5·8	5·7	7·6	8·4	8·0	11·5
1955–70	4·0	3·9	8·4	5·9	5·8	10·3	8·0	7·7	10·9

Source: The Growth of World Industry 1938–1961, International Analyses and Tables, 1938–62, U.N., New York, 1965 and 1970 (p. 178). Vol. I. *General Industrial Statistics.*

1962–6: *Monthly Bulletin of Statistics,* U.N., New York, 1966 and 1967, November. (Special table: A.)

Annex V/3A

INDEX NUMBERS OF INDUSTRIAL PRODUCTION IN DEVELOPING COUNTRIES BY MAIN REGIONS

$(1950 = 100)$

Year	Industry total	Total	Mining		
			of which		
			Coal	Ores	Crude oil and natural gas
I.S.I.C.	1–3, 51	1	11	12	13
AFRICA (excluding South Africa)					
1938	—	76·2	44·8	82·6	6·3
1948	—	82·5	72·4	84·0	50·0
1950	100·0	100·0	100·0	100·0	100·0
1955	—	133·3	172·4	130·6	131·3
1960	—	—	148·3	165·3	—
1965	—	—	110·3	157·3	—
1970	—	—	—	—	—
LATIN AMERICA					
1938	54·0	55·9	73·5	92·2	42·1
1948	90·5	91·5	100·0	96·8	89·5
1950	100·0	100·0	100·0	100·0	100·0
1955	131·7	142·3	130·8	148·4	142·1
1960	177·7	189·7	141·1	182·8	196·4
1965	195·2	206·7	157·3	178·1	221·0
1970	264·8	256·3	224·9	216·3	269·6
ASIA (excluding Japan)					
1938	80·0	70·8	92·2	116·8	48·5
1948	90·9	76·3	90·6	76·4	73·5
1950	100·0	100·0	100·0	100·0	100·0
1955	141·8	100·0	123·4	131·4	82·3
1960	221·8	172·1	198·4	144·9	179·3
1965	256·3	199·9	242·1	155·0	213·2
1970	368·3	306·6	271·9	190·6	343·9

Annex V/3B
MANUFACTURING

Year	Manufacturing total	Light industry	Heavy industry	Electrical energy and gas
I.S.I.C.	2–3	20–26 28–30, 39	27, 31–38	51
AFRICA (excluding South Africa)				
1938	—	—	—	29·7
1948	—	—	—	75·7
1950	100·0	100·0	100·0	100·0
1955	—	—	—	199·9
1960	—	—	—	340·5
1965	—	—	—	391·8
1970	—	—	—	—
LATIN AMERICA				
1938	54·7	59·4	47·2	44·0
1948	90·6	91·9	86·8	86·0
1950	100·0	100·0	100·0	100·0
1955	129·6	121·6	143·3	150·0
1960	174·9	147·3	218·8	228·0
1965	190·6	156·7	247·1	276·0
1970	260·7	199·7	365·5	449·3
ASIA (excluding Japan)				
1938	81·1	87·0	69·2	57·9
1948	92·4	96·3	82·7	89·5
1950	100·0	100·0	100·0	100·0
1955	150·9	153·6	140·4	181·5
1960	228·2	214·7	250·0	336·8
1965	264·0	240·6	305·8	426·2
1970	358·5	313·4	447·4	786·3

Annex V/3C

INDEX NUMBERS OF INDUSTRIAL PRODUCTION BY MAIN REGIONS: SELECTED INDUSTRIES

Year	Food industry	Textile industry	Paper industry	Chemical industry	Non-ferrous minerals	Metallurgy	Metal-working industry
I.S.I.C.	20–22	23	27	31–32	33	34	35–38
AFRICA (excluding South Africa)							
1938	—	—	—	—	—	66·1	—
1948	—	—	—	—	—	83·1	—
1950	100·0	100·0	100·0	100·0	100·0	100·0	100·0
1955	—	—	—	—	—	129·2	—
1960	—	—	—	—	—	210·7	—
1965	—	—	—	—	—	209·2	—
1970	—	—	—	—	—	—	—
LATIN AMERICA							
1938	58·8	54·7	48·2	48·0	38·3	55·5	44·7
1948	89·7	95·2	85·7	84·0	81·6	87·3	93·6
1950	100·0	100·0	100·0	100·0	100·0	100·0	100·0
1955	125·0	117·8	137·4	152·0	141·6	130·1	144·6
1960	157·3	133·3	194·6	236·0	189·9	177·7	246·7
1965	166·1	133·3	226·7	276·0	206·6	196·8	278·6
1970	213·9	160·2	—	411·5	299·8	272·8	413·4
ASIA (excluding Japan)							
1938	77·3	111·7	65·0	72·1	64·1	88·0	60·0
1948	89·4	105·8	80·0	86·0	69·2	73·3	93·3
1950	100·0	100·0	100·0	100·0	100·0	100·0	100·0
1955	128·8	170·5	370·0	92·3	171·8	117·3	226·6
1960	169·7	215·6	660·0	154·3	307·7	217·3	433·3
1965	186·3	237·2	790·0	178·4	371·8	269·3	556·6
1970	261·5	306·2	—	270·0	568·5	375·5	764·2

Source: The Growth of World Industry 1938–1961, International Analyses and Tables, U.N., New York, 1966. Monthly Bulletin of Statistics, U.N., November 1966. Vol. I, General Industrial Statistics, U.N., New York, 1965 and 1970 edition. New York 1972.

I*

Annex V/4

AVERAGE GROWTH RATES OF PRODUCTION AND EMPLOYMENT, 1963–71

Country	Production				Employ-ment
	Industry total	Mining	Manufac-turing	Electrical Energy and gas	Manufac-turing
I.S.I.C.	1–3, 511, 512	1	2–3	511, 512	2–3
Argentina	8·1	7·3	7·9	10·1	—
Brazil	7·9*	15·2*	6·7*	—	1·1
Ceylon	5·4†	2·8†	5·2†	—	—
Chile	—	1·9	4·2	—	–0·8
Colombia	6·0*	4·3*	6·1*	7·9†	0·6*
Ecuador	—	—	12·4*	—	1·0
Egypt	5·3*	19·4*	3·5*	8·6*	—
El Salvador	—	—	10·0	10·3	—
Guatemala	5·2	—	3·7	11·0	1·8
India	4·6	2·8	4·2	11·4	—
Iran	14·7	14·9	12·5	22·2	—
Mexico	8·6	2·9	8·8	12·0	—
Pakistan	6·1	3·6	6·4	—	—
Peru	—	—	6·7*	7·7*	3·1*
Philippines	6·6	11·6	5·7	9·3	1·1
Senegal	3·1	11·8	1·0	6·9	—
Singapore	—	—	8·6	—	—
South Korea	20·1	4·8	21·2	21·6	9·3
Tunisia	3·6	1·6	3·8	6·6	—
Turkey	12·2†	7·1†	13·6†	12·5*	—
Venezuela	2·8	2·1	5·1	11·4	2·0
Zambia	3·0	1·4	12·6	5·9	—

Source: *The Growth of World Industry*, 1970 edn., Vol. I. *General/Industrial Statistics 1960–1969*, U.N., New York, 1972. *U.N. Monthly Bulletin of Statistics*, April 1973.
* 1963–9.   † 1960–6.

Annex V/5

STRUCTURE OF INDUSTRY BY VALUE ADDED IN DEVELOPED CAPITALIST AND DEVELOPING COUNTRIES

I.S.I.C.	As percentage of industrial production					As percentage of manufacturing production								
	1	2–3	51	20–26, 28–30, 39	27, 31–38	20–22	23	24	25–26	27	31–32	33	34	35–38
	Mining	Manu-facturing	Elec-trical energy and gas	Light industry	Heavy industry	Food industry	Textile industry	Textile and leather garments	Wood industry	Paper industry	Chemical industry	Non-ferrous minerals	Metal-lurgy	Metal-working industries
DEVELOPED CAPITALIST COUNTRIES														
1948	9·6	86·6	3·8	42·2	57·8	14·6	6·1	5·7	5·0	3·5	7·8	4·2	10·4	31·9
1961	6·8	87·6	5·6	35·9	64·1	12·1	4·6	4·5	3·9	3·7	11·6	4·1	8·1	36·6
AFRICA (excluding South Africa)														
1948	33·3	63·5	3·2	62·5	37·5	28·9	10·9	6·0	—	1·1	6·9	4·5	6·8	18·2
1961	—	—	—	55·6	44·4	26·1	10·7	6·1	—	2·3	9·7	5·6	8·9	17·9
LATIN AMERICA														
1948	18·7	78·2	3·1	64·7	35·3	28·3	14·0	—	—	1·7	10·9	4·8	6·9	11·0
1961	18·3	77·3	4·4	54·1	45·9	26·2	9·8	—	—	2·2	15·3	5·8	7·3	15·3
ASIA (excluding Japan)														
1948	19·0	79·0	2·0	72·1	27·9	27·4	22·3	—	—	0·6	13·3	2·2	4·2	7·6
1961	18·4	78·2	3·4	63·9	36·1	23·5	15·0	—	—	1·1	11·1	4·0	5·1	14.8

Source: *The Growth of World Industry 1938–1961, International Analyses and Tables*, U.N., New York, 1965, pp. 242–5.

Annex V/6A
STRUCTURE OF MANUFACTURING BY VALUE ADDED
(*total manufacturing* = 100)

I.S.I.C.		Food-stuffs	Bever-ages	Tobacco	Textile industry	Textile garments
		20	21	22	23	24
Brazil	1969	12·8	2·7	1·5	10·1	2·8
Ceylon	1969	16·9	5·7	8·6	10·5	5·4
Chile	1967	15·6	4·9	3·4	13·2	2·8
Colombia	1968	15·5	14·4	4·6	15·2	2·7
Cyprus	1969	18·3	17·4	3·9	3·9	9·0
Dominican Rep.	1967	49·1	14·6	9·8	3·0	0·8
Ecuador	1969	25·9	11·5	1·0	12·5	0·5
Egypt	1968	20·6	1·7	5·2	30·2	0·2
Ethiopia	1969	27·1	14·4	3·8	30·4	0·2
Ghana	1967	4·0	13·7	18·0	11·0	4·1
Honduras	1968	23·4	26·4	6·3	3·6	3·0
India	1966	10·9	0·6	2·0	22·6	0·2
Iran	1968	20·1	1·6	8·6	17·3	10·4
Jamaica	1969	28·0	8·4	4·8	— 8·5 —	
Jordan	1968	16·2	2·5	4·8	5·6	5·3
Kenya	1969	16·7	9·9	4·1	5·9	1·5
Lybia	1969	13·7	10·1	38·0	5·0	5·0
Mauritius	1969	63·3	5·0	4·1	1·4	—
Nigeria	1968	13·4	15·8	7·8	18·1	—
Panama	1969	29·6	11·1	5·6	0·6	5·6
Peru	1969	24·3	7·9	2·7	8·4	2·9
Philippines	1969	23·7	8·4	8·3	6·3	2·2
Singapore	1969	8·1	3·6	2·7	1·8	2·3
South Korea	1969	6·9	7·5	8·8	15·3	3·0
Southern Rhodesia	1968	13·6	6·9	4·4	7·8	8·2
Turkey	1968	15·6	4·6	15·4	14·3	0·1
Uganda	1969	20·0	6·4	4·7	20·9	1·4
Zambia	1968	13·6	13·2	3·3	2·3	6·2

Annex V/6B

I.S.I.C.		Wood and wood products	Furniture	Paper industry	Printing industry	Rubber industry	Chemical industry	Petrol and coal
		25	26	27	28	30	31	32
Brazil	1969	2·6	1·6	2·7	3·0	2·1	—15·9—	
Ceylon	1969	—1·5—		3·4	0·1	4·3	11·3	1·7
Chile	1967	1·9	0·8	3·2	3·1	2·1	8·5	—
Colombia	1968	1·0	0·8	3·0	2·9	2·6	14·5	4·1
Cyprus	1969	1·8	4·1	0·8	4·8	1·0	4·7	—
Dominican Rep.	1967	2·0	0·7	2·1	1·4	1·0	5·5	—
Ecuador	1969	2·6	0·5	3·8	4·5	2·6	11·0	10·2
Egypt	1968	0·2	0·3	2·3	2·0	1·7	12·7	3·1
Ethiopia	1969	2·5	0·7	0·2	2·2	0·6	2·2	2·4
Ghana	1967	13·2	1·3	2·7	4·4	0·6	8·5	5·5
Honduras	1968	11·2	0·9	0·9	2·7	1·2	8·0	—
India	1966	0·6	0·5	2·1	2·5	2·2	10·0	1·9
Iran	1968	—2·6—		0·5	1·5	2·4	4·5	0·7
Jamaica	1969	2·2	4·5	—7·7—		2·5	7·2	—
Jordan	1968	0·4	6·7	0·6	4·0	0·3	6·2	14·1
Kenya	1969	2·3	0·9	1·7	4·8	1·0	7·0	6·0
Lybia	1969	1·2	0·6	—	4·2	—	13·2	1·2
Mauritius	1969	0·4	1·2	0·1	2·5	0·6	2·2	—
Nigeria	1968	1·7	0·7	1·0	2·6	4·1	9·4	2·4
Panama	1969	2·7	3·6	2·7	6·9	0·3	6·6	—
Peru	1969	1·2	1·6	1·2	2·8	1·9	9·1	7·2
Philippines	1969	4·6	0·6	2·6	2·9	2·6	11·7	5·3
Singapore	1969	5·8	0·9	1·2	4·8	7·2	5·3	17·5
South Korea	1969	2·9	0·5	2·4	3·0	1·8	12·9	8·1
Southern Rhodesia	1968	2·3	1·9	2·7	4·6	2·4	11·8	—
Turkey	1968	0·7	0·1	1·8	1·3	1·9	5·5	11·9
Uganda	1969	3·4	0·2	0·6	2·9	1·2	2·6	—
Zambia	1968	7·2	0·7	0·4	6·3	1·7	7·3	0·3

Annex V/6C

I.S.I.C.		Non-ferrous minerals	Metal-lurgy	Metal products	Mach-inery	Elec-trical equip-ment	Trans-port equip-ment	Other manu-factur-ing products
		33	34	35	36	37	38	39
Argentina	1957	4·1	5·6	5·5	4·5	6·3	6·7	1·5
Brazil	1969	5·8	—11·4—		6·0	6·3	8·6	1·7
Ceylon	1969	2·6	1·3	5·2	5·1	2·9	1·9	1·4
Chile	1967	3·9	11·4	5·7	2·9	4·2	6·9	2·6
Colombia	1968	3·9	—	5·1	1·2	3·1	2·2	—
Cyprus	1969	11·9	—	6·4	3·2	0·3	0·6	1·2
Dominican Rep.	1967	4·7	0·2	1·2	0·2	0·4	1·2	—
Ecuador	1969	5·5	0·6	3·2	—	2·1	0·6	0·4
Egypt	1968	4·4	5·4	3·3	1·8	2·8	1·0	0·3
Ethiopia	1969	5·8	2·7	1·1	—	0·1	—	0·1
Ghana	1967	1·7	0·9	3·5	—	0·6	4·0	0·7
Honduras	1968	6·5	—	3·5	0·3	0·2	—	—
India	1966	4·5	12·6	3·2	6·2	5·1	10·0	1·7
Iran	1968	10·1	2·0	5·8	0·6	3·3	5·8	1·3
Jamaica	1969	8·8	—13·9—					—
Jordan	1968	15·6	—7·6—		0·1	1·2	1·7	
Kenya	1969	6·7	—	6·0	0·9	5·5	16·3	1·1
Lybia	1969	5·8	—	5·7	—	0·2	—	1·5
Mauritius	1969	2·5	—	0·8	2·0	0·8	8·5	1·2
Nigeria	1968	4·3	—7·7—		0·2	0·6	2·0	—
Panama	1969	8·4	1·4	5·5	0·4	0·6	0·3	—
Peru	1969	4·3	9·7	2·6	2·0	2·7	3·8	—
Philippines	1969	4·9	2·8	4·5	0·8	3·2	3·2	1·1
Singapore	1969	3·3	2·8	6·2	2·3	5·7	14·8	2·2
South Korea	1969	6·1	3·8	2·4	2·0	3·6	6·0	2·5
Southern Rhodesia	1968	5·4	5·9	7·4	3·7	3·0	6·4	—
Turkey	1968	5·2	9·8	3·0	2·6	1·9	3·5	0·4
Uganda	1969	7·9	19·9	5·3	0·8	0·6	5·0	0·1
Zambia	1968	10·9	6·7	11·1	4·9	1·9	1·5	0·5

Source: The Growth of World Industry 1953–1965, National Tables, U.N., New York, 1967 and 1970. Vol. I. General Industrial Statistics 1960–69, U.N., New York, 1972.

Annex V/7A

CONTRIBUTION OF INDUSTRY TO NATIONAL INCOME (G.N.P.)

I.S.I.C.		Industry 1–3, 511, 512	of which Manufacturing 2–3
Argentina	1960	31	29
	1969	31	28
Brazil	1960	19	18
	1968	21	19
Burma	1953	11	10
	1967	10	9
Ceylon	1960	9	8
	1969	11	10
Chile	1960	34	23
	1970	40	28
Colombia	1960	23	18
	1969	22	18
Cyprus	1960	—	—
	1970	19	11
El Salvador	1960	16	15
	1969	21	20
Ethiopia	1960	6	6
	1969	10	10
Honduras	1960	13	11
	1969	16	13
India	1960	15	13
	1969	15	13
Iraq	1960	47	10
	1963	43	9
Iran	1960	26	25
	1963	34	32
Jamaica	1960	22	12
	1969	25	13
Jordan	1960	8	6
	1968	12	9
Kenya	1960	—	—
	1970	14	12

Annex V/7A (*cont.*)

I.S.I.C.		*Industry* *1–3, 511, 512*	*of which* *Manufacturing* *2–3*
Malawi	1960	6	6
	1968	9	8
Mexico	1960	30	26
	1970	29	23
Pakistan	1960	10	9
	1967	11	10
Paraguay	1960	18	17
Philippines	1960	18	16
	1970	19	16
South Korea	1960	17	14
	1970	24	21
Syria	1960	19	—
	1969	18	—
Thailand	1960	14	13
	1969	18	14
Tanzania	1960	21	—
	1970	24	22
Tunisia	1960	15	12
	1969	20	13
Uruguay	1960	21	—
	1969	24	22

Source: The Growth of World Industry 1953–1965 and *1970*, National Tables. U.N., New York, 1967, 1971.

INDEX

INDEX